PowerScore®

GMAT

READING
COMPREHENSION
BIBLE

A Comprehensive System for Attacking
GMAT Reading Comprehension!

PowerScore®
TEST PREPARATION

Published by
PowerScore Publishing
57 Hasell Street
Charleston, SC 29401

Authors: David M. Killoran
             Jon M. Denning

Manufactured in Canada
07 29 20 20

ISBN: 978-0-9846583-8-1

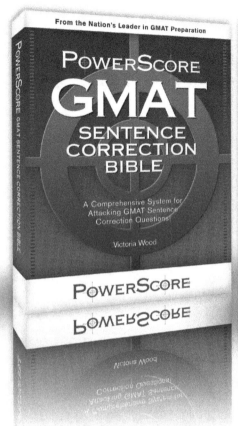

CONTENTS

CHAPTER ONE: INTRODUCTION

CHAPTER TWO: THE BASICS OF READING COMPREHENSION

CHAPTER THREE: VIEWSTAMP PASSAGE ANALYSIS

Chapter Four: Passage Elements and Formations

Chapter Five: The Questions And Answer Choices

CHAPTER SIX: PUTTING IT ALL TOGETHER

CHAPTER SEVEN: PRACTICE PASSAGES

CHAPTER EIGHT: TEST READINESS

GLOSSARY

About PowerScore

PowerScore is one of the nation's fastest growing test preparation companies. Founded in 1997, PowerScore offers GMAT, GRE, LSAT, SAT, and ACT preparation classes in over 150 locations in the U.S. and abroad. Preparation options include In Person courses, Accelerated courses, Live Online courses, On Demand courses, private tutoring, and admissions consulting. For more information, please visit our website at powerscore.com or call us at (800) 545-1750.

About the Authors

Dave Killoran, a graduate of Duke University, is an expert in test preparation with over 20 years of experience teaching classes for graduate school admissions tests. In addition to having written PowerScore's renowned *GMAT Critical Reasoning Bible* and many other popular publications, Dave has overseen the preparation of thousands of students and founded two national test preparation companies.

Jon Denning, a graduate of the Georgia Institute of Technology, oversees product creation and instructor training for all of the exam services PowerScore offers. He is also a Senior Instructor with 99th percentile scores on the LSAT, GMAT, GRE, SAT, and ACT, and for the past 15 years has assisted thousands of students in the college, graduate, and law school admissions processes.

Chapter One:
Introduction

Chapter One: Introduction

POWERSCORE®
TEST PREPARATION

Introduction

Welcome to *The PowerScore GMAT Reading Comprehension Bible*. We congratulate you on your savvy purchase—you now own the most advanced book ever published for GMAT Reading Comprehension! The purpose of this book is to provide you with a powerful and comprehensive system for attacking the various types of Reading Comprehension passages and questions that appear on the Graduate Management Admission Test (GMAT). By carefully studying and correctly applying the techniques we employ, we are certain that you will increase your GMAT Verbal score.

In an effort to clearly explain the fundamental principles of the Reading Comprehension section, this book contains substantial discussions on how to deconstruct the passages as you read, how to identify and attack the questions, and how to successfully avoid the traps set by the test makers. In doing so, we recommend techniques and approaches that have been tested in our live and on-demand preparation classes, through individual tutoring, and on the GMAT itself.

In order to effectively and efficiently apply our methods, we strongly recommend that you:

- Carefully read and re-read each of the concept discussions;

- Look at the explanation for the correct answer choice as well as the explanations for the incorrect answer choices once you have finished each question or example;

- Closely examine each problem and determine which elements led to the correct answer, and then study the analyses provided in the book and check them against your own work;

- Track every question that you miss or that you struggle with, and record each instance of difficulty in a performance tracker file or notebook.

By doing so, you will greatly increase your chances of quickly recognizing and reacting to key RC elements and ultimately maximizing your score.

If you are looking to further improve your GMAT score, we also recommend that you pick up copies of the renowned PowerScore GMAT Critical Reasoning Bible and GMAT Sentence Correction Bible. When combined with the Reading Comprehension Bible, you will have a formidable methodology for attacking the Verbal portion of the test. The other GMAT Bibles are available through our website at powerscore.com and at fine retailers.

This book also contains a variety of focused drills and exercises that supplement the discussion of techniques and question analysis. The drills help strengthen specific skills that are critical for GMAT excellence; for this reason they are as important as the GMAT questions themselves. In the answer keys to these drills we will often discuss important GMAT points, so we strongly advise you to read through all explanations even if you answered the question correctly.

Please note that this book is intended primarily not as a practice guide, but rather as a preparation guide. The purpose of the book is to teach you techniques and strategies, and we use a variety of examples and drills to that end. For practice questions, we strongly recommend picking up the Official Guides from GMAC, the makers of the GMAT. Those books contain hundreds of released GMAT questions that are perfect for trying out the approaches taught in this book.

How GMAT Studying is Different Than "Regular" Studying

Studying for the GMAT is different than studying for a history or chemistry test. In those disciplines, when you learn a fact or formula there is often a direct and immediate increase in your score on the exam. However, GMAT Reading Comprehension is not a fact-based measure; it is a test of reading and reasoning processes, so the correlation between learning an idea and seeing an instantaneous score improvement is not as strong.

In a sense, it is like learning to drive a car: even after you learn the rules of the road and the mechanics of the vehicle, the first several times you attempt to drive you are probably not a good driver at all. Nothing feels familiar or comes easily, and you are more likely a menace on the road than anything else (we certainly were!). But with time and proper practice—and a healthy dose of patience—you eventually reach a state of comfort, possibly even expertise, so that now getting behind the wheel is entirely natural and intuitive. Learning to routinely beat the GMAT Verbal section is no different!

Many of the tools we talk about in this book are fundamental to the GMAT, but they take time to integrate into how you approach the test, so at first they may seem slow and unwieldy. It will get better! For the time being, focus more on learning the ideas, and less on how they impact your practice test results. Once you have completed most of the book, you should shift into a practice testing mode that will allow you to work with the techniques and to make them second nature. This practice will cement the ideas and provide the greatest scoring impact.

A Note About Timing

As will be discussed in more detail later, time pressure is one of the defining challenges of taking the GMAT. Thus, when studying GMAT questions, there can be an overwhelming urge to focus on the clock. But for now you must resist that impulse. When you are first learning new concepts, take your time to understand what is being said and focus on the mechanics of how to apply the techniques presented. Don't worry about your pace! Once you have internalized the concepts and methodology, then you can start slowly working on timing as an element of your approach. The old adage about learning to walk before you can run applies perfectly to GMAT preparation, so concentrate more on how key strategies and ideas work than on your initial speed.

Additional Resources

MBA.com is the official website of the makers of the test, and they provide a variety of online resources and updates. As such, we strongly suggest that all *GMAT Reading Comprehension Bible* students visit www.mba.com on a frequent basis. This is also the website to visit in order to register for the test and to get information about your specific test center.

Because access to accurate and up-to-date information is critical, we have devoted a section of our website to *GMAT Reading Comprehension Bible* students. This free online resource area offers supplements to the book material, answers questions posed by students, and provides updates as needed. There is also an official book evaluation form that we strongly encourage you to use.

The exclusive *GMAT Reading Comprehension Bible* online area can be accessed at:

 **powerscore.com/grcb**

If we can assist you in your GMAT preparation in any way, or if you have any questions or comments, please do not hesitate to contact us via email at:

 **gmatbibles@powerscore.com**

We look forward to hearing from you!

A Brief Overview of the GMAT ━━━

The Graduate Management Admission Test is accepted for admission at over 2000 business schools worldwide. According to the Graduate Management Admission Council (GMAC), the makers of the test, "The GMAT is specifically designed to measure the verbal, quantitative, and writing skills of applicants for graduate study in business. It does not, however, presuppose any specific knowledge of business or other specific content areas, nor does it measure achievement in any particular subject areas."

The GMAT is given in English, and consists of four separately timed sections. The following tables break down those four sections, the question types in each, and the amount of time per section:

When you take an actual GMAT, you must present an ID. They will also take your picture and digitally scan your palm print pattern. These steps are taken in order to increase test security and to eliminate problems.

Analytical Writing Assessment		
Analysis of an Argument	30 minutes	1 question

Integrated Reasoning		
Graphics Interpretation		
Two-Part Analysis	30 minutes	12 questions
Table Analysis		
Multi-Source Reasoning		

Quantitative Section		
Data Sufficiency	62 minutes	31 questions
Problem Solving		

Verbal Section		
Critical Reasoning		
Reading Comprehension	65 minutes	36 questions
Sentence Correction		

On the following pages, we will examine each section in more detail.

GMAT Section Types

Analytical Writing Assessment

The Analytical Writing Assessment (AWA) consists of one 30-minute essay. The essay topic is called Analysis of an Argument.

The AWA was developed in 1994 in response to requests from business schools to add a writing component to the GMAT. Studies had shown that strong writing and communication abilities are critical for strong business performance, and business schools wanted to have a means of assessing candidates' communication abilities. According to GMAC, "The AWA is designed as a direct measure of your ability to think critically and to communicate your ideas...The Analysis of an Argument task tests your ability to formulate an appropriate and constructive critique of a specific conclusion based upon a specific line of thinking."

The Analytical Writing Assessment essay is initially scored on a 0 to 6 scale in half-point increments by two readers—one human reader, and one machine reader. The two scores are averaged to produce a final score for the essay.

The Integrated Reasoning Section

The Integrated Reasoning section was introduced in June 2012 in response to surveys that indicated what business schools felt were important skills for incoming students.

Twelve questions are presented in one of four formats: Graphics Interpretation, Two-Part Analysis, Table Analysis, and Multi-Source Reasoning. The questions focus on your data-handling skills, and feature unique elements of computer interaction. For example, you must synthesize and evaluate information from a variety of sources, organize and combine information in order to understand relationships, and manipulate information in order to solve problems.

A separate Integrated Reasoning score from 1 to 8 in single-point increments is produced based on your performance in this section.

The Quantitative Section

The Quantitative section of the GMAT is comprised of multiple-choice questions that cover mathematical subjects such as arithmetic, algebra, and geometry. There are two question types—Problem Solving and Data Sufficiency.

Problem Solving questions contain five separate answer choices, each of which offers a different solution to the problem. On a typical test, approximately 18-20 of the 31 Quantitative section questions will be in the Problem Solving format.

Data Sufficiency questions consist of a question followed by two numbered statements. You must determine if the numbered statements contain sufficient information to solve the problem—individually, together, or not at all. Each Quantitative section typically contains approximately 11-13 Data Sufficiency questions, and this type of problem is unique to the GMAT and can be exceptionally challenging.

The Verbal Section

The GMAT Verbal section is a test of your ability to read for content, analyze argumentation, and to recognize and correct written, grammatical errors. Accordingly, there are three types of problems—Reading Comprehension, Critical Reasoning, and Sentence Correction.

Reading Comprehension questions examine your ability to analyze large amounts of material for content and understanding. Usually four passages are presented that range up to 350 words in length, and each passage is accompanied by 3 to 5 questions. Passage topics are drawn from a variety of areas, including business, science, politics, law, and history.

Critical Reasoning questions present a short argument followed by a question such as: "Which of the following weakens the argument?" "Which of the following parallels the argument?" or "Which of the following must be true according to the argument?" The key to these questions is understanding the reasoning types and question types that frequently appear. Within the Verbal Section you will encounter approximately 10 to 14 Critical Reasoning questions.

For more help with Critical Reasoning questions, consult the PowerScore GMAT Critical Reasoning Bible.

Each Sentence Correction problem presents a sentence containing an underlined section. Five answer choices follow the problem, each suggesting a possible phrasing of the underlined section. The first answer is a repeat of the original underlined section, and the remaining four are different from the original. Your task is to analyze the underlined section and determine which of the answers offers the best phrasing.

Section Order

The test makers allow you some flexibility in the order in which you take each section of the test. You can choose one of three options for the section order on your GMAT:

Although the two 8-minute breaks are optional, you should always take the entire break time in order to avoid fatigue.

Option 1	Option 2	Option 3
Analytical Writing	Verbal	Quantitative
Integrated Reasoning	(First Break)	(First Break)
(First Break)	Quantitative	Verbal
Quantitative	(Second Break)	(Second Break)
(Second Break)	Integrated Reasoning	Integrated Reasoning
Verbal	Analytical Writing	Analytical Writing

So which order should you select? There is no one right answer for this, as everyone has different strengths and preferences. Some students want to get their weakest section out of the way or tackle it first when their brain is rested and ready; others may take their strongest section first to help build confidence. While preparing for the exam, experiment with different section orders and see which you prefer.

Experimental Questions

About 15% of the questions on the GMAT are experimental, with roughly 3 in Integrated Reasoning, 3 in Quant, and 6 in Verbal.

During the GMAT you will encounter questions that will not contribute to your score. These questions, known as "experimental" or "pre-test" questions, are used on future versions of the GMAT. Unfortunately, you will not be informed during the test as to which questions do not count, so you must give your best performance on each question.

The GMAT CAT Format

As opposed to the traditional paper-and-pencil format used by many other tests, the GMAT is administered on a computer. Consequently, only one question at a time is presented, the order of questions is not predetermined, and the test actually responds to your answers and shapes the exam in order to most efficiently arrive at your proper score. This format is known as a Computer Adaptive Test, or CAT.

For example, the first question in the Verbal or Quantitative section will be a medium difficulty question. If answered correctly, the computer will supply a somewhat harder question on the assumption that your score is somewhere above that level. If this next question is answered correctly, the following question will again be more difficult. This process continues until a question is missed. At that point, the test will supply a somewhat easier question as it tries to determine if you have reached your score "ceiling." By increasing or decreasing the difficulty of the questions based on prior response, the test attempts to quickly pinpoint your appropriate score level and then confirm that level. Consequently, the first several questions are used to broadly establish your general scoring range:

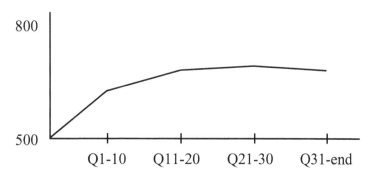

In the diagram above, correct responses to the first several questions lead to significant jumps in score, whereas later questions make smaller adjustments. A strong beginning followed by a weak finish will produce a higher score than a weak beginning followed by a strong finish. For this reason it is essential that your performance early in the section be as strong as possible, even if this requires using more than the average time allotted per question.

Special GMAT CAT Considerations

The CAT format has certain features that appreciably alter the testing experience:

- The CAT format does not allow you to "skip" a question; you cannot leave a question blank nor can you come back to a question. In order to move forward in the test you *must* answer the question on the screen. If you do not know the answer, you must make an educated guess. And since the test adapts to your previous responses, once you complete a question, you cannot return to that question.

- You cannot write on the computer screen, but you will be given a booklet of five "noteboards," which are basically spiral-bound laminated sheets of legal-sized paper. You may not erase your notes, but you can request additional noteboards.

- Facility with a computer is clearly an advantage; fast typing is also an advantage in the Analytical Writing Section where your response must be typed into the computer.

- The test penalizes examinees who do not finish all of the questions in a section. Thus, since the number of questions answered is incorporated into the calculation of scores, it is helpful that you complete every question in each section, even if you must guess on questions in order to do so. In other words, an incorrect response is better than no response.

- The results of your test (excluding the Writing score) are available at the conclusion of the exam.

Question Difficulty

Complicating the GMAT CAT scoring system is that question difficulty affects your overall score. Each question is assigned a predetermined "weight," and more difficult questions have a greater weight. Consequently, it is important that you answer difficult questions and not just "skip" any question that appears difficult. Answering fifteen easy questions will produce a lower score than answering fifteen difficult questions.

General Pacing

Since completing every question in a section is critical, pacing is of the utmost importance. Based purely on the number of questions and the total time per section, the following lists the average amount of time you can spend per question:

Integrated Reasoning Section	12 questions, 30 minutes
Average time per question	*2 minutes, 30 seconds*
Quantitative Section	31 questions, 62 minutes
Average time per question	*2 minutes, 0 seconds*
Verbal Section	36 questions, 65 minutes
Average time per question	*1 minute, 48 seconds*

Score-Specific Pacing

The following references provide alternate Quantitative and Verbal pacing strategies depending on desired score.

Basic Quantitative Strategy for various scoring ranges:		
700-800	Complete every question	average of just under 2 minutes per question
600-690	Attempt to complete every question	average of 2 minutes, 15 seconds per question, keep enough time to guess on uncompleted questions
500-590	Attempt to complete at least 75% of questions	average of 2 minutes, 35 seconds per question, keep enough time to guess on uncompleted questions

Basic Verbal Strategy for various scoring ranges:		
700-800	Complete every question	average of 1 minute, 45 seconds per question
600-690	Attempt to complete every question	average of 2 minutes per question, keep enough time to guess on uncompleted questions
500-590	Attempt to complete at least 75% of questions	average of 2 minutes, 20 seconds per question, keep enough time to guess on uncompleted questions

However, since the questions at the start of each section are more critical than later questions, a greater amount of time than the average can be allotted to the early questions, and then the pace can be accelerated as the section proceeds.

Timing and Practice

Not all of your practice needs to be timed, particularly as you develop foundational skills in Reading Comprehension. With that said, you do need to be prepared for the actual test, and the GMAT is, of course, time constrained.

A timer can be quite helpful as you develop your reading skills and begin to establish a comfortable Reading Comprehension speed, fast enough to maximize efficiency, but slow enough to allow sufficient retention of information from the passage. The timer allows you to make sure you are maintaining your ideal pace.

When you become a registered user at mba.com, you will be able to download free practice software that includes two full practice tests, and we recommend that you take a full practice test as you begin your preparation, for exposure to the types of questions and time constraints that you will be contending with on test day. Keep in mind, however, that your initial score provides little indication of your potential score; consider the first practice test an introduction to the GMAT and an initial mental endurance workout.

Computers and Noteboards

Taking a standardized test on a computer is an unusual experience. The natural tendency to mark up the page is thwarted since you cannot write on the computer screen. Consequently, the five noteboards provided by the on-site administrator are an important aid to a strong test performance. You may not erase your work, but you can request more noteboards during the test if you run out of space.

During the pre-test tutorial, or at the very beginning of your first section, use part of one noteboard to quickly draw out the following chart:

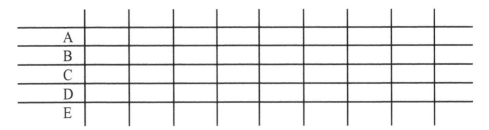

As you progress through each question, you can use the chart to keep track of eliminated answer choices as is necessary.

For example, if you are certain answer choices (A) and (C) are incorrect in problem #2, simply "X" them out on the chart:

	2							
A	X							
B								
C	X							
D								
E								

In this fashion you can overcome the inability to physically mark out answer choices on the computer screen.

You should also familiarize yourself with GMAT CAT computer controls since computer aptitude is clearly an advantage. The test is given on standard computers, and the free GMATPrep Software contains test tutorials to help you gain experience with the GMAT computer controls. In addition, in the Analytical Writing Section, your typing ability affects overall performance, and thus you must have at least basic typing skills.

GMAT Practice Tests vs. the GMAT CAT

Reading Comprehension questions are a bit different from the other GMAT question types in a few ways. Critical Reasoning questions appear one by one, each concerned with a single stimulus that is generally only a few lines long. The same goes for Sentence Correction questions, and for all of the questions in the Quantitative section. With GMAT Reading Comprehension, several questions are attached to the same passage, and you have to read a (relatively) lengthy passage before you can even attack the first question presented.

Mastery of the GMAT requires a comfort working with the presentation of a computer-based test. Familiarize yourself with the CAT as you prepare, to help ensure that there are no surprises on test day!

To allow students to familiarize themselves with the types of questions and concepts tested on the GMAT, GMAC publishes the Official Guide and has made several practice tests from previous administrations available for purchase as well. We strongly recommend that you make use of such materials; practicing with questions from previous GMATs can be a very effective way to prepare. As a general rule, what you see on their practice tests should provide a fairly accurate reflection of the actual exam, but you should be aware that with regard to Reading Comprehension in particular, what you see in the Official Guide will be a bit different from what you can expect to encounter on test day.

Since the test makers don't explicitly list the various ways in which the computer adaptive test will diverge from what you may have seen on practice tests, they are listed below for your consideration and review:

Passage Presentation

GMAT Reading Comprehension passages are presented on a computer screen, so you should avoid the habit of making notations directly on, within, or near the passage when you are working with paper practice materials. If you were to develop a reliance on underlining key information, for example, that could work against you on test day since you cannot underline words on the screen.

Number of Questions per Passage

Passages found in the GMAC practice tests and in the Official Guide are generally followed by three to eight questions, but you will not see any single passage accompanied by eight questions on test day. Instead, for any given passage the CAT tends to have a larger pool of questions from which just a few (generally three or four) are selected, based on the performance of the individual test taker.

Question Presentation

When a Reading Comprehension passage is presented on the GMAT, the computer format provides access to the passage on one side of the screen, with the questions presented, one at a time, on the other side. This means that you will not have the opportunity to assess the questions as a group or decide which question to do first, nor will you have any advanced notice of the number of questions that will follow any given passage.

Number of Questions and Passages per Section

The tests that have been released have included three Reading Comprehension passages accompanied by 18 to 23 questions. On test day, you can probably expect to see four passages accompanied by about three or four questions each, for a total of 12-15 Reading Comprehension questions in total.

Referenced Excerpts

Often, GMAT Reading Comprehension questions refer to specific terms or phrases from within a given passage. In the Official Guide, you will see such terms and excerpts referenced as follows:

The author uses the term "undaunted" in line 23 most probably to emphasize that

The passage suggests which of the following about the "traditional approach to patient care" on line 39?

On the real GMAT, when Reading Comprehension questions refer to words or phrases from the passages, those excerpts will not be referenced with line numbers. Instead, they will be highlighted in color within the passage.

The practice passages provided in the Official Guide and in released practice tests can be very helpful as you practice with the types of passages and questions that you will encounter on the GMAT. But as we have discussed, what you will be seeing on test day will be just a little different from what you may have seen in your official practice materials. If you know what to expect, though, these slight divergences shouldn't be *too* stressful. None of these differences should play a substantial role in your conceptual approach to Reading Comprehension, but awareness of these distinctions can be very helpful as you develop a familiarity and comfort with the test, and can be vital to achieving your highest potential score.

The GMAT Scoring Scale ■■■■■■■■

Every GMAT score report contains five sections:

- An Integrated Reasoning Score—on a scale of 1 to 8
- A Quantitative Score—on a scale of 6 to 51
- A Verbal Score—on a scale of 6 to 51
- A Total Score—on a scale of 200 to 800
- An Analytical Writing Assessment Score—on a scale of 0 to 6

The Quantitative and Verbal scores are combined to create the Total Score, which is given in 10-point increments. The Total Score is the one most familiar to GMAT test takers, and presented on the famous 200 to 800 scale, with 200 being the lowest score and 800 the highest score.

The Integrated Reasoning Score is scaled in 1-point increments, and does not contribute to your Total Score.

The Analytical Writing Assessment essay is initially scored on a 0 to 6 scale (in half-point increments) by two readers—one human reader, and one machine reader (basically, a computer scoring program). The two scores are averaged to produce a final score for your essay. Approximately 90% of all test takers receive a score of 3.5 or higher.

Your AWA score has no effect on your Total Score.

The GMAT Percentile Table ▬▬▬▬

It is important not to lose sight of what the GMAT Total Score actually represents. The 200 to 800 test scale contains 61 different possible scores. Each score places a student in a certain relative position compared to other test takers. These relative positions are represented through a percentile that correlates to each score. The percentile indicates where the test taker ranks in the overall pool of test takers. For example, a score of 700 represents the 88th percentile, meaning a student with a score of 700 scored better than 88 percent of the people who have taken the test in the last two years. The percentile is critical since it is a true indicator of your positioning relative to other test takers, and thus business school applicants.

It is important to remember that you do not have to answer every question correctly in order to receive an excellent GMAT score. There is room for error, and accordingly you should never let any single question occupy an inordinate amount of your time.

Charting out the entire percentage table yields a rough "bell curve." The number of test takers in the 200s and 700s is very low (only 12% of all test takers receive a score in the 700s; only 3% in the 200s), and most test takers are bunched in the middle, comprising the "top" of the bell. In fact, approximately two-thirds of all test takers score between 400 and 600 inclusive.

The median score on the GMAT scale is roughly 560. The median, or middle score is the score at which approximately 50% of test takers have a lower score and 50% of test takers have a higher score.

The Use of the GMAT ██████████████

The use of the GMAT in business school admissions is a complex, and often controversial, process. At most schools an "admissions index" consisting of your GMAT score and your undergraduate grade point average is used to help determine your standing relative to other applicants, and a sufficiently high admissions index virtually guarantees your admission. This means that your GMAT score is one of the most important determinants of the type of school you can attend.

However, for all the significance of the GMAT, the exam is not without its flaws. As a standardized test currently given in a computer adaptive format there are a number of valuable skills that the GMAT cannot measure, including listening skills, note-taking ability, perseverance and work ethic, and many more. GMAC is aware of these limitations and on a regular basis they caution all business school admissions offices against using GMAT scores as the *sole* admission criterion.

Still, because the test ultimately produces a quantified and easily-compared result for each student, the tendency to rank applicants is strong. Fortunately, once you get to business school the GMAT is largely forgotten. For the time being consider the test a temporary, but surmountable hurdle you must overcome in order to reach your ultimate goal.

For more information on the GMAT, or to register for the test, contact the Graduate Management Admission Council at their website at www.mba.com.

Chapter Two:
The Basics of Reading Comprehension

Chapter Two: The Basics of Reading Comprehension

The Reading Comprehension Passages

GMAT Reading Comprehension passages can be based on a variety of topics from the social sciences, the physical or biological sciences, humanities, or business related fields such as economics or marketing. While you may be unfamiliar with some passage topics, the Official Guide states that "neither the passages nor the questions assume knowledge of the topics discussed." Each passage is accompanied by questions that require you to interpret the passage, apply information from the passage, or draw inferences from your reading of the passage. These questions are presented on a split computer screen, allowing the reading passage to remain visible on the left side of the screen, while the associated question and answer choices appear on the right.

The GMAC does not provide exact information about the number of passages that may appear on any given test, nor the basis on which the adaptive test selects passages or questions; the Official Guide merely indicates that "the number of questions associated with each passage may vary." With that said, our research indicates that you can expect to see three or four passages on the test (and in rare cases, five). These passages are divided into two types: shorter passages, under 200 words, comprised of one to three paragraphs (test takers often encounter two or three such passages on the GMAT) and longer passages of up to 350 words that include three to five paragraphs (most test takers can expect to see one or two such passages on the test).

Note that the number of questions that may accompany any given passage in released tests does not reflect a clear correlation with the length of the passage itself (longer passages are sometimes followed by as few as three questions, while shorter passages are in some cases followed by as many as eight). Our research, however, suggests that on the actual GMAT, shorter passages are often accompanied by three questions, with longer passages often followed by four. Keep in mind, though, that given the adaptive nature of the test and the limited information provided by the GMAC, there is no way to predict with complete certainty how many Reading Comprehension passages or questions you will see when you take the GMAT; as you consider your ideal pace, remember to remain somewhat flexible, as the test makers provide no guarantees!

The total number of Reading Comprehension questions in a given Verbal section varies, but will be between 12 and 15, spread over three or four passages (rarely five, though GMAC makes no promises to the contrary). Answering each question obviously requires more than merely reading the question prompt, which is why the time per point earned on a RC question is relatively high (it averages out to be between 1 ½ and 2 minutes per point, depending on your reading speed).

As discussed previously, the amount of time you spend on a given Reading Comprehension passage will vary depending on its length, complexity, and the number of questions that follow:

A. *Length*. According to GMAC, passage length cannot exceed 350 words. You are likely to come across short and long passages, each of which requires a different allocation of time (see table below).

B. *Complexity*. Overly technical passages or passages covering complex or unfamiliar topics will require a somewhat slower pace for complete comprehension.

C. *Questions*. Test makers often write six to eight questions for each passage, but usually only present three or four of those on the Computer Adaptive Test. Since not every piece of information provided in the passage will be critical, it is imperative to focus on those aspects of the passage that are most likely to be relevant to the questions that will follow.

Proper pacing technique in reading comprehension requires an active, aggressive approach to the text; your goal should be to have a general understanding of structure, viewpoints, purpose, tone, etc., rather than focus on each and every detail presented in the passage (when local questions require detailed information, you can always refer to the relevant portion of the passage). Despite the variability of passage length, difficulty, and number of questions per passage, it can be helpful to keep a few benchmark numbers in mind. The ideal reading speed for the GMAT is somewhere in the range of 125-150 words per minute (WPM). The benchmarks below are provided for comparative purposes only: use them as a rough guide as you develop your own ideal reading speed for the test.

Passage Type	Word Count	Reading Pace	Time per Passage	Number of Questions	Time per Question
Short	roughly 150-200	Faster	1 ½ min	3-4	1 ½ min
Short	roughly 150-200	Slower	2 min	3-4	1 min
Long	roughly 250-350	Faster	3 min	3-4 (rarely 5)	1 ½ min
Long	roughly 250-350	Slower	3 ½ min	3-4 (rarely 5)	1 min

You have 65 minutes to complete the Verbal section, or about one minute 48 seconds per question on average, but that average does not account for the time you will need to read the passages. If you can complete each question in about a minute on average, that should leave roughly three minutes to complete a longer passage, and a little over two minutes to finish a shorter passage. Of course, the amount of time you spend on each passage set will vary with the length and reading level of the passage, as well as the complexity of the accompanying questions. We recommend that you develop a flexible pacing strategy as you determine your optimal reading speed and increase your familiarity with the types of passages and questions that you will encounter on test day.

Why Reading Comprehension?

Each portion of the GMAT verbal section is designed to test abilities required of students earning a Master of Business Administration degree, or MBA. The Critical Reasoning questions measure your skills in argumentation and logic. The Sentence Correction questions test your ability to understand and apply the complex rules of English grammar. Reading Comprehension passages and questions test skills particularly important to business school students and professionals. MBA candidates are required to read significant portions of dense text throughout their studies, and business professionals must often be prepared to do the same in the normal course of business.

The Section Directions

Each Reading Comprehension passage is prefaced by the following directions:

> "The questions in this group are based on the contents of a passage. After reading the passage, choose the best answer to each question. Answer all questions following the passage on the basis of what is stated or implied in the passage."

Because these directions precede each Reading Comprehension passage, you should familiarize yourself with them now. Once the GMAT begins, *never* waste time reading the directions for any section.

Let us examine these directions more closely. Consider the following sentence: "Answer all questions following the passage on the basis of what is stated or implied in the passage." Thus, the test makers indicate that you are to use the statements of the author of the passage to prove and disprove answer choices. You do not need to bring in additional information aside from the typical ideas that the average American would be expected to believe on the basis of generally known and accepted facts.

For example, you would be expected to understand the *basics* of how the weather works, or how supply and demand works, but not the specifics of either. Please note this does not mean that the GMAT cannot set up scenarios where they discuss ideas that are extreme or outside the bounds of common knowledge, such as a passage about a difficult scientific or legal concept. The test makers can and do discuss complex or obscure ideas; in these cases, they give you context for the situation by providing additional, explanatory information.

Always be sure to read every answer choice before making a selection. If you read only one or two answer choices and then decide you have the correct one, you could end up choosing an answer that has some merit but is not as good as a later answer. One of the test makers' favorite tricks is to place a highly attractive wrong answer choice immediately before the correct choice in the hopes that you will pick the wrong answer and then move to the next question without reading any of the other answer choices.

Passage Topics

Reading Comprehension passages are drawn from a wide variety of disciplines, including science, business, and humanities. Thus, you will typically encounter passage sets with widely varying topical matter.

Please note that the topic of the passage is not necessarily indicative of the level of difficulty. That is, some Science passages are easy, some are difficult. The same goes for Business related passages, Humanities passages, etc. In the next chapter we will discuss how to attack any type of passage, and we will discuss how the underlying structure of passages can be analyzed regardless of the passage topic. Topic is examined here so that you understand the nature of what you will be reading. In some cases, knowing the topic can help you make informed decisions about the viewpoints that will be presented therein, and in many cases students perform better when passage subject matter is familiar to them.

What's Really Being Tested?

When you consider the section directions and the nature/topics of the passages, it becomes clear that the exam makers are really testing two basic concepts: your ability to understand what was said and your short-term memory. Neither of those tasks sounds very challenging because, after all, we work with each one every single day, so how difficult could these passages be? In practice, however, the difficulty can be quite high, especially because these tasks often involve working with unfamiliar topics under intense time pressure.

We'll soon be discussing tools to make each task easier, but in the meantime take a moment to understand the way in which you are being tested, and how important it is for you to know what was said and to be able to remember where the author said it. Part of the process of preparing for this challenge is knowing what you need to do, and the earlier you lock on to the concepts that underlie this section, the easier Reading Comprehension will ultimately become for you.

Approaching the Passages

Every Reading Comprehension passage set contains two separate parts: the passage on one side of the screen, and the questions and answer choices on the other. When examining the two parts for the first time, students sometimes wonder about the best general strategy for attacking the passages: Should I skim the passage? Should I read just the first and last sentence of each paragraph? Should I look at the first question beforehand?

The answer is that your basic strategy should be to:

Read the passage in its entirety and then attack the questions.

What this means is you should first read the entire passage with an eye towards capturing its main ideas, viewpoints, tone, and structure, and then proceed to the questions. Although this may seem like a reasonable, even obvious, approach, we mention it here because some GMAT texts advocate skimming the passage.

We will discuss how to systematically break down each passage shortly.

With that in mind, let us take a moment to discuss some of the various reading approaches that you *might* consider using, but should avoid:

1. **DO NOT merely skim the passage**, then do each question, returning to the passage as needed.

   In theory, it might seem that skimming could add some degree of efficiency, but in practice this is not the case. In fact, this approach actually reflects a fundamental misunderstanding of the nature of the Reading Comprehension passages.

   Skimming might be sufficient to absorb lighter materials, such as newspaper or magazine articles, but that is because those types of passages are written with simplicity in mind. A newspaper editor wants readers to know half the story by the time they have read the headline, and magazines put the most attention-grabbing pictures on their covers; these publications are trying to draw you in, to entice you to make a purchase or form a belief. The makers of the GMAT, on the other hand, are well aware that they are dealing with a captive audience; they do not feel any pressure to entertain (as you may have noticed), and thus passages are chosen based on completely different criteria.

For many, skimming is a natural reaction to a time-constrained test, but unfortunately the test makers are well aware of this tendency—the passages they use are chosen in part because they evade quick and simple analysis. In practice, the time "saved" on the front end by skimming a passage is more than lost on the back end. In answering the questions the skimmer invariably finds the need to constantly go back and re-read, and is often not sufficiently familiar with the passage structure to locate relevant reference points quickly.

2. **DO NOT read just the first and last sentence of each paragraph** of the passage and then do each question, returning to the passage as needed.

This type of "super-skimming" is also tempting—the prospect of breezing through the passages quickly picking up the big picture ideas is appealing, after all—but again, GMAT passages unfortunately are not constructed to allow for this technique: this shorthand and ineffective approach is based in part on the common misconception that the main idea of every paragraph appears in the first or last sentence. While this may occasionally hold true, we will see that this is far from guaranteed. After all, the makers of the GMAT are extremely sharp, and certainly familiar with these common, shortcut approaches. So naturally many passages will not follow this general rule—the test makers do not like for passages to fall victim to such a simple, formulaic analysis.

This approach is basically an even more simplistic and fruitless variation of skimming that provides neither substantive knowledge of the information in the passage nor familiarity with the structure sufficient to locate important reference points later on.

The bottom line is that your reading approach must be maximally effective for all passages. The flawed strategies above, although perhaps effective in some limited contexts, do not consistently produce solid results, and thus they should *not* be part of your basic approach to each passage.

Basic Passage Strategy

Having discussed some common practices to avoid, let us now consider the proper way to attack a GMAT passage. The following is the *basic* approach to use, and in subsequent chapters we will expand on these points. So, for now, simply consider this the broad template you should use to attack each passage:

1. Read the passage for an understanding of structure and detail, for viewpoints and for themes, and for the author's tone. Take notes (on your noteboard) as needed to help you better understand what is being said.

2. Focus on understanding what is being said in each sentence and paragraph, which means you cannot skim or read so fast the words make little sense. At the end of each paragraph, pause briefly and consider what you have just read, and mentally distill the key points of that paragraph into a quick summary that translates the text into simpler terms. Note too how the paragraphs fit together to create the overall passage structure.

3. After reading the passage, stop for a moment and consider the entirety of the author's message and what you've been told, as well as by whom (the viewpoints expressed). You can be explicit in your analysis rather than worrying about "reading between the lines" at this point.

4. As you move to the questions, expect to occasionally look back to the passage, but attempt to only do so when necessary to confirm your answers.

These are the primary steps to a proper approach to the Reading Comprehension passages; each step will be discussed in greater detail shortly.

Your Focus While Reading

Have you ever reached the second, or even third paragraph of an article or reading passage and suddenly realized that you had no idea what you had just been reading? Many students have had this uncomfortable experience at some point. How are we able to read with our eyes while our minds are elsewhere? Ironically, it is our familiarity with the act of reading that has allowed many to develop the "skill" to do so without 100% focus. This approach might be fine for the morning newspaper, a favorite magazine, or an email from a friend, but these writings tend to be more simply composed and unaccompanied by difficult questions. GMAT passages, on the other hand, are chosen for their tendency to elude this type of unfocused approach. Faced with this type of reading, many people "zone out" and lose concentration. Thus, your state of mind when approaching these passages is extremely important.

Giving yourself the simple instruction, "read the passage," allows your mind too much free rein to wander as your eyes gloss over the words. Instead, you should take a more active approach, breaking down the passage as you go, creating something of a running translation, and effectively mentally outlining the passage, as we will discuss further in the coming pages.

Yes, it can be difficult to focus for long stretches of time, but you must train yourself through practice to keep your concentration at as high a level as possible. This last point is key: you must regularly practice a focused attack when you are reading to ensure an optimal performance.

When starting a section, keep the following tips in mind:

- Channel any nervous energy into intensity.

- Enjoy reading the passages—make them into a game or learning exercise. And regularly remind yourself that you *do* enjoy it (even if it feels a bit contrived).

- If you lose focus, immediately pause, take a deep breath, refocus, and then return more intently to the task at hand.

- Read aggressively, not passively. Actively engage the material and think about the consequences of what you are reading. The passage was written for a reason, what is it?

GMAT reading is unlike the reading most people engage in on a day-to-day basis. For example, newspapers and magazines, and even most novels, are written with an eye towards presenting the material in the clearest and most interesting fashion possible. LSAT Reading Comprehension passages, on the other hand, are not written in this manner. They are often written in an academic style that is, at times, intentionally dense and complex.

We will talk more on the following pages about the mentality described here, but note that each of these recommendations applies not just to the GMAT, but to your non-GMAT reading behavior as well! To fully develop and internalize this process, we strongly encourage you to become a routine daily reader of all manner of academic text—whether online or hardcopy—such as articles and content found in The Economist, National Geographic, Wired, Scientific American, The Wall Street Journal, and any other sources of reasonably dense passages. Make it a habit to scrutinize at least one or two articles daily, approaching them exactly as you would a GMAT passage, and you'll find your Reading Comprehension performance naturally improves as a result!

Finally, that last bullet is particularly critical, as it introduces a technique at the heart of any successful reading performance: Active Reading. In fact, this concept is so central to the techniques outlined in this book that we will examine it directly and at length later in the chapter (including relevant drills to help you hone your skills), and return to it as a part of every subsequent passage discussion.

Your Attitude While Reading

Many students approach the Reading Comprehension passages with some anxiety, concerned about the prospect of reading dense passages with difficult structures and unfamiliar terminology. Couple that concern with the generally dull nature of most passages and it's little wonder people's minds have a tendency to wander.

To combat this potential disinterest, maintaining the proper mindset is vital. Simply put, concerns about boredom or anxiety can quickly become self-fulfilling prophecies in Reading Comprehension. To perform well then, you must avoid a negative attitude and you must instead approach the passages with a positive, energetic, and enthusiastic attitude. This upbeat approach is something that all high-scorers maintain, and is something that you can learn to create if you do not have it already.

A positive attitude is perhaps the most underrated factor in GMAT success. Virtually all high-scoring students expect to do well on the GMAT, and this mind set helps them avoid distractions during the exam, and overcome any adversity they might face.

How can you make the passages more interesting and turn them into a positive experience? Here are two common methods:

- Many students approach the passages as academic learning exercises and hope to find some fun new fact or interesting information (don't laugh, it happens often!). When you begin reading with the expectation that you will learn something new, the passage becomes easier to read and more engaging.

- Some students approach the passages as puzzles to solve, as if they have been challenged to navigate a maze of sorts (and this is a fairly accurate description). For certain personalities, the idea of a beatable challenge stimulates their competitive nature and makes it easier for them to focus.

The ideas above are not the only ways to make the reading more enjoyable, and you may have your own method. Regardless, the key is to look at these passages as an exercise to enjoy (rather than suffer through). The truth of the matter is that if you do not try to enjoy reading the passages or get some value from them, you will be hard-pressed to perform at your best.

Some students get annoyed by the academic style of writing of the exam, but this is just part of the test. The passages in this section are not meant to be easy, and the test makers know that the way the passages are written and constructed can be off-putting to many students. You must simply ignore this situation, and take on the passages as a challenge.

Note too that while strong readers obviously have many advantages on this test, becoming a more proficient reader has significant value in other contexts, as well. As you practice applying the approaches discussed in this book, keep in mind that they are applicable to reading in general, and not meant solely to help you achieve a high GMAT score (even if that is the *main* goal)!

Understanding the *Type* of Difficulty in the Passages

There is a widespread misconception among test takers that because one's reading level is difficult to improve (having been developed over many years), one's performance on the Reading Comprehension passages is also unlikely to change. But this belief reflects a common misunderstanding that GMAT Reading Comprehension passages address deep concepts that are inherently challenging, and thus initial reading ability invariably determines performance. Fortunately, this is not accurate!

First, while some of the concepts can be unusual or challenging, keep in mind that passage authors only have about a half of a page to get their points across (350 words or fewer), and thus are limited as to the degree of depth that can be reached. This is not to say that these passages are simple, but that the challenge often comes from sources other than broad conceptual difficulty or deep topical analysis. And no matter what, everything you need to know to answer the questions is there in the passage.

Second, the GMAT is designed not only as a test of conceptual abilities—in many cases it is also a test of intimidation. So, how do the test makers ensure that the passages are challenging? Sometimes by choosing subjects that seem daunting; many passages are based on esoteric topics, or filled with sophisticated-sounding scientific or technical terms. It is vital that you avoid intimidation as a response to words or phrases which you have never seen. Since the makers of the GMAT do not expect or require outside knowledge with regard to Reading Comprehension passage topics, unfamiliar terms or phrases will almost always be surrounded by context clues. These issues will be covered further in our discussion of reading strategy; for now the key point is to understand that unfamiliar words or phrases do not necessarily make a passage any more conceptually difficult, as long as you do not allow these novel terms or phrases to overwhelm you. Stay confident, remain undaunted by such language, and try to see the basic ideas within the passage as you read.

On the following pages are two drills that test and reinforce the ability to simplify dense text into more understandable and accessible language.

Concept Drill

Language Simplification Drill I

Read each of the following sentences, and in the space that follows rephrase each in a simpler, more efficient writing style. *Answers begin on page 37*

> Example: The law protects executives from incurring personal liability for their conduct while working for their companies, but such indemnification rights are not unlimited.
>
> Basic Translation:
> *The law protects executives for their conduct, but only up to a point.*

1. The jurors will probably not be inclined to acquiesce to the defendant's plea for mercy.

   Basic Translation: _____
   _____
   _____
   _____

2. Expensive machinery is rarely, if ever, a necessary precondition for facilitation and enhancement of the manufacturing process.

   Basic Translation: _____
   _____
   _____
   _____

3. While there is some wisdom behind prohibiting the use of non-renewable resources, such an injunction does not preclude the use of renewable resources.

   Basic Translation: _____
   _____
   _____
   _____

Language Simplification Drill I

4. The Prime Minister's recent announcement reaffirms his party's long-standing belief that a policy of nuclear deterrence is generally incompatible with long-lasting peace.

Basic Translation: _____

_____

_____

_____

5. The requirement to document all tax-deductible expenses imposes a heavy burden on some taxpayers, though it does not obviate the need for compliance with all other provisions of the tax code as well.

Basic Translation: _____

_____

_____

_____

6. We strongly oppose the allocation of healthcare spending from the public to the private sector, which not only contradicts the government's alleged reluctance to increased private sector spending, but also threatens to disrupt continuity of care and deprive the public of medical services.

Basic Translation: _____

_____

_____

_____

Language Simplification Drill I

7. Unless the candidate clarifies his recent statements, his position on several integral issues will be likely the subject of widespread misinterpretation.

Basic Translation: _____

_____

_____

_____

8. The use of complicated wording as an overall literary technique does not always detract from the intended meaning of the text, though the ironic prevalence of this approach in some lowbrow literary journals raises important questions about the degree to which complexity of language may be correlated with simplicity of thought.

Basic Translation: _____

_____

_____

_____

Language Simplification Drill I Answer Key—page 34

1. *The jurors will probably not be inclined to acquiesce to the defendant's plea for mercy.*

Jurors will probably not be merciful to the defendant.

2. *Expensive machinery is rarely, if ever, a necessary precondition for facilitation and enhancement of the manufacturing process.*

Manufacturing does not require expensive machinery.

3. *While there is some wisdom behind prohibiting the use of non-renewable resources, such an injunction does not preclude the use of renewable resources.*

The ban against using non-renewable resources allows for the use of renewable resources.

4. *The Prime Minister's recent announcement reaffirms his party's long-standing belief that a policy of nuclear deterrence is generally incompatible with long-lasting peace.*

The Prime Minister restated his party's belief that the strategy of nuclear deterrence is not compatible with long term peace.

5. *The requirement to document all tax-deductible expenses imposes a heavy burden on some taxpayers, though it does not obviate the need for compliance with all other provisions of the tax code as well.*

One must comply with all provisions of the tax code; documenting one's tax-deductible expenses is not enough.

6. *We strongly oppose the allocation of healthcare spending from the public to the private sector, which not only contradicts the government's alleged reluctance to increased private sector spending, but also threatens to disrupt continuity of care and deprive the public of medical services.*

The author is unhappy with the current government. The government claims not to want increased private sector spending, but now healthcare spending has been shifted from the public to the private sector. According to the author, this has deprived some people of medical services.

Language Simplification Drill I Answer Key

7. *Unless the candidate clarifies his recent statements, his position on several integral issues will be likely the subject of widespread misinterpretation.*

   If the candidate doesn't clarify what he intended to say, many people will probably misinterpret his recent statements.

8. *The use of complicated wording as an overall literary technique does not always detract from the intended meaning of the text, though the ironic prevalence of this approach in some lowbrow literary journals raises important questions about the degree to which complexity of language may be correlated with simplicity of thought.*

   Complicated wording might convey the intended meaning of the text, though complex language may often reflect much simpler concepts.

Language Simplification Drill II

Now that you've practiced with shorter samples of challenging language, the following is an optional advanced drill designed to hone your skills of translation. Your goal once again is to simplify the language in each example, relaying the same basic ideas in a more straightforward manner. Note: This drills should be taken as an untimed exercise; we suggest that you take as much time as necessary to develop and reinforce this valuable skill. *Answers begin on page 45*

Example:

Many of the notably acerbic comments regarding the author's latest work were made by critics who sadly lacked the intellectual wherewithal necessary to understand the nuanced message of the beautifully written, epic tome. Unfortunately, the efforts of many of these purported sophisticates to break through the esoteric language often used by the academic writer were met, evidently, with limited success.

Basic Translation:
Some critiques were harsh, because critics tried but couldn't understand the author's big book.

1. Recent scholarship on the role of Eskimo women in ritual practice often relies on the dubious assumption that female participation in this activity merely supported the male role. Such interpretations of complementarity not only undervalue the distinctly unique and indispensable role of women in ritual practice, but also impose a decidedly patriarchal viewpoint upon its subject.

    Basic Translation: _____
    _____
    _____
    _____

2. Comprehensive plans are statements of local governments' objectives and standards for future land development, including distribution of population, density, and infrastructure. Because such plans are usually prepared by experts, the standards they set are often overly technocratic for the complex and ever-changing area of urban planning. As a result the practical enforceability of these standards remains somewhat dubious in some of the fastest-growing municipalities.

    Basic Translation: _____
    _____
    _____
    _____

Language Simplification Drill II

3. Professor Lavin's simplistic interpretation of Hieronymus Bosch's disquieting religious paintings is more revealing of the professor's own inadequacies than of those that allegedly plagued the subject of his critique. Indeed, Lavin's attempts to explain Bosch's style as the result of a mental illness are as hackneyed as they are predictable, symptomatic of the cultural conventions to which many contemporary historians inadvertently cling.

Basic Translation: _____

_____

_____

_____

4. The recently introduced city tax on cigarettes seeks to curb smoking by imposing a significant financial disincentive on people who choose to continue smoking. Some critics have contended that the tax can inadvertently lead to a counterproductive effect, because many residents resort to buying cigarettes in bulk from vendors outside the city. Studies show, however, that smoking trends correlate rather poorly with smokers' perception of the quantity of cigarettes available to them at any given time. These critics' fears are therefore unwarranted.

Basic Translation: _____

_____

_____

_____

5. One of the writer's major critiques of Western theater targets its dialogue as a text-bound performance whose compulsory repetition is devoid of spontaneity and therefore lacking in true meaning. The compulsion to repeat the text, however, can yield different interpretations, as the dialogue through which characters convey their versions of the written text can itself be a source of spontaneity in the performance of that text.

Basic Translation: _____

_____

_____

_____

Language Simplification Drill II

6. Under some common law jurisdictions, for an offer and acceptance to constitute a valid contract the acceptance of the offer must meet and correspond with the offer in every respect, including the manner in which each is made. Not every variance between offer and acceptance, however, should render the intended acceptance ineffective or preclude formation of a contract, because acceptance can assume a variety of forms.

    Basic Translation: _____

    _____

    _____

    _____

7. One of the main goals of a criminal justice system is to optimize the control of crime by devising a set of punishments whose magnitude is sufficient to deter a reasonable person from committing any given crime. Although deterrence is an intuitively compelling strategic goal, there is a growing skepticism about the deterrent effect of criminal law itself. For instance, rather than imposing draconian sentencing guidelines for illegal drug users, there is a strong deterrence argument in favor of a public health doctrine that depicts the consequences of using such substances in order to discourage their use.

    Basic Translation: _____

    _____

    _____

    _____

8. Lawmakers argue that governance results from a fundamentally normative project of deliberation and consent. However, the modalities of deliberation and contractual obligation depend not upon the stability of civil government but rather on its occasional failure to deliver upon the promise it creates. Granted, such failures can be rightfully viewed as temporary setbacks, but they eventually occasion the discourse that is a hallmark of a well-functioning democracy.

    Basic Translation: _____

    _____

    _____

    _____

Language Simplification Drill II

2

9. In the absence of a statute providing otherwise, the admitting physician at McLean Hospital was under no legal obligation to render professional services to Jack Johnson, who was not a patient of the hospital at the time he arrived there. Regardless of whether one finds doctrinal or moral grounds for establishing a duty to treat, neither the existence of a license law nor the possession of a license to practice medicine can be construed as instruments that enlarge a physician's duty in regard to accepting an offered patient, because such laws are essentially a preventive, not a compulsory, measure.

Basic Translation: _____

_____

_____

_____

10. There is little credibility to the claim that even a politically polarized nation can distinguish between legitimate calls to action and the voices of messianic demagoguery. To speak without listening is an exercise in futility, for no matter how informed or erudite the views, they are bound to fall on deaf ears. Unfortunately, the same cannot be said about shouting.

Basic Translation: _____

_____

_____

_____

Language Simplification Drill II

11. Scholars of Antonin Artaud often argue that the dramatic effects of the satirical genre were not entirely consistent with his philosophy of truth and illusion. Whereas satire uses humor to ridicule the topical issues of the day, for Artaud the only "truths" worth deriding are supposedly those that cannot be proven as such, and may, in fact, be false. It would be too facile to assume, however, that by imbuing his plays with futuristic elements and absurd plot lines, Artaud drew a line between illusion and reality, or—worse—protected the sanctity of politics from satire's corrosive effects. A play need not be credible to be topical. As a skilled dramaturge, Artaud blurred the distinction between the boundaries we take for granted, often staging them as conditions for their mutually assured destruction.

Basic Translation: _____

_____

_____

_____

12. Socrates defines timocracy as a regime closest to, but decidedly inferior to, aristocracy. However, the language used to differentiate them makes such proximity both essential and unsettling. The surprise emerging from the passage on timocracy lies precisely in a dialectic whose attainment of regime derivation and differentiation depends on a certain failure to obliterate difference and faction as constitutive elements of either regime. In seeing both regimes as mutually constitutive and co-extensive, rather than oppositional or mutually exclusive, Socrates inadvertently questions the valorized difference between the two.

Basic Translation: _____

_____

_____

_____

Language Simplification Drill II

13. Scientists who reject the notion that excessive exposure to sunlight in tropical areas increases the risk of melanoma cannot reliably conclude that their theories cannot be disproved. Granted, none of the studies showing a correlation between ultraviolet radiation and skin cancer were conducted in tropical areas, and many of them failed to control for exposure to other potential carcinogens such as diet and smoking. Nevertheless, lack of evidence for a particular claim should not be interpreted as evidence undermining that claim.

Basic Translation: _____

_____

_____

_____

14. More than a theory of governance proscribing the framework of a rather fragile social contract, Kobe's ideology describes the quintessence of a social contract that rescues us from the vicissitudes of anarchy. By relying upon the modality of retrospection, Kobe achieves his goal from the very vantage point it seeks to address—the vantage point of the modern constitutional state. Admittedly, such an ideology is a work of contradictions that resists a simple explanation, revealing in form as well as content a profound struggle with the contingency of its time. But this is true of most, if not all, doctrinal texts.

Basic Translation: _____

_____

_____

_____

Language Simplification Drill II Answer Key—page 39

As you consider the answers below, keep in mind that your responses need not match them exactly. If your basic translations look a bit different, that's fine—again, the basic goal is to practice taking challenging language and expressing the same ideas in a more straightforward and comprehensible way.

1. *Recent scholarship on the role of Eskimo women in ritual practice often relies on the dubious assumption that female participation in this activity merely supported the male role. Such interpretations of complementarity not only undervalue the distinctly unique and indispensable role of women in ritual practice, but also impose a decidedly patriarchal viewpoint upon its subject.*

   The study of Eskimo women often underestimates their unique and important role in ritual practice, wrongly portraying them from a patriarchal perspective as just supporting the men.

2. *Comprehensive plans are statements of local governments' objectives and standards for future land development, including distribution of population, density, and infrastructure. Because such plans are usually prepared by experts, the standards they set are often overly technocratic for the complex and ever-changing area of urban planning. As a result the practical enforceability of these standards remains somewhat dubious in some of the fastest-growing municipalities.*

   Local governments' comprehensive plans for future development may be too rigid to apply to some types of urban land development, an area that is always changing.

3. *Professor Lavin's simplistic interpretation of Hieronymus Bosch's disquieting religious paintings is more revealing of the professor's own inadequacies than of those that allegedly plagued the subject of his critique. Indeed, Lavin's attempts to explain Bosch's style as the result of a mental illness are as hackneyed as they are predictable, symptomatic of the cultural conventions to which many contemporary historians inadvertently cling.*

   The professor's interpretation of Bosch's religious paintings, as having resulted from mental illness, is too simplistic, revealing the professor's own shortcomings, not those of the painter.

4. *The recently introduced city tax on cigarettes seeks to curb smoking by imposing a significant financial disincentive on people who choose to continue smoking. Some critics have contended that the tax can inadvertently lead to a counterproductive effect, because many residents resort to buying cigarettes in bulk from vendors outside the city. Studies show, however, that smoking trends correlate rather poorly with smokers' perception of the quantity of cigarettes available to them at any given time. These critics' fears are therefore unwarranted.*

   Critics fear that the city tax on cigarettes might encourage people to smoke more, not less, because smokers would start buying cigarettes in bulk. These fears are thus unjustified.

Language Simplification Drill II Answer Key

5. *One of the writer's major critiques of Western theater targets its dialogue as a text-bound performance whose compulsory repetition is devoid of spontaneity and therefore lacking in true meaning. The compulsion to repeat the text, however, can yield different interpretations, as the dialogue through which characters convey their versions of the written text can itself be a source of spontaneity in the performance of that text.*

The writer's critique of Western theater is too harsh, because the same text can be performed and interpreted differently.

6. *Under some common law jurisdictions, for an offer and acceptance to constitute a valid contract the acceptance of the offer must meet and correspond with the offer in every respect, including the manner in which each is made. Not every variance between offer and acceptance, however, should render the intended acceptance ineffective or preclude formation of a contract, because acceptance can assume a variety of forms.*

In some jurisdictions, common law requires an offer to be in the same form as an acceptance, but not every variation weakens the validity of the contract.

7. *One of the main goals of a criminal justice system is to optimize the control of crime by devising a set of punishments whose magnitude is sufficient to deter a reasonable person from committing any given crime. Although deterrence is an intuitively compelling strategic goal, there is a growing skepticism about the deterrent effect of criminal law itself. For instance, rather than imposing draconian sentencing guidelines for illegal drug users, there is a strong deterrence argument in favor of a public health doctrine that depicts the consequences of using such substances in order to discourage their use.*

Stricter punishments do not deter criminals as much as we think. It may be better to discourage illegal drug use by showing its effects on one's health.

8. *Lawmakers argue that governance results from a fundamentally normative project of deliberation and consent. However, the modalities of deliberation and contractual obligation depend not upon the stability of civil government but rather on its occasional failure to deliver upon the promise it creates. Granted, such failures can be rightfully viewed as temporary setbacks, but they eventually occasion the discourse that is a hallmark of a well-functioning democracy.*

Deliberation and consent are both the cause, and the effect, of effective civil governance. Even stable governments occasionally fail to deliver on their promises, which generates public discourse. Such a discourse eventually leads to deliberation and consent—hallmarks of a well-functioning democracy.

Language Simplification Drill II Answer Key

9. *In the absence of a statute providing otherwise, the admitting physician at McLean Hospital was under no legal obligation to render professional services to Jack Johnson, who was not a patient of the hospital at the time he arrived there. Regardless of whether one finds doctrinal or moral grounds for establishing a duty to treat, neither the existence of a license law nor the possession of a license to practice medicine can be construed as instruments that enlarge a physician's duty in regard to accepting an offered patient, because such laws are essentially a preventive, not a compulsory, measure.*

    The doctor was under no obligation to treat Jack, because the law does not compel doctors to treat every patient who shows up at their door. The law is meant to prevent unlicensed doctors from practicing medicine, rather than compel licensed doctors to do the same.

10. *There is little credibility to the claim that even a politically polarized nation can distinguish between legitimate calls to action and the voices of messianic demagoguery. To speak without listening is an exercise in futility, for no matter how informed or erudite the views, they are bound to fall on deaf ears. Unfortunately, the same cannot be said about shouting.*

    A polarized nation cannot distinguish legitimate calls to action from messianic demagoguery. Unfortunately, the voices of demagoguery are much louder than the voices of reason.

11. *Scholars of Antonin Artaud often argue that the dramatic effects of the satirical genre were not entirely consistent with his philosophy of truth and illusion. Whereas satire uses humor to ridicule the topical issues of the day, for Artaud the only "truths" worth deriding are supposedly those that cannot be proven as such, and may, in fact, be false. It would be too facile to assume, however, that by imbuing his plays with futuristic elements and absurd plot lines, Artaud drew a line between illusion and reality, or—worse—protected the sanctity of politics from satire's corrosive effects. A play need not be credible to be topical. As a skilled dramaturge, Artaud blurred the distinction between the boundaries we take for granted, often staging them as conditions for their mutually assured destruction.*

    Scholars think that Artaud's plays focus on the absurd, and as such cannot be taken seriously as political satire. However, the author believes that the two are not mutually exclusive, because a play can be politically relevant even if it's not entirely credible.

Language Simplification Drill II Answer Key

12. *Socrates defines timocracy as a regime closest to, but decidedly inferior to, aristocracy. However, the language used to differentiate them makes such proximity both essential and unsettling. The surprise emerging from the passage on timocracy lies precisely in a dialectic whose attainment of regime derivation and differentiation depends on a certain failure to obliterate difference and faction as constitutive elements of either regime. In seeing both regimes as mutually constitutive and co-extensive, rather than oppositional or mutually exclusive, Socrates inadvertently questions the valorized difference between the two.*

Socrates believes that timocracy is inferior to aristocracy. However, the two regimes are similar enough. Socrates' rhetoric reveals that neither regime is perfect or whole (i.e. he fails "to obliterate difference and faction as constitutive elements of either regime"), even as he attempts to differentiate between the two.

13. *Scientists who reject the notion that excessive exposure to sunlight in tropical areas increases the risk of melanoma cannot reliably conclude that their theories cannot be disproved. Granted, none of the studies showing a correlation between ultraviolet radiation and skin cancer were conducted in tropical areas, and many of them failed to control for exposure to other potential carcinogens such as diet and smoking. Nevertheless, lack of evidence for a particular claim should not be interpreted as evidence undermining that claim.*

Some scientists think that excessive exposure to sunlight does not cause melanoma, because the evidence supporting such a causal relationship is murky. They assume that nobody can prove them wrong, because the evidence showing a causal connection is murky, but that doesn't mean anything.

14. *More than a theory of governance proscribing the framework of a rather fragile social contract, Kobe's ideology describes the quintessence of a social contract that rescues us from the vicissitudes of anarchy. By relying upon the modality of retrospection, Kobe achieves his goal from the very vantage point it seeks to address – the vantage point of the modern constitutional state. Admittedly, such an ideology is a work of contradictions that resists a simple explanation, revealing in form as well as content a profound struggle with the contingency of its time. But this is true of most, if not all, doctrinal texts.*

Kobe wrote a theory of governance that recommends a certain social contract, namely, the modern constitutional state. He writes from the "vantage point [he] seeks to address," suggesting that Kobe resides in a state in which that contract is already established. The author concedes that there are some contradictions in Kobe's work, but dismisses such criticism because such contradictions are not unique to Kobe.

Reading Speed and Returning to the Passage

The amount of time that you spend reading the passage has a direct effect on your ability to comfortably complete all of the questions. At the same time, the makers of the GMAT have certain expectations about the level of knowledge you should retain when you read a passage. Many questions will test your knowledge of small, seemingly nitpicky variations in phrasing, and reading carelessly is GMAT self-destruction. Thus, every test taker is placed at the nexus of two competing elements: the need for speed (caused by the timed element) and the need for accuracy (caused by the detailed reading requirement). How well you manage these two elements strongly determines how well you perform.

Although it may sound rather mundane, the best approach is to read each passage at the high end of your normal reading speed. If possible, you should try to step it up a notch or two, while recognizing that reading too quickly will cause you to miss much of the detailed information presented in the passage and may even force you to reread much of the text.

One fortunate thing to be aware of as you read is that you do not need to remember every single detail of the passage! Instead, you simply need to remember the basic structure of the passage so you will know where to look, if required, when answering the questions. We will cover this in more detail when we discuss passage structure.

So what's the ideal reading time? Everyone's reading speed is different, but the fastest readers tend to complete each passage in somewhere around one and half to two minutes (depending in part on passage length, and on passage complexity). Readers moving at a more deliberate pace may finish the passage in around two and a half or three minutes, but once your reading time per passage exceeds the three minute mark, the likelihood of being able to complete the full section drops considerably.

In the coming chapters we will focus on improving your GMAT reading ability. Improving in this area will, in part, consist of learning what to look for when reading the passages. Once your ability improves, you will be able to move through the passages and questions more quickly. For now however the focus centers less on target speed and more on improving your overall GMAT reading ability, in large part by teaching you what to look for when reading the passages.

Remember to practice with on-screen passages! Anything that might affect your reading speed and retention should be considered as you prepare.

2

In seeking to increase reading speed, some students ask us about speed reading courses. In our extensive experience, speed reading techniques do not work on GMAT passages because of the way they are written and constructed. GMAT passages are written in a detailed style filled with built-in traps and formations, and speed reading techniques are not designed to detect these elements.

Please note though that the primary aim of this book is not to make you a *faster* reader (your natural reading speed has been developed over many years and is hard to increase by itself in a short period of time). Instead, as you become more adept with effective approaches to the passages, you will be able to attack the passage sets far more proficiently. The goal here is to make you a *better* reader with a greater knowledge of what to look for, and this will inevitably result in increased speed.

Unknowns and Uncertainty

One of the keys to GMAT Reading Comprehension is to accept the fact that you will not be able to know every detail of the passage. In the prior section we talked about reading speed and how this affects your information pickup and recall, and we made the point that you do not *need* to have perfect recall of the facts of the passage. But, it's also the case that it's not really *possible* to remember every detail.

GMAT passages are written in a way where there is a significant amount of jumbled information and often conflicting viewpoints, as well as intentionally convoluted sentences. These sections of text can be difficult to understand, and often readers pass through with a sense that they have missed certain elements. This is okay and should not cause you alarm or undue concern! The reasons this situation is acceptable are as follows:

1. You have the time and opportunity to return to the passage

    Every reader will return to the passage at some point while answering the questions to confirm that his or her knowledge of the text is correct. Thus, if a segment of the passage is unclear, you will have an opportunity to return to it if and when you are asked about it.

No reader can remember every single detail of the passage, so do not be concerned if some elements are unclear. Instead, expect that to occur, and move forward without delay. You will have time to return to review the text if needed.

2. The rest of the passage and the questions will help teach you about difficult sections

    In the typical Reading Comprehension passage set, there is information in the remainder of the passage and even in the questions that can help shed light on challenging passage sections. In some instances, this information can help decode portions you read but did not initially understand or that you'd forgotten.

3. The segment in question may not be tested directly and is unlikely to be the central piece of the passage

    Of course, you may not be asked about the unclear section of text at all! And even if you are, it is rarely the most important part of the passage (overly-complex text may serve as nothing but a distraction).

Understanding that you won't pick up every detail releases you from the pressure of perfection. You can move more quickly through the text because you won't fear sections that aren't 100% clear to you.

If you approach the section with the realization that at times you will not be able to pick up and recall every single piece of information, this reduces the pressure and stress on you as a reader (and allows you to go faster). When you encounter a segment that is not entirely clear to you, don't panic; simply note it (either mentally or on your noteboard) and then return to it later if needed.

As readers we are trained to attempt to fully understand and analyze every word and sentence we come across, but the GMAT is constructed in a way that at times thwarts that goal. So, do not become overly concerned if you can't figure something out on your first pass, and in fact expect that to occur at times.

Active Reading and Anticipation

As noted earlier in this chapter when discussing your focus while reading, the best readers read actively. That is, they engage the material and consider the implications of each statement as they read. They also use their involvement in the material to constantly anticipate what will occur next in the passage. This type of reading takes focus and a positive attitude, as discussed previously, but it also takes practice.

The first part
of this book
is devoted
to examining
the theory of
approaching
the passages
and questions,
whereas the
second part
of the book
is focused on
applying those
techniques
and analyzing
passage
elements.

Let us take a moment to examine several short sections of text, and use them to highlight the idea of how active reading leads to anticipating what comes next:

> Governmental reforms, loosening of regulations, and the opening of markets each played a role in fueling China's economic growth over the last quarter-century.

After reading this section, one could deduce that there are a number of directions this passage could go. For example, a detailed analysis of each of the three listed factors in the economic growth could be presented, or further implications of the growth could be discussed. Let's add the next two sentences—which complete this paragraph—and see where the author takes us:

> Governmental reforms, loosening of regulations, and the opening of markets each played a role in fueling China's economic growth over the last quarter-century. Within the economy, the two most important segments
> (5) are industry and agriculture. However, industry has grown at a significantly faster pace than agriculture.

If you were reading this passage, when you reached this juncture you should have a fairly good idea of the possible directions the author can take with the *next* paragraph. Consider for a moment the information that has been presented thus far:

- Three factors were named as playing a role in China's economic growth over the last quarter-century.

- The economy is stated to have two key segments.

- One of those two segments is said to have grown at a much faster rate than the other segment.

Clearly, the logical direction to take at this point would be to either explain why industry has grown at a faster rate or why agriculture has grown at a slower rate, or both. There does seem to be a slightly higher likelihood that the author will focus on industry because the exact phrase used was, "industry has grown at a significantly faster pace than agriculture," and this phrasing puts the emphasis on "industry."

Let's see which direction the author chose:

> Governmental reforms, loosening of regulations, and the opening of markets each played a role in fueling China's economic growth over the last quarter-century. Within the economy, the two most important segments
> (5) are industry and agriculture. However, industry has grown at a significantly faster pace than agriculture.
> The growth in industry has occurred largely in the urban areas of China, and has been primarily spurred by a focus on technology and heavy manufacturing. This
> (10) emphasis, however, has not come without costs.

Not surprisingly, the author chose to address the industrial side of the economic growth, in this case by focusing on the segments within industry that have been the most important. Of course, as you continue to read, being correct thus far in your predictions should not cause you to stop reading actively. As the passage progresses you should continue to "look ahead" mentally. For example, the last sentence in the text above suggests that the next topic of discussion will be the costs associated with the industrial economic growth.

As a reader, anticipating what will come next in the passage is a habit you should seek to cultivate. By constantly thinking about the possible directions the author can take, you will gain a richer perspective on the story being told and be better prepared for the twists and turns most passages exhibit. Of course, at times, you might be incorrect in your prediction of what will come next. This is not a problem—you will still be able to absorb what is presented and there is no associated time loss. Simply put, there are tremendous benefits gained from reading actively.

On the following pages are two Active Reading Drills, each of which provides an opportunity to practice recognizing and reacting to context clues in GMAT Reading Comprehension passages; in the next chapter we move on to full passage analysis.

Active Reading Drill I

The following drill is presented to reinforce the valuable habit of reacting to identifiable verbal cues. Most students are likely to be familiar with the meanings of common transitional words such as "furthermore" and "however," but again, the most effective readers are responsive when they see these sorts of transitions, actively predicting the passage's next lines. After each of the following examples, take a moment to consider what is likely to come next in the passage, and write down your expectations. *Answers begin on page 59*

1. After developing her initial hypothesis, early studies yielded consistently positive results; in fact,…

    _____

    _____

    _____

    _____

    _____

2. As a result of his childhood accomplishments, Rhee found many opportunities that would have been inaccessible to lesser known talents. Notwithstanding his early successes,…

    _____

    _____

    _____

    _____

    _____

3. Martindale was generally scorned by his contemporaries, who characterized him as an artist who lacked the imagination to create anything truly original, as well as the self-awareness to perceive his own shortcomings. Modern critics, however…

    _____

    _____

    _____

    _____

    _____

Active Reading Drill I

4. Many American constitutional scholars argue that in making legal determinations, the Supreme Court should comply whenever possible with the original intent of the drafters of the Constitution. At the same time,...

_____

_____

_____

_____

_____

5. Most experts in the field who were first told of Dr. Jane's hypothesis were initially skeptical, but...

_____

_____

_____

_____

_____

6. Jackson found these challenges nearly insurmountable. In fact...

_____

_____

_____

_____

7. Despite strong objections to the proposed legislation...

_____

_____

_____

_____

Active Reading Drill I

8. While the movement had encountered resistance at first, eventually...

_____
_____
_____
_____

9. It was indeed true that many of the men had volunteered for the difficult mission, but...

_____
_____
_____
_____

10. Unlike the complex language that pervaded the writer's first three novellas...

_____
_____
_____
_____

11. The general mood at the conference was lighthearted. However...

_____
_____
_____
_____

12. On one side of the debate were those who had been directly affected by the storm...

_____
_____
_____
_____

Active Reading Drill I

13. As the journey progressed, unfortunately for all those involved, conditions did not improve...

_____

_____

_____

_____

14. Since the corporation rescinded its proposal to build a distribution center on the edge of town, the zoning commission's sole reason for approving the variance required by the proposal was gone. With this in mind,...

_____

_____

_____

_____

15. The cold case detective assigned to review the investigation file began to notice several inconsistencies between the crime scene photographs and the original investigator's notes describing the scene. For instance,...

_____

_____

_____

_____

16. On one hand, the non-profit's treasurer was relieved to discover that it was not the organization's charismatic president who had embezzled the $125,000 missing from the organization's bank account. On the other hand,...

_____

_____

_____

_____

Active Reading Drill I

17. Last year, the school board wasted valuable tax dollars buying the football team new uniforms and equipment. Meanwhile,...

_____
_____
_____
_____

18. While it may be true that the government's newly announced passenger car fuel economy standards will enable vehicles meeting those standards to travel farther on a tank of gas,...

_____
_____
_____
_____

19. Early in the 20th century, astronomers discovered that the light emitted from nearly all observable stars was shifted into the red part of the color spectrum, meaning that the stars were moving away from Earth. In other words,...

_____
_____
_____
_____

20. Historical data suggests that no one-term representative of the minority party will be able to successfully sponsor important legislation during the representative's first term in office. Even so,...

_____
_____
_____
_____

Active Reading Drill I Answer Key—page 54

1. *After developing her initial hypothesis, early studies yielded consistently positive results; in fact,...*

   In this case, the words "in fact" tell us that the next information provided will likely continue to support the positive results yielded by early studies.

2. *As a result of his childhood accomplishments, Rhee found many opportunities that would have been inaccessible to lesser known talents. Notwithstanding his early successes,...*

   "Notwithstanding," which basically means "in spite of," tells us that the passage is about to take a turn; although Rhee did apparently enjoy early success, we are soon likely to be told of some challenge(s) that appeared in spite of Rhee's early achievements and opportunities.

3. *Martindale was generally scorned by his contemporaries, who characterized him as an artist who lacked the imagination to create anything truly original, as well as the self-awareness to perceive his own shortcomings. Modern critics, however...*

   The word "however" in this example is a clear indication that there is contrast between contemporaries' characterizations and those of modern critics, so it is likely that modern critics are going to have nicer things to say about Martindale.

4. *Many American constitutional scholars argue that in making legal determinations, the Supreme Court should comply whenever possible with the original intent of the drafters of the Constitution. At the same time,...*

   If taken out of context, "at the same time" might appear to continue a thought, but the phrase is often more akin to "on the other hand." Here, the author begins by telling us that, according to many, Supreme Court decisions should be based on the Constitution's original intent. "At the same time" is likely in this case to be followed by some limitation on the advisability of this notion (e.g., "At the same time, many facets of modern life were not envisioned by the founders.")

5. *Most experts in the field who were first told of Dr. Jane's hypothesis were initially skeptical, but...*

   "But" is a fairly common clue that the passage is about to take a new turn. If we are told of skepticism at first, followed by "but," then it is likely that the author is about to discuss how the hypothesis was confirmed, or possibly how Dr. Jane was able to overcome the initial skepticism of the experts.

6. *Jackson found these challenges nearly insurmountable. In fact...*

   "In fact" will lead into a continuation of the previous thought. From here, the author will likely discuss the difficulty or nature of the aforementioned challenges.

Active Reading Drill I Answer Key

7. *Despite strong objections to the proposed legislation...*

   Since this sentence begins with the term "despite," a directional change should follow--perhaps a discussion of those who supported the legislation (in spite of others' objections) or of the subsequent success of the legislation (in spite of previous objections).

8. *Although the movement had encountered resistance at first, eventually...*

   The word "although" in this example indicates that there is contrast--in this case, between the resistance initially encountered, and eventually...most likely some degree of acceptance.

9. *It was indeed true that many of the men had volunteered for the difficult mission, but...*

   In this case, the word "but" tells us that a turn is coming: next, the author might discuss some of those others who *didn't* volunteer ("...but many chose not to go"), qualify the willingness of those who did volunteer ("...but they weren't very happy about it"), or perhaps a level of difficulty that was surprising despite expectations.

10. *Unlike the complex language that pervaded the writer's first three novellas...*

    The straightforward language in this example indicates that the author will likely now discuss the writer's change, to more straightforward language.

11. *The general mood at the conference was lighthearted. However...*

    As alluded to in this drill's directions, the word "however" provides a clear indication that the author's discussion is about to shift to a less lighthearted subject.

12. *On one side of the debate were those who had been directly affected by the storm...*

    Since this sentence begins with the perspective from one side of the debate, the author will likely go on to provide information about those on the other side of the debate.

13. *As the journey progressed, unfortunately for all those involved, conditions did not improve...*

    At this point the author will most likely continue to discuss the worsening conditions for the unfortunate journey.

Active Reading Drill I Answer Key

14. *Since the corporation rescinded its proposal to build a distribution center on the edge of town, the zoning commission's sole reason for approving the variance required by the proposal was gone. With this in mind,...*

The phrase "with this in mind" indicates that the author may proceed to tell us that the zoning commission will reject the proposed variance, an action consistent with the removal of the commission's only reason for approving it.

15. *The cold case detective assigned to review the investigation file began to notice several inconsistencies between the crime scene photographs and the original investigator's notes describing the scene. For instance,...*

Here, the author begins by alluding to a relatively broad category of information, the several inconsistencies between the crime scene photographs and the investigator's notes. By beginning the next sentence with "For instance," the author signals the appearance of a description of at least one of those inconsistencies.

16. *On one hand, the non-profit's treasurer was relieved to discover that it was not the organization's charismatic president who had embezzled the $125,000 missing from the organization's bank account. On the other hand,...*

In this case, it appears that the evidence satisfied the treasurer that the president had not embezzled the money. However, the money was taken by someone. It is most likely that the sentence beginning with "On the other hand" will conclude with an expression of the treasurer's concern that they still do not know who embezzled the money.

17. *Last year, the school board wasted valuable tax dollars buying the football team new uniforms and equipment. Meanwhile,...*

The author's word choice in the first sentence provides a hint as to what is likely to follow the word "meanwhile." By saying the school board "wasted" the "valuable" tax dollars, the author implies there was a better use for those funds. We can expect that the author will tell us about some other, more pressing need that could have been addressed with the money spent on uniforms and equipment.

Active Reading Drill I Answer Key

18. *While it may be true that the government's newly announced passenger car fuel economy standards will enable vehicles meeting those standards to travel farther on a tank of gas,...*

In this example, the author begins with a concession, that the new fuel economy standards achieve the desired effect of increasing fuel efficiency for compliant cars. However, we can predict that the author will continue by pointing out some trade-off or unintended consequence of the new standards that calls into question the wisdom of such regulation.

19. *Early in the 20th century, astronomers discovered that the light emitted from nearly all observable stars was shifted into the red part of the color spectrum, meaning that the stars were moving away from Earth. In other words,...*

Here, the author describes a scientific discovery that could be confusing to the reader, such that the reader may not fully comprehend the implication of the discovery that nearly all of the observable stars are moving away from Earth. The phrase "in other words" indicates that the author will restate the implication of the discovery to make it more accessible to the reader. Here, the author will tell us that the discovery indicates that the universe is expanding.

20. *Historical data suggests that no one-term representative of the minority party will be able to successfully sponsor important legislation during the representative's first term in office. Even so,...*

The author's presentation of historical data indicates that it is highly unlikely that a representative of such short tenure would be able to introduce important legislation and have it be approved by the legislative body. The term "even so" implies that the following information will discuss some positive impact that such a representative may have, whether it is a specific representative who may actually be successful in sponsoring important legislation, or a generalized statement of the positive contribution such a representative can make.

Active Reading Drill II

The following drill is intended to further reinforce the habit of reacting to verbal cues, noting in particular the different directions indicated by subtle shifts in the language. After each of the following examples, write down your predictions about what is likely to come next. *Answers begin on page 68*

2

1. It was to be one of the tallest buildings in the world, and the size and scope of the project would present many unique challenges. As the building continued, issues with the construction of the massive structure were numerous...

    A) Incredibly, though...

    _____
    _____
    _____
    _____

    B) Challenges included...

    _____
    _____
    _____
    _____

    C) As a result...

    _____
    _____
    _____
    _____

Active Reading Drill II

2. Having planned extensively for a variety of different emergency situations, including both hurricanes and flash floods, city officials had considered themselves well-prepared for just such an emergency.

A) Thankfully...

_____

_____

_____

_____

B) Unfortunately...

_____

_____

_____

_____

C) Some, however, were not quite so confident;

_____

_____

_____

_____

Active Reading Drill II

2

3. At the time of its publication, McMillan's first novel was lauded by many as one of the most important literary works of the era,

A) but in retrospect...

_____

_____

_____

_____

B) and critics continue to praise the work's insights;

_____

_____

_____

_____

C) although several of McMillan's contemporaries took issue with this characterization...

_____

_____

_____

_____

Active Reading Drill II

4. The proposal was intended to provide a compromise that would be considered equitable by all concerned parties, but some who learned of the changes opposed the new plan.

A) Regardless,...

_____
_____
_____
_____

B) Indeed,...

_____
_____
_____
_____

C) These opponents claimed...

_____
_____
_____
_____

Active Reading Drill II

5. The strike went on for months, and some wondered whether it would go on indefinitely. Management seemed completely intractable, and the union had no intention of giving up on what the group considered to be very reasonable demands.

A) Making matters worse,..

_____

_____

_____

_____

B) Eventually, though...

_____

_____

_____

_____

C) , such as...

_____

_____

_____

_____

Active Reading Drill II Answer Key—page 63

Once again, do not be concerned if your predictions do not perfectly match those discussed below; the most important function of this exercise is to reinforce the habit of using context clues while reading the passage.

1. *It was to be one of the tallest buildings in the world, and the size and scope of the project would present many unique challenges. As the building continued, issues with the construction of the massive structure were numerous...*

   A) Incredibly, though...

   This example opens with a discussion of a difficult construction project with numerous issues. "Incredibly, though" tells us that the next statement will be surprising in light of the project's many difficulties.

   B) Challenges included...

   "Challenges included" is a very straightforward context clue that says "here comes a list of challenges." Lists, of course, are always worth noting when working through any Reading Comprehension passage, and if you were to see this excerpt in an actual passage, you could probably count on at least one question that deals with this list.

   C) As a result...

   "As a result" is a phrase that generally precedes the discussion of an effect, so what follows these words will be a mention of some outcome caused by the numerous construction issues.

Active Reading Drill II Answer Key

2. *Having planned extensively for a variety of different emergency situations, including both hurricanes and flash floods, city officials had considered themselves well-prepared for just such an emergency.*

A) *Thankfully...*

This one begins with the fact that city officials felt prepared for a particular emergency—this could potentially go in several directions. "Thankfully" leads into a positive outcome of some sort, maybe that they were indeed prepared, or perhaps that their preparations were not put to the test.

B) *Unfortunately...*

"Unfortunately" does not suggest a positive direction—maybe the officials were not as prepared as they thought, or perhaps they were presented with a different type of emergency.

C) *Some, however, were not quite so confident;*

This example takes a slightly different direction. Since the sentiment begins, "Some, however, were not quite so confident;" followed by a semicolon, the author is possibly about to begin a discussion about either those people who were less confident, or the reasons for that lack of confidence.

3. *At the time of its publication, McMillan's first novel was lauded by many as one of the most important literary works of the era,*

A) *but in retrospect...*

The author begins in this example by presenting the fact that McMillan's novel was released to widespread acclaim. This introduction deals specifically with the time of the novel's publication, so when it is followed by "but in retrospect," that is a clear indication that the author is perhaps about to turn away from the positive initial reaction, perhaps to more critical perspectives.

B) *and critics continue to praise the work's insights;*

Rather than taking a new direction, this example would lead to a continuation of the discussion of critical praise.

C) *although several of McMillan's contemporaries took issue with this characterization...*

This is a clear indication that a shift in direction has come—the author will now most likely turn the discussion either to those contemporaries or their specific criticisms.

Active Reading Drill II Answer Key

4. *The proposal was intended to provide a compromise that would be considered equitable by all concerned parties, but some who learned of the changes opposed the new plan.*

   A) Regardless,...

   In this example we see an early directional shift: the proposal was intended to be fair, but some opposed the new plan. The word "regardless" probably indicates a shift back, away from those opponents (i.e. "without regard for those opponents...") possibly leading to the fact that the proposal would remain in place, despite the opponents.

   B) Indeed,...

   "Indeed" generally continues a sentiment, so in this example the author will probably further discuss those who opposed the plan.

   C) These opponents claimed...

   This example will clearly lead into a discussion of the specific claims of opponents against the referenced proposal.

5. *The strike went on for months, and some wondered whether it would go on indefinitely. Management seemed completely intractable, and the union had no intention of giving up on what the group considered to be very reasonable demands...*

   A) Making matters worse,...

   Here the author discusses a long standing strike in which both sides are apparently committed to their agendas. "Making matters worse" tells us that the author is about to discuss further factors detrimental to the situation.

   B) Eventually, though...

   The word "though" implies a turnaround, and in this context we can probably expect to read about how they were able to overcome the strike.

   C) , such as...

   "Such as" follows the reference to reasonable demands, so the author is about to list examples of those demands.

Chapter Three:
VIEWSTAMP Passage Analysis

Chapter Three: VIEWSTAMP Passage Analysis

What to Read For ▐▬▬▬▬▬▬▬▬

Thus far we've discussed some of the basic ideas behind how to approach the passages, mostly focusing on the mindset you need to adopt when attacking each passage set. Let's now turn to the specific elements you must look for while reading.

One of the points in the last chapter was that your reading speed does not determine your final RC score. This isn't to suggest you do not need to change anything about how you read! Instead, the focus is on *how* you read and what you look for as you read. In other words, it's not about reading faster but about reading better.

To achieve the goal of reading better, you must concentrate on the basic passage elements that generate the majority of questions. These identifiable elements are not difficult to understand, but they are easy to lose in the thicket of information that is a Reading Comprehension passage. So, to help you track those elements you should ask yourself a set of questions while reading, and at the end of the passage you should be able to answer each of the following:

3

- What is the Main Point of the text? What's the author driving at?

- What is the author's purpose or goal in presenting this information?

- Which groups are speaking or are talked about in the passage? In other words, who said what?

- What's the tone or attitude of each group? Angry? Disappointed? Neutral?

- What is the basic position or argument of each group? Nothing complex, more along the lines of, "The environmentalists are for the passage of the bill and the opponents think the bill will hurt the economy. The author is neutral."

- Last, but not least, what's the structure of the passage? Can you make a mental map of where the ideas appear in the passage and how they fit together?

The questions here are fairly simple, and once you are used to considering them as you read they become quite easy to remember.

Note too that many RC test questions will be answered directly as you satisfy the inquiries listed here.

We will examine each point in detail on the following pages, but these basic questions help distill the passage information into a simple, usable format that allows you to effectively attack the questions. With that in mind, let's talk about the mental tool we use to help keep those questions straight: VIEWSTAMP.

What is VIEWSTAMP? ▐███████████

The basic questions on the previous page all relate to the primary elements that generate the questions for every GMAT Reading Comprehension passage. With the time pressure and overall complexity involved in RC passages sometimes one can forget to think about these simple questions, so we use the acronym VIEWSTAMP to help you remember each item.

The acronym uses letters from each of these six critical components:

VIEW = the different **VIEW**points in the passage
S　　 = the **S**tructure of the passage
T　　 = the **T**one of the passage
A　　 = the **A**rguments in the passage
M　　 = the **M**ain Point of the passage
P　　 = the **P**urpose of the passage

The major elements listed above help map the overall framework of the reading comprehension passages you will see on the GMAT. Regardless of the topic or the length of a passage, your task will be to take note of the information provided (sometimes considering various viewpoints), draw inferences, and understand what the author is trying to achieve. Noting these integral elements as you assess each passage is crucial to your increased efficiency and accuracy in attacking the questions that follow a Reading Comprehension passage.

Ultimately, VIEWSTAMP is a mental tracking tool that focuses your attention on the ideas and elements most likely to produce questions.

Analyzing the Passage Using VIEWSTAMP ▐███████████

In its basic form, VIEWSTAMP is a mnemonic device that helps remind you of what to look for in each passage. But in practice we use this device as a diagnostic instrument that helps us constantly apply a rigorous analysis to each paragraph of the passage. Thus, it is important to discuss exactly when and how to ask these questions, and what to look for as a satisfactory response.

When to Apply VIEWSTAMP

VIEWSTAMP is designed to be a constant companion as you move through the passage. You are always looking for the presence of each element, and at the end of *each paragraph* you should consider the main elements of what you just read as well as what information relates to the VIEWSTAMP goals. Seek to understand not just *what* the author said in the paragraph, but *why* the author made those statements. What's the greater point that's being presented? How does each element function in service of that point?

This paragraph-by-paragraph analysis culminates when you finish the last paragraph, at which point you should have a relatively good sense of what was said, and by whom. As you conclude your reading, pause to make sure you have all of the information straight. If you do not, you risk being swayed by clever answer choices with tempting but inaccurate phrasing. So, if you are at all uncertain about something that feels significant, take a moment to lock down the facts!

How to Apply VIEWSTAMP

One of the keys of applying VIEWSTAMP is to not seek too much detail for each item. An excessive amount of detail will slow you down, and become hard to juggle mentally. Instead, what you want is a very generalized answer to each question. We'll go into the details of each element in the remainder of this chapter, but for now think about each question as a broad query seeking a single sentence answer if possible.

For example, consider the idea of the main point of a passage. While GMAT Reading Comprehension passages are all unique, in every instance you can summarize the main point in a sentence or two at most. So, at the end of the passage when you are looking to answer the question of what is the main point, keep your answer simple and broadly encompassing of the entirety of the text. You do not need to summarize every few sentences or go into the nuances of each passage; fine shades of meaning are not useful at this level because they are too easy to forget. Thus, a hypothetical main point summary such as the following would fail our goal:

> The passage argues for the adoption of the new Geisen-Tremaine standards for measuring educational progress among American schoolchildren because these standards take into account cultural and socioeconomic factors that can impact some students more than others. The author pays particular attention to the deficiencies of current measures in addressing underprivileged youth achievement.

It's not that this first summary is bad; it's actually quite good. The problem is that it's not a distillation of the essence of the passage, and if you apply this level of detailed analysis to each element within the passage, you won't have a simple analysis but instead an extremely complicated analysis that might be difficult to remember.

Instead, seek something along these lines:

> The main point is that the new standards for measuring the progress of American schoolchildren should be adopted.

This second summary, while short and relatively generalized, would allow you to answer any question about the primary purpose or main point of the passage (which are questions that appear frequently), and would also clue you in to the author's overall intent and belief set. The keys are clarity and simplicity since those will provide maximum recall when you are attacking the questions.

Now, the natural question to ask is: won't a broad summary leave me vulnerable to questions about details or specific sections of the passage? The happy answer is No. When you encounter specific questions you have free rein to return to the passage text, and in fact you are encouraged to do so. Every high scorer returns to the passage to confirm information because there are simply too many details in the passage to remember in full. This process is made easier because one of the elements being tracked is Structure, so when you encounter a detail question and must return to the passage your already-existing structural knowledge of where to find the information will help you move more quickly and decisively.

So, at the *end* of each passage you should be able to briefly summarize the six elements within VIEWSTAMP in short, succinct sentences. If you cannot accomplish this goal, you will likely struggle with some or all of the questions. As you practice reading passages, constantly ask yourself these questions, and seek to refine your approach until you are comfortable with each of the points.

Finally, consider your analysis of the six elements to be fluid: it will change from passage to passage. In some passages certain elements will appear earlier than others, and in some cases you might determine an element very early on whereas in another passage you may need to wait until the end of the passage to make a judgment. For example, in one passage the author's attitude might be identifiable right from the beginning whereas in another passage that attitude might not be clear until near the end. Do not try to impose a rigid order onto your reading; instead react to what the test makers give you: the variation in how information is presented in the passage will require you to be flexible in how you read. Your goal as a reader using VIEWSTAMP is not to read each passage in a fixed and unyielding way, but rather to track the six elements and react to them when they appear. In this way, you can adapt to any passage structure and formation, and thereby attack any set of questions successfully!

1. Viewpoint Identification and Analysis

A viewpoint is the position or perspective of a person or group. On the GMAT, Reading Comprehension passages may contain one viewpoint, or might reflect two (or more) different perspectives. These viewpoints can be the author's or those of groups discussed by the author.

As you read, you *must* identify each viewpoint that is presented in the passage. This is a fairly easy process—whenever a new group or individual viewpoint is discussed, simply note its appearance. Because viewpoints can be presented at any time, your analysis of viewpoints will not be concluded until you finish reading the passage.

Consider the following opening paragraph of a passage, and seek to identify the various viewpoints present:

This section discusses the "VIEW" in VIEWSTAMP. The "VIEW" stands for Viewpoints.

3

In economics, Pareto optimality occurs in systems where no allocative change can be made to advantage one party without disadvantaging another party. If such a change could be made,
(5)   then the change would be a Pareto improvement; when no further Pareto improvements can be made, the system reaches Pareto optimality. While elements of the Pareto principle can be useful in understanding the efficiency of a
(10)   system, application of such principles to the allocation of public resources would not yield equitable or socially desirable results.

Number of Viewpoints: 1

Lines 1-7: No Specific Viewpoint. The opening content in Lines 1-7 is not viewpoint specific; although these statements are provided by the author, the information only serves to provide context for the remainder of the paragraph, and does not take a specific view of the subject that can be assigned to any party.

Lines 8-12: Author: This excerpt does not provide multiple viewpoints; it is simply the author's presentation of information about Pareto systems. Note that lines 1-7 provide contextual information that could be classified as No Specific Viewpoint, but in this item we include them in the author's viewpoint because the remainder of the paragraph continues on with a definable viewpoint assigned to the author.

Many Reading Comprehension passages begin with a Viewpoint Neutral discussion that provides context for the passage.

Test takers might ask, "What is the value of tracking all of the viewpoints in a given Reading Comprehension passage?" There are several important reasons:

1. Tracking the viewpoints will help you disentangle the mass of information contained in every Reading Comprehension passage.

2. Within the questions, you will be asked to identify the viewpoints presented in the passages and to differentiate between those viewpoints. Answer choices will often present different viewpoints in order to test your ability to distinguish between groups.

In the paragraph on the previous page we encountered only the author's view. When multiple views are presented, however, they often appear "back-to-back," so the test makers can assess your ability to compare and contrast different views in close proximity. When test takers fail to distinguish these separate views they are far more prone to missing questions that test the difference between these viewpoints.

In the prior example paragraph, the sole view is presented very clearly and is easy to identify. Unfortunately, viewpoints will not always be presented with such clarity. Consider the following opening paragraph from a different sample passage:

An opinion presented without reference to any group is typically the author's perspective.

Patent laws are thought to have originated in Italy, but legal history professors have convincingly shown that the concept of patents existed as far back as the third century in ancient Greece.
(5) Despite the long legal history of patents, recent commentators have suggested that their use should be either abolished or curtailed significantly. They argue that social and technological changes have surpassed the
(10) capacities of the patent system, and instead of being an engine of expansion, patent laws are now more commonly used as a means of suppression.

Number of Viewpoints: 3

Lines 1-4: Author. By using the word "convincingly" to describe the view of Legal History Professors, the author indicates that he or she agrees with the idea that the concept of patents has existed as far back as third century Greece. Note that Line 1 could be assigned to No Specific Viewpoint, but because Line 1 addresses the origin of patent laws—an origin that is expressly addressed by the author in Line 2—Line 1 is thus included in the author's viewpoint.

Lines 2-4: Legal History Professors. This group demonstrated that the concept of patents has existed as far back as the third century in ancient Greece, an idea with which the author agrees.

Lines 6-12: Recent Commentators. The Commentators believe that the use of patents should be restricted or eliminated.

Of course, not all viewpoints are presented in separate sentences. In an effort to confuse test takers, the test makers sometimes introduce two viewpoints in a single sentence, as in the following example:

> While the proponents of the Futurism art movement
> believed that the past was an era to be ignored, some
> critics assert that, ironically, for the Futurists to break
> from the past would have required a more thorough
> (5) understanding of history on their part.

In the sentence above, two views are introduced: that of the proponents of Futurism, and that of the critics of Futurism. However, although the sentence contains two opposing views, tracking those elements is no more difficult than when the views are presented in separate sentences. Again, we will discuss notating the views in a later section.

When we begin our discussion of the questions that typically accompany GMAT passages, we will revisit the importance of a viewpoint-based analysis. In the meantime, always remember to identify the various viewpoints that you encounter in a Reading Comprehension passage. The drill that follows is designed to help practice and reinforce this important habit.

VIEWSTAMP Analysis: Viewpoint Identification Drill

Each of the following items presents a paragraph. Read each item and identify the viewpoints present. Then, in the spaces that follow each paragraph, fill in the proper line references and respective viewpoints. *Answers begin on page 89*

3

Passage 1:

Federal rules of evidence have long prohibited the presentation in court of many types of "hearsay" (evidence recounted second-hand, rather than reported directly by a witness), based on the notion

(5)   that only the most readily verifiable evidence should be allowed consideration by any court in making its determinations. Dr. Kinsley has argued, however, that the rules of evidence as currently written are unacceptably overreaching, precluding

(10)   the use of too many types of evidence whose value would far outweigh any associated detriment if allowed court admissibility. But modern hearsay rules have been written with good reason.

Lines: _____

Viewpoint: _____

Lines: _____

Viewpoint: _____

Lines: _____

Viewpoint: _____

VIEWSTAMP Analysis: Viewpoint Identification Drill

Passage 2:

In the years which preceded Roger Bannister's
record breaking performance, it was widely
believed that the human body was not equipped to
complete a mile-long run in under four minutes;
(5)   human lungs, many leading experts asserted, could
never deliver sufficient oxygen, and the heart
could not undergo such physical stress. Bannister,
undeterred, believed that he could reach the goal
that he had set in 1952.

Lines: _____

Viewpoint: _____

Lines: _____

Viewpoint: _____

Passage 3:

Friedman suggested monetary manipulation to
bring the supply and demand for money to an
artificial equilibrium, but, as Margaret Thatcher and
many others have since learned, the application of
(5)   these principles in the real world often brings about
results contrary to those predicted from the ivory
towers of abstract economic theory.

Lines: _____

Viewpoint: _____

Lines: _____

Viewpoint: _____

VIEWSTAMP Analysis: Viewpoint Identification Drill

<u>Passage 4</u>:

        The first cardiac pacemaker was the brainchild of
John Hopps, a Canadian electrical engineer who, in
1941, while researching hypothermia and the use
of heat from radio frequencies to restore
(5)   body temperature, found that mechanical or
electrical stimulation can restart a heart that has
stopped under conditions of extreme cold. The
earliest versions of the pacemaker were heavy
pieces of equipment which were far too large for
(10)   implantation, and instead had to be rolled on
wheels and kept attached to the patient at all times.
Modern science has seen a striking decrease in the
size of these devices, which are now small enough
to be surgically placed under the skin, allowing
(15)   them to remain virtually undetectable externally.

Lines: _____

Viewpoint: _____

VIEWSTAMP Analysis: Viewpoint Identification Drill

<u>**Passage #5**</u>:

On the other side of the interpretation debate are those who believe that the Constitution was meant to be a "living document," whose proper construction would readily adapt to an evolving
(5)   nation. Judges who subscribe to this perspective are often referred to by strict constructionists as judicial activists who are trying to take law-making power away from the legislative branch of the government. These judges, however, consider
(10)   themselves interpreters, not activists. The framers specifically allowed for constitutional amendment, and afforded significant power to the judicial branch; they felt that the Constitution was to provide a framework but would have to adapt to a
(15)   changing nation.

3

Lines: _____

Viewpoint: _____

Lines: _____

Viewpoint: _____

Lines: _____

Viewpoint: _____

Lines: _____

Viewpoint: _____

VIEWSTAMP Analysis: Viewpoint Identification Drill

Passage #6:

Critics often accuse Primo Levi of providing a
historically incomplete account of the Holocaust in
his last book, *The Drowned and the Saved* (1986).
While technically correct, such accusations reveal

(5)   a fundamental failure to understand the role of
memory—and forgetting—in Levi's outstanding
work. Levi regards human memory as a "marvelous
but fallacious" instrument, given the inherent
subjectivity of personal narration: time can alter

(10) memory, and false memories can emerge. As many
psychologists agree, this can be particularly true of
traumatic memories. Trauma can often limit precise
recall of an injurious experience, and its severity
is often predictive of memory status. From that

(15) perspective, the critics are correct: as a survivor
of unimaginable horrors, Levi is unlikely to
provide a reliably detailed account of his personal
experiences. But he never meant to: *The Drowned
and the Saved* is, above all, an introspective

(20) account of survival.

Lines: _____

Viewpoint: _____

Lines: _____

Viewpoint: _____

Lines: _____

Viewpoint: _____

Lines: _____

Viewpoint: _____

Lines: _____

Viewpoint: _____

VIEWSTAMP Analysis: Viewpoint Identification Drill

<u>Passage #7</u>:

        One needs only to look at the vast body of
    literary criticism produced during the Cold War
    to realize that, as Abbott Gleason aptly observes
    in his introduction to George Orwell's *Nineteen*
(5) *Eighty-Four* (1949), Orwell's novel "has come
    to be regarded as one of the great exposes of the
    horrors of Stalinism." *Nineteen Eighty-Four* has
    indeed transcended its historical occasion, its
    themes persisting as ubiquitous elements of popular
(10) culture, political debate, and literary criticism
    even after the end of the Cold War. History has
    transformed the fictional paradigms contained in
    the novel into an allegory of its own factual reality,
    an allegory that describes a shared experience
(15) by staying embedded in the collective American
    unconscious. If—as Walter Benjamin observes in
    his essay, "The Storyteller"—storytelling is the
    lost art of the twentieth century, Orwell manages to
    find that art precisely at those moments of dramatic
(20) narration when censorship and alienation seem
    most oppressive, didactic, and deafening.

        Lines: _____

        Viewpoint: _____

        Lines: _____

        Viewpoint: _____

3

VIEWSTAMP Analysis: Viewpoint Identification Drill

Passage #8:

Designed by American architect Frank Lloyd
Wright in the early 1920's, the Hollyhock House
was an odd addition to the suburban landscape of
East Hollywood. Critics deplored its abandonment
(5)　of traditional principles of Western architecture,
noting the clear inconsistency with its Anglo-
Colonial and Beaux-Arts neighbors. Because its
exterior walls tilted back at 85 degrees, many
felt that the Hollyhock House looked more like a
(10)　Mayan temple than a residential building.

Indeed, the Hollyhock House lacked the typical
air of domesticity expected of it. Nevertheless,
the monumental nature of its form should not
have caused such consternation. Although the
(15)　geometrically abstract hollyhock motif dominates
the exterior and the interior spaces of the house,
it also creates a rare sense of cohesion between
the two. Thanks to the symmetrical leaves
spaced evenly along its stem, the hollyhock also
(20)　establishes an allegorical connection between the
hilly landscape of Southern California and the
building's ornamental design. In sharp contrast
with their predecessors, many modern-day
architects now see the building as organically
(25)　inseparable from the Olive Hill on which it sits,
casting a much more favorable light on Frank
Lloyd Wright's ingenious design.

Lines: _____

Viewpoint: _____

Lines: _____

Viewpoint: _____

Lines: _____

Viewpoint: _____

VIEWSTAMP Analysis: Viewpoint Identification Drill

<u>**Passage #9**</u>:

What is "canon"? Scholars typically label as "canonical" those works of Western literature that have the greatest artistic merit. Critics often complain that canonicity is inherently subjective,
(5) often biased in favor of those who have the power and authority to define what "artistic merit" actually is. Even if the canon does not serve political interests overtly, their argument goes, it provides a perspective that is inherently
(10) exclusionary, if not oppressive.

What such debates fail to acknowledge is that the canon is as much about the past as it is about the present. It creates a fantasy of origin, a shared beginning that has survived the passage
(15) of time thanks to the timeless truth we imagine is contained in it. Much like the painted table in the antique shop, its nicks and chips precious signs of its antiquarian value, the canon provides a compensatory myth whose ambiguities only
(20) contribute to its stature of a classic. They do so by inviting a plethora of interpretations that seek to settle, once and for all, the "real" meaning of the text. The classic is itself a deeply disjointed work that both invites and resists interpretation,
(25) its contradictions exhibiting not a mere lack of adequate philosophical analysis, but rather the symptoms of contingency and incommensurability inherent in its own genealogy.

Lines: _____

Viewpoint: _____

Lines: _____

Viewpoint: _____

Lines: _____

Viewpoint: _____

VIEWSTAMP Analysis: Viewpoint Identification Drill

Passage #10:

For centuries, historians have regarded Vasari's *Life of Michelangelo*, originally published in 1550, as the primary source of information about the marble statue *David*. According to Vasari,
(5) Michelangelo completed the statue in 1504 from a large block of marble previously owned by Piero Soderini, then *gonfaloniere* for life in the city of Florence. Soderini had offered the project to several other Florentine sculptors before offering it
(10) to Michelangelo, Vasari claims, and the numerous attempts at carving the statue had rendered the block of marble virtually unsalvageable.

Although direct proof of Vasari's account was unattainable, he offered enough details to lend
(15) his argument a semblance of rigor. By 1840, however, the consensus among experts was that *David*'s provenance had little to do with Piero Soderini. A newly uncovered document dating back to 1476 showed that it was the Overseers of
(20) the Office of Works of the Duomo (the *Operai*) who commissioned the marble *David* to several sculptors—first to renowned Florentine sculptor Agostino di Duccio, and twelve years later to a younger artist, Antonio Rossellino. The Operai
(25) intended the statue to be part of the century-old "Prophet-project," a monumental series of twelve Old Testament-themed sculptures which would adorn the buttresses of Florence's cathedral church. Unfortunately, Agostino and Rossellino made
(30) little progress for over a decade, prompting the Operai to commission the piece to the 26-year old Michelangelo. Documents from the Duomo dating back to 1501 explicitly refer to the statue's intended purpose and style, leaving no doubt that
(35) Vasari's earlier accounts were factually incorrect.

Lines: _____

Viewpoint: _____

Lines: _____

Viewpoint: _____

Lines: _____

Viewpoint: _____

VIEWSTAMP Analysis: Viewpoint Identification Drill Answer Key—page 80

Passage #1:

Lines 1-7: This section is not attributed to any particular party, so it must come from the author. As this portion is purely informational, there is no tone at this point.

Lines 7-12: This is the perspective of Dr. Kinsley. By using the term "unacceptably," Kinsley appears to have a fairly strong negative opinion about the breadth of hearsay prohibitions as currently written.

Lines 12-13: This excerpt is also not attributed to anyone, so it is the author at this point who takes issue with Kinsley's argument, asserting that the hearsay rules have a reasonable foundation.

Passage #2:

Lines 1-7: In the beginning of this paragraph, the author apprises us of a widely held belief about the body's limitations, followed by a more specific attribution of related assertions to many leading experts.

Lines 7-9: Here the author makes the switch to the perspective of Bannister. There is not too much attitude reflected here, although Bannister is characterized as fairly confident.

Passage #3:

Lines 1-3: The first two lines provide Friedman's suggestion as a simple presentation of information.

Lines 3-7: This portion, which is not specifically attributed to anyone else, provides the perspective of the author, who takes a very negative attitude, clearly reflected in the reference to the "ivory tower theory." The author is not a fan of Friedman's suggestion of monetary manipulation.

Passage #4:

Lines 1-15: This excerpt does not provide multiple viewpoints; it is simply the author's presentation of information about the history of the cardiac pacemaker and its inventor. As is sometimes the case with science passages, this selection reflects a relatively neutral tone.

VIEWSTAMP Analysis: Viewpoint Identification Drill Answer Key

<u>Passage #5:</u>

<u>Lines 1-5</u>: This is the viewpoint of the "living document" proponents, and the tone is fairly matter-of-fact.

<u>Lines 5-9</u>: Here the author presents the perspective of the strict constructionists, who take a negative tone with regard to the "living document" judges.

<u>Lines 9-10</u>: At this point we are presented with the perspective of the so-called "judicial activists," who believe that they are simply offering interpretations rather than newly made laws.

<u>Lines 10-12</u>: Here we are provided with information about the beliefs of the framers, with an attitude that lends more support to the idea of the Constitution as a living document.

<u>Passage #6:</u>

<u>Lines 1-4</u>: The viewpoint presented here is that of the critics, who accuse Levi of providing an incomplete account of the Holocaust.

<u>Lines 4-7</u>: This section is crucial: the author concedes that the critics are "technically correct," but takes a strong stance against their position. The author also embraces Levi's book as an "outstanding work."

<u>Lines 7-11</u>: This excerpt clarifies Levi's viewpoint.

<u>Lines 11-14</u>: A new viewpoint is introduced—that of psychologists.

<u>Lines 14-20</u>: The author elaborates on her earlier claim about why the critics are "technically correct," but fail to grasp the purpose of Levi's account. We also learn more about Levi's purpose, as understood by the author.

<u>Passage #7:</u>

<u>Lines 1-7</u>: This excerpt introduces Gleason's views on George Orwell. The author quotes Gleason, suggesting an overlap of viewpoints.

<u>Lines 7-16</u>: This section elaborates on the author's interpretation of *Nineteen Eighty-Four*. The attitude is scholarly, the views—erudite.

<u>Lines 16-21</u>: The author mentions Walter Benjamin, but the reference only serves to lend further credibility to the author's own views regarding Orwell.

VIEWSTAMP Analysis: Viewpoint Identification Drill Answer Key

Passage #8:

Lines 4-10: Introduce the critics' viewpoint, which is critical of the Hollyhock House.

Lines 12-14: This is the author's main point. The author concedes that the building is not as "domestic" as expected, but views the critics as too harsh.

Lines 22-27: Juxtapose the critics' views mentioned in the first paragraph to those of modern-day architects.

Passage #9:

Lines 1-3: Define "canon" from a scholarly perspective.

Line 3-10: Outline the critics' argument against canonicity.

Line 12-28: Introduce and elaborate on the author's perspective regarding canonical works.

Passage #10:

Line 1-4: Introduce Vasari's importance to historians.

Line 4-12: Outline Vasari's version of events regarding the provenance of Michelangelo's *David*.

Line 13-15: Imply the author's position regarding Vasari's historical account: it *seems* rigorous (but probably isn't).

Line 15-17: Introduce the experts' position, which is in direct disagreement with Vasari's.

Lines 24-28: Mention the *Operai*'s purpose for commissioning the piece, which functions as evidence for the author's main point.

Lines 32-35: Re-assert the author's main point: Vasari's account is factually incorrect.

2. Passage Structure

This section discusses the "S" in the VIEWSTAMP acronym. The "S" stands for Structure.

Many students, when they first begin working with Reading Comprehension passages, attempt to remember every single detail of the passage. Given the limits of human short-term memory and the test's intensive time pressure, this is an impossible task. Fortunately, it is also an unnecessary one. Built into your test taking strategy should be the expectation that you will frequently return to the passage during the questions to confirm and disconfirm answer choices.

When taking the GMAT CAT, understanding the structure of a passage for quick reference can be particularly important, since there is no way to take notes directly on the passage.

In order to successfully return to the passage, however, you must attempt to identify the underlying logical structure of the passage as you read. This will help you quickly find information once you begin to answer the questions. For example, some passages open by stating the background of a thesis that will be challenged later in the passage. In the following paragraphs the author will then present an alternative viewpoint to the thesis and perhaps specific counterexamples which provide support for the alternative view. Awareness of this general structure will allow you to reduce the time you spend searching for information when you refer back to the text.

Fortunately, identifying the logical structure of a passage does not require any training in logic or logical terminology. You simply need to be able to describe in general terms the order in which things are presented in the passage. This is most often connected to specific paragraphs, as in, "The first paragraph introduces the jury unanimity requirement, and then presents the viewpoints of the critics of unanimity. At the start of the second paragraph, the author takes a strong position that jury unanimity is essential. The second and third paragraphs support that position— paragraph two states that the costs of hung juries are minimal, and paragraph three states that requiring unanimous verdicts leads to fairer verdicts and thus fairer trials." With a brief synopsis such as this one, you could confidently return to the passage as needed. Question about the critic's position? Most likely the answer will be found in the first paragraph. Question about verdict fairness? Most likely the answer will be found in the last paragraph.

Don't worry that you will not be able to recall every detail. The answers to every problem are already on the page, and thus your task is simply to be able to identify the correct answer, not to remember every single thing about the passage.

Your structural analysis should be general enough to be mentally retained, while still providing enough basic detail to serve as a guide when you return to the passage. Also keep in mind that if you need to refresh your memory, you can glance at your notes for clues.

Of course, the Viewpoint Analysis approach we discussed before will also help you identify and track the structure of the passage, since understanding the views of the various players assists in your ability to understand the passage as a whole. Identifying the main point and author's tone will also make this task easier.

VIEWSTAMP Analysis: Structure Identification Drill

Moving on to the "Structure" portion of the VIEWSTAMP analysis, your objective in this drill is to determine what the author accomplished in each one of the following paragraphs as concisely as possible, yet with enough detail to serve as a practical guide when you return to the passage in responding to a question. *Answers begin on page 96*

1. The artistic style of Vincent Van Gogh, the Dutch master Post-Impressionist painter born in 1853, is defined by passionate brush strokes and the bold use of symbolic color. Van Gogh's body of work is expansive, given his relatively short creative life. Recent evidence, however, suggests that as many as 100 works previously attributed to Van Gogh may not be authentic. This shocking number has prompted leading scholars to ask why Van Gogh has been forged more than any other modern master.

   Paragraph summation:_____
   _____
   _____
   _____
   _____

2. *On War*, the posthumously published seminal work of military theorist Carl von Clausewitz (1780-1831), is regarded as an effort, unique in its time, to marry the concepts of political and military strategy. Guided by the principle that war is "simply the expression of politics by other means," Clausewitz rejected a succession of preceding works of military theory for being focused too heavily on practical, geometrical, and unilateral considerations. In short, Clausewitz sought a unified theory of war that encompassed both the practical considerations of conducting war and the constant, reciprocal application of intelligent forces that permit military genius to rise above the fixed rules of traditional military doctrine.

   Paragraph summation:_____
   _____
   _____
   _____
   _____

VIEWSTAMP Analysis: Structure Identification Drill

3. Harriet Tubman was born a slave in Maryland in 1819 or 1820. Having suffered vicious beatings as a child, she escaped north to Philadelphia when she was approximately thirty years old. Over the next several years, Tubman learned the duties of a conductor on the Underground Railroad, a network of people and secret places used to help slaves escape to non-slave holding territories, and to freedom. During this time she worked tirelessly, devoid of fear for her personal safety, to help others escape as she had done. Through her work, Tubman became acquainted with other figures whose words and actions would echo down through history, telling both her story and their own.

    Paragraph summation:_____
    _____
    _____
    _____
    _____

4. The emergence of the Euro-American presence in the Osage territory, however, had deleterious effects that extended beyond just the devastating use of military force. Prior to the cultural influence of the Euro-American political leadership, Osage tradition required that any decision made by the Osage as a people had to be unanimous. Recurring contact with the leadership structure of Western civilizations quickly began to change the Osage culture, and with troubling results. The strength of the traditional Osage system of unanimity was that each individual was bound to every major decision, and internal strife once a decision had been made was rare.

    Paragraph summation:_____
    _____
    _____
    _____
    _____

VIEWSTAMP Analysis: Structure Identification Drill

5. Forensic handwriting analysis, a pattern matching discipline in which an examiner compares a "known" handwriting sample to the handwriting on a "questioned" document to determine whether the person who created the known sample also wrote the questioned document, has been the subject of ongoing and vigorous debate within the legal community. Granted the status of "expert testimony," such forensic analysis is an infrequently used but often powerful evidentiary tool employed by prosecutors to convince juries of a defendant's guilt. But, should such evidence even be admissible at trial? The answer to this question begins with another question: is forensic handwriting analysis a science? Recent federal appellate court decisions are split on this issue, which is critical to the determination of the proper legal standard to be used by trial courts in ruling on the admissibility of forensic handwriting evidence.

Paragraph summation:_____

_____

_____

_____

_____

6. In the early 1950s, a diagnosis of autism—a broad term used to describe developmental brain disorders resulting in difficulties in social interaction and communication, both verbal and non-verbal, and also resulting in repetitive behaviors—almost always meant a life of institutionalization for the person diagnosed, beginning in childhood and lasting throughout the rest of the person's life. Temple Grandin, born in the late 1940s, was herself diagnosed with autism in 1950. As a child, Grandin did not speak until she was more than three years old, communicating only through screams and other non-verbal vocalizations. Despite these disadvantages, Grandin went on to earn a doctorate in animal science and to invent a livestock restraint system used for the humane handling of nearly half of the cattle in North America. One key to Dr. Grandin's success was a symptom of her autism: she is a photo-realistic visual thinker who can construct and examine complex designs in her mind before they are constructed, just as someone might examine a photograph of the built object, and down to the last detail.

Paragraph summation:_____

_____

_____

_____

_____

VIEWSTAMP Analysis: Structure Identification Drill Answer Key—page 93

1. *The artistic style of Vincent Van Gogh, the Dutch master Post-Impressionist painter born in 1853, is defined by passionate brush strokes and the bold use of symbolic color. Van Gogh's body of work is expansive, given his relatively short creative life. Recent evidence, however, suggests that as many as 100 works previously attributed to Van Gogh may not be authentic. This shocking number has prompted leading scholars to ask why Van Gogh has been forged more than any other modern master.*

    This excerpt introduces the artist Van Gogh, as well as the question of why his works are so often forged. As this paragraph seems to begin a discussion rather than complete one, it would likely be the introductory paragraph in a longer passage.

2. *On War, the posthumously published seminal work of military theorist Carl von Clausewitz (1780-1831), is regarded as an effort, unique in its time, to marry the concepts of political and military strategy. Guided by the principle that war is "simply the expression of politics by other means," Clausewitz rejected a succession of preceding works of military theory for being focused too heavily on practical, geometrical, and unilateral considerations. In short, Clausewitz sought a unified theory of war that encompassed both the practical considerations of conducting war and the constant, reciprocal application of intelligent forces that permit military genius to rise above the fixed rules of traditional military doctrine.*

    In this paragraph the author discusses Clausewitz, a military theorist who uniquely combined military and political theory. This example might appear as an entire short passage or could also be the introductory paragraph within the structure of a longer passage.

3. *Harriet Tubman was born a slave in Maryland in 1819 or 1820. Having suffered vicious beatings as a child, she escaped north to Philadelphia when she was approximately thirty years old. Over the next several years, Tubman learned the duties of a conductor on the Underground Railroad, a network of people and secret places used to help slaves escape to non-slave holding territories, and to freedom. During this time she worked tirelessly, devoid of fear for her personal safety, to help others escape as she had done. Through her work, Tubman became acquainted with other figures whose words and actions would echo down through history, telling both her story and their own.*

    Here the author discusses the apparent subject of the passage, Harriet Tubman; the role of this excerpt within a larger passage would be to recount some of the details of the Underground Railroad and the part played by Tubman..

VIEWSTAMP Analysis: Structure Identification Drill Answer Key

4. *The emergence of the Euro-American presence in the Osage territory, however, had deleterious effects that extended beyond just the devastating use of military force. Prior to the cultural influence of the Euro-American political leadership, Osage tradition required that any decision made by the Osage as a people had to be unanimous. Recurring contact with the leadership structure of Western civilizations quickly began to change the Osage culture, and with troubling results. The strength of the traditional Osage system of unanimity was that each individual was bound to every major decision, and internal strife once a decision had been made was rare.*

This paragraph discusses the Euro-American culture's negative impact on the Osage people, specifically the undermining of the Osage tradition of requiring unanimity in decisions affecting the whole people. The appearance of the term "however" in the first sentence tells us that this is at least the second paragraph in a larger passage, and the end of the paragraph suggests further discussion to come, so this would likely appear structurally as a middle paragraph in a three or four paragraph passage.

3

5. *Forensic handwriting analysis, a pattern matching discipline in which an examiner compares a "known" handwriting sample to the handwriting on a "questioned" document to determine whether the person who created the known sample also wrote the questioned document, has been the subject of ongoing and vigorous debate within the legal community. Granted the status of "expert testimony," such forensic analysis is an infrequently used but often powerful evidentiary tool employed by prosecutors to convince juries of a defendant's guilt. But, should such evidence even be admissible at trial? The answer to this question begins with another question: is forensic handwriting analysis a science? Recent federal appellate court decisions are split on this issue, which is critical to the determination of the proper legal standard to be used by trial courts in ruling on the admissibility of forensic handwriting evidence.*

This paragraph introduces both the subject of forensic handwriting analysis and the issue of whether this study is a science. This excerpt might stand alone as a short passage, but likely leads to a subsequent passage expanding upon the as yet undecided issue of admissibility.

VIEWSTAMP Analysis: Structure Identification Drill Answer Key

6. *In the early 1950s, a diagnosis of autism—a broad term used to describe developmental brain disorders resulting in difficulties in social interaction and communication, both verbal and non-verbal, and also resulting in repetitive behaviors—almost always meant a life of institutionalization for the person diagnosed, beginning in childhood and lasting throughout the rest of the person's life. Temple Grandin, born in the late 1940s, was herself diagnosed with autism in 1950. As a child, Grandin did not speak until she was more than three years old, communicating only through screams and other non-verbal vocalizations. Despite these disadvantages, Grandin went on to earn a doctorate in animal science and to invent a livestock restraint system used for the humane handling of nearly half of the cattle in North America. One key to Dr. Grandin's success was a symptom of her autism: she is a photo-realistic visual thinker who can construct and examine complex designs in her mind before they are constructed, just as someone might examine a photograph of the built object, and down to the last detail.*

This paragraph relays a significant amount of information regarding Dr. Temple Grandin, who overcame a diagnosis of autism to become an accomplished inventor, in part by turning a symptom of her condition (photorealistic visual thought) into an asset. From a structural standpoint, this example is long enough that it could be an entire passage; the subject is introduced and discussed at length, and the end of the excerpt allows for the possibility (although it does not suggest the need) for further discussion in a subsequent paragraph.

3. Tone of the Author

The author's tone, or attitude, is revealed through the author's choice of words in the passage. For example, is the author indifferent? Critical? Convinced? Hopeful? Skeptical? To determine the author's tone, you should pay close attention to any clues about how the author feels about the subject under discussion. Does the author seem certain or unsure, positive or negative?

In the vast majority of passages, GMAT authors tend not to be extreme in their opinions. Since most passages are drawn from academic or professional publications, the authors attempt to offer reasoned, tempered arguments in support of their position, hoping to sway the average reader. In doing so, they often present counterarguments and acknowledge the position of the other side. This fact does not mean that they cannot have strong opinions; it just means that they will not use extremely passionate or fiery language. Thus, one does not often see an author whose tone would be described as "jubilant," "tempestuous," or "depressed."

Note also that tone is representative of the passage as a whole, and not just of a single section. An author who exhibited strong support for a position throughout a passage but then at the very end of the passage acknowledged that critics existed would not be said to be "concerned" or "negative." In other words, the tone exhibited in the last few lines would not override or outweigh the positive support that the author displayed earlier. Instead, such a section would simply modify the overall tone of the author to something along the lines of "reasoned optimism" or "positive but realistic."

Clearly, the author is not the only one who may express a distinct tone. Each viewpoint group can have a tone as well, but determining that tone can sometimes be far more difficult because other positions are filtered through the author's words. That is, the author chooses all of the text in the passage, so the viewpoint of each group is harder to discern at times because non-author views are given to you secondhand. This typically results in a limited range of tones, so, although an author's tone can be quite complex, usually the tone of other viewpoint groups is less so, and can often be reduced to a simple agree/disagree position. Thus, while you must know the viewpoint of each group in the passage, as far as attitude, you are primarily concerned with the attitude of the author.

Let us analyze a few excerpts and examine the idea of tone further.

Questions that refer to highlighted portions of text on the GMAT often ask about the purpose of a particular word or phrase the author chose to use; understanding the author's tone is vital to complete comprehension of a passage.

Most GMAT authors do not display a very extreme attitude or tone.

Consider the following section of text:

> There are signs that the animosity between the two
> companies is diminishing.

In the section above, the author's attitude towards the occurrence appears to be neutral. The information is presented factually, and no valuation of the diminishing animosity is provided. Consider, however, how this passage would read if one additional word were inserted:

> Fortunately, there are signs that the animosity between
> the two companies is diminishing.

With the addition of "fortunately," the author's attitude towards the occurrence is now clear—the diminishment of the animosity is a positive occurrence. Other word choices would obviously have a different effect. For example, choosing "unfortunately" instead of "fortunately" would reverse the author's position on the diminishing disagreement .

Of course, GMAT passages are comprised of more than a single sentence, and sometimes no indicator words are present. The following text segment typifies how a passage can begin:

> Hydraulic fracturing, or "fracking," is the practice
> of introducing pressurized fluids into rock
> layers—such as those in shale—in order to assist
> in the removal of petroleum and natural gas from
> (5) the rock strata. While fracking has increased the
> recovery of oil and gas from US reserves and has
> provided economic growth in areas of the country
> that had been depressed, the environmental risks
> are unquestionably cause for concern. Groundwater
> (10) contamination is the primary threat, because
> fracking fluids can migrate into water supplies.
> Other threats exist as well, including air pollution
> and toxic waste. These concerns need to be
> addressed if fracking is allowed to continue.

Tone: Cautious; Concerned.

The author admits that fracking has provided some benefits, including economic growth and an increase in energy production. However, the author also notes that there are concerns, and that these concerns need to be addressed if fracking is to continue. "Concerned" and "Cautious" would thus be the best descriptors.

Here is another example:

In the months following the 1919 Paris Peace
Conference, a special commission drafted the
Covenants for the League of Nations. Later, in
June of that same year, 44 nations signed the
(5)   Covenant, effectively establishing the League
of Nations. In early 1920, the first League
council meeting was held, with representatives
from each of the signatory nations in attendance.

Tone: Neutral; Factual; Explanatory.

The tone of this paragraph is very matter-of-fact. And, indeed, the
paragraph is a simple recitation of facts, devoid of any emotionally
charged words or opinion indicators.

Because tracking viewpoints and tone is such a critical ability, the next
several pages contain a drill that will help test and strengthen your ability
to identify various viewpoints and their accompanying tones.

The makers of
the test say
that the GMAT
"measures
your ability to
understand,
analyze and apply
information
and concepts
presented in
written form."

3

VIEWSTAMP Analysis: Tone Identification Drill

Connecting with the author to understand his or her perspective is vital to a full understanding of a Reading Comprehension passage. Read each of the following paragraphs, and identify and briefly describe the attitude or tone of the author while reading. *Answers begin on page 105*

3

Passage #1:

While often maligned by political commentators of the 1970s, the early success of the Five Year Plans for the Soviet economy is indisputable. After languishing for decades economically, in
(5)   just 13 years under Plan stewardship the Russian economy suddenly produced double-digit growth.

Tone: _____

Passage #2:

In an attempt to produce the results desired by the manufacturer, the glyphosate test results were manually manipulated, including fabrication of data tables and falsification of
(5)   data. These fraudulent practices endangered millions of lives, and the punishments handed down—minor jail terms and fines—were intolerably low. Such reprehensible behavior demanded harsher punitive action in order to
(10) deter other scientists from engaging in the same behavior.

Tone: _____

VIEWSTAMP Analysis: Tone Identification Drill

Passage #3:

The works of Maya Angelou reflect a passion for living and a breathtaking range of life experience. Her dazzling 1969 autobiographical work, *I Know Why the Caged Bird Sings*, rightly brought her
(5)   worldwide recognition and fame, but "author" was just one of many artistic endeavors at which she excelled; she was also an acclaimed poet, playwright, screenwriter, editor, dancer, narrator, journalist, broadcaster, composer, actor, producer,
(10)   and director.

Tone: _____

3

Passage #4:

The legal system of Yemen has traditionally been weak and disorganized. Although Sharia (the religious law of Islam) is the constitutionally mandated source of Yemeni law, in practice the
(5)   system is administered by the Supreme Judicial Council (SJC). The SJC appoints judges (and can remove them at will), leading to an uncertain system prone to corruption, harassment, and manipulation. While many attempts to reform the
(10)   judiciary have been made in recent years, real reform remains unlikely, and Yemen is liable to continue to suffer without genuine rule of law.

Tone: _____

Concept Drill

VIEWSTAMP Analysis: Tone Identification Drill

<u>Passage #5</u>:

In the aftermath of the Great Depression, the Glass-Steagall Act of 1933 reformed the American banking system. Later congressional actions weakened Glass-Steagall until, ultimately,
(5) significant sections were repealed in 1999. These developments directly lead to the financial meltdown of the late 2000s, an event that affected millions of citizens. However, with the recent shift in voter attitudes, I am certain that changes will
(10) be made to the current banking statutes that will result in greater stability and sustained economic growth.

Tone: _____

<u>Passage #6</u>:

West Indian manatees are aquatic mammals that inhabit the Caribbean and US Southeastern coastal area. The large, slow-moving manatee has an inquisitive nature and amiable temperament, and
(5) presents no threat to humans. For a number of years, manatee populations have been decreasing, and encounters with humans or man-made refuse is often the cause. For example, fast-moving watercraft regularly strike these gentle mammals,
(10) sometimes killing them and often inflicting serious injury. In other instances, discarded fishing gear such as hooks, sinkers, and monofilament line, is ingested by the curious manatee, causing distress and sometimes agonizing death. We should do
(15) more to save the manatee from this inhumane treatment.

Tone: _____

VIEWSTAMP Analysis: Tone Identification Drill Answer Key—page 102

Note that this drill seeks to assist you in identifying the tone present in written statements. Writing down one or two descriptor words is intended to assist you in concisely encapsulating the tone. This is *not* to suggest that you should constantly write down tone descriptors while reading.

Also, the descriptors provided in the answer key are general descriptors. If you provided a different term, that is acceptable as long as your answer is in the general vicinity of the answer provided. For example, if the answer key uses "congratulatory" as the tone, and you answered "complimentary," then that would still be correct.

Passage #1:

While often maligned by political commentators of the 1970s, the early success of the Five Year Plans for the Soviet economy is indisputable. After languishing for decades economically, in
(5)   just 13 years under Plan stewardship the Russian economy suddenly produced double-digit growth.

Tone: Positive; Impressed.

The author's general tone is a very positive one, reflecting that the author was impressed by the early achievements of the Five Year Plans. The author first establishes this tone by setting up a comparison to political commentators, who often criticized the Plans. Then, by using the phrases such as "early success is…indisputable" and "in just 13 years…suddenly produced," the author indicates that the achievements of the Soviet economy are particularly notable and worth consideration. Specifically, the strength of the term "indisputable," and the use of the qualifier "just" are the main indications of the author's attitude, and what distinguishes this sentence from a simple reporting of the facts.

VIEWSTAMP Analysis: Tone Identification Drill Answer Key

<u>Passage #2:</u>

In an attempt to produce the results desired by the manufacturer, the glyphosate test results were manually manipulated, including fabrication of data tables and falsification of
(5)   data. These fraudulent practices endangered millions of lives, and the punishments handed down—minor jail terms and fines—were intolerably low. Such reprehensible behavior demanded harsher punitive action in order to
(10)   deter other scientists from engaging in the same behavior.

Tone: Critical; Disapproving; Near Outrage.

The second and third sentences in this segment provide the most information about the tone of this passage. "Fraudulent practices endangered millions" indicates the severity of the issue (consider how the meaning of the sentence would change if "fraudulent" and "endangered" were changed to milder terms). "Intolerably low" indicates that the author feels that what has occurred was unacceptable in the extreme. "Reprehensible" is a very clear and forceful description of the actions, indicating that the author feels strongly about the issue in a negative manner. And finally, "demanded" is again a very strong descriptor. Thus, at the least the author's tone is critical and disapproving, and possibly approaching outrage.

VIEWSTAMP Analysis: Tone Identification Drill Answer Key

Passage #3:

> The works of Maya Angelou reflect a passion for
> living and a breathtaking range of life experience.
> Her dazzling 1969 autobiographical work, *I Know*
> *Why the Caged Bird Sings*, rightly brought her
> (5) worldwide recognition and fame, but "author" was
> just one of many artistic endeavors at which she
> excelled; she was also an acclaimed poet,
> playwright, screenwriter, editor, dancer, narrator,
> journalist, broadcaster, composer, actor, producer,
> (10) and director.

Tone: Enthusiastic; Appreciative; Adulatory.

The author's attitude towards Angelou's work is extremely complimentary. Phrases such as "breathtaking range," "dazzling 1969 autobiographical work," "rightly brought her worldwide recognition," and "just one of many artistic endeavors at which she excelled" indicate not just respect, but an attitude closer to adoration or adulation.

VIEWSTAMP Analysis: Tone Identification Drill Answer Key

<u>Passage #4</u>:

The legal system of Yemen has traditionally been weak and disorganized. Although Sharia (the religious law of Islam) is the constitutionally mandated source of Yemeni law, in practice the
(5)   system is administered by the Supreme Judicial Council (SJC). The SJC appoints judges (and can remove them at will), leading to an uncertain system prone to corruption, harassment, and manipulation. While many attempts to reform the
(10) judiciary have been made in recent years, real reform remains unlikely, and Yemen is liable to continue to suffer without genuine rule of law.

Tone: Negative; Pessimistic; Doubtful.

The description of the Yemeni legal system is unquestionably negative ("uncertain system prone to corruption, harassment, and manipulation"), and the author closes with a series of pessimistic statements: "real reform remains unlikely" and "liable to continue to suffer."

<u>Passage #5</u>:

In the aftermath of the Great Depression, the Glass-Steagall Act of 1933 reformed the American banking system. Later congressional actions weakened Glass-Steagall until, ultimately,
(5)   significant sections were repealed in 1999. These developments directly lead to the financial meltdown of the late 2000s, an event that affected millions of citizens. However, with the recent shift in voter attitudes, I am certain that changes will
(10) be made to the current banking statutes that will result in greater stability and sustained economic growth.

Tone: Optimistic; Confident.

The first 8 lines of the passage suggest that the author may take a rather negative view of the subject, but this is only because the events under discussion are, by definition, negative. In Lines 8-12, however, the author displays a confident and optimistic attitude that changes will be made: "I am certain that changes will be made...that will result in greater stability and sustained economic growth."

VIEWSTAMP Analysis: Tone Identification Drill Answer Key

<u>Passage #6</u>:

West Indian manatees are aquatic mammals that
inhabit the Caribbean and US Southeastern coastal
area. The large, slow-moving manatee has an
inquisitive nature and amiable temperament, and
(5)   presents no threat to humans. For a number of
years, manatee populations have been decreasing,
and encounters with humans or man-made refuse
is often the cause. For example, fast-moving
watercraft regularly strike these gentle mammals,
(10)   sometimes killing them and often inflicting serious
injury. In other instances, discarded fishing gear
such as hooks, sinkers, and monofilament line, is
ingested by the curious manatee, causing distress
and sometimes agonizing death. We should do
(15)   more to save the manatee from this inhumane
treatment.

3

Tone: Sympathetic; Compassionate.

This can be a challenging passage. However, the author uses a number of words to humanize
the manatees, and repeatedly refers to them in positive terms ("inquisitive," "amiable,"
"gentle," "curious," "agreeable") while at the same time referring to their suffering in more
extreme ways ("serious injury," "distress and agonizing death," "inhumane"). This fact, coupled
with the closing statement that "we should do more" for the manatee, suggests that the author's
attitude in this segment is one of sympathy and compassion towards the manatees. If you felt
that the last sentence had an air of indignance or outrage to it, that is not a misinterpretation,
either. The author certainly seems to be calling for action on the basis of an inhumanity,
although the "should" (instead of "must" or "I demand") ratchets down the level of rhetoric.

4. Passage Argumentation

Identifying viewpoints and tone is critical to getting a generalized feel for how a passage unfolds. GMAT Reading Comprehension passages often consist of premises and conclusions just as in the Critical Reasoning section, and understanding the arguments will help to clarify the details. Consider the arguments presented in the example below and the brief discussion that follows.

> Michelangelo was apprenticed to painter Domenico Ghirlandiao at age 13, before creating any of his seminal works. As a result, many art historians believe that Ghirlandiao
> (5) played a pivotal role in the artistic development of Michelangelo. Some critics, however, counter that Michelangelo's inherent talent would have similarly developed at any of the academies at the time, and that Ghirlandiao was
> (10) simply a stepping stone. These critics argue that the Medici played a far greater role in Michelangelo's development, as they were his patrons and commissioned a number of his works. While acknowledging that the Medici were
> (15) more significant in Michelangelo's career, the opposition notes that it was Ghirlandiao who introduced Michelangelo to the Medici, when the Medici asked Ghirlandiao to supply his two best pupils, and that Ghirlandiao gave up Michelangelo
> (20) before the young artist's apprenticeship was up.

<u>Lines 3-6 and Lines 14-20: Many Art Historians</u>. This group believes that Ghirlandiao played a critical role in the rise of Michelangelo. Later in the passage, the "opposition" is referenced. Since the Critics disagreed with the Many Art Historians, this reference to the "opposition" can be linked back to the Many Art Historians. Note that the Many Art Historians do not disagree that the Medici were important; they just argue that Ghirlandiao was important as well.

<u>Lines 6-13: Critics</u>. The Critics believe that Ghirlandiao was a minor piece in Michelangelo's life, and that the Medici were more significant.

Arguments that are presented in a GMAT Reading Comprehension passage should always be noted, as they will almost certainly be the subject of questions that follow the passage.

On the next page begins a drill that provides practice taking note of passage argumentation.

VIEWSTAMP Analysis: Argument Identification Drill

Read each of the following paragraphs, and note any identifiable arguments while reading. In the space provided, identify each argument by the line reference. *Answers begin on page 115*

Passage #1:

Incentivization has recently become a hotly
debated topic. On one side of the debate are
theorists who believe that the use of incentives
is fraught with dangers, including unintended
(5) side effects that could lead to the distortion of
our social values and goals. On the other side
of the debate are pragmatists who insist that,
while such dangers exist and are legitimate
concerns, there is no other feasible way to
(10) induce needed social changes.

3

Number of Arguments: _____

Argument Line References: _____

_____

_____

_____

_____

_____

_____

_____

_____

_____

VIEWSTAMP Analysis: Argument Identification Drill

Passage #2:

The Universal Declaration was a needed list of fundamental human rights drawn up in 1946 after consultation with leading politicians and philosophers from around the world. While the
(5) responses from those thinkers were surprisingly consistent, putting those human rights into practice was controversial. An early criticism came from cultural relativists, who argued that the concept of rights derived from western individualism, and
(10) was thus a form of western cultural imperialism. These criticisms were unwarranted, however. As the critics of the cultural relativists noted, each culture does not contain a wholly separate set of values, but rather sets of values that at times
(15) intertwine, and many of the values that the cultural relativists attributed solely to western thinking were also present within non-western cultures. Further, critics contended, relativists ignored the fact that even individual countries
(20) have no single uniform culture, but rather large numbers of sub-cultures blended together to create the whole.

Number of Arguments: _____

Argument Line References: _____

_____

_____

_____

_____

_____

_____

_____

_____

_____

_____

VIEWSTAMP Analysis: Argument Identification Drill

<u>**Passage #3**</u>:

Neutrinos are subatomic particles, similar to
electrons but lacking an electrical charge. In a
recent scientific controversy, experimental results
indicated that neutrinos were able to travel faster
(5)   than the speed of light, a violation of Einstein's
theory of special relativity. While some researchers
hailed the results as a breakthrough with profound
implications for the future, other researchers
immediately questioned the credibility of the
(10)   reported findings.

3

Number of Arguments: _____

Argument Line References: _____

_____

_____

_____

_____

_____

_____

_____

_____

_____

_____

Concept Drill

VIEWSTAMP Analysis: Argument Identification Drill

Passage #4:

The swift emergence of bitcoin (a peer-to-peer, digital currency that permits electronic payments between strangers without third-party intervention) as a form of currency has left
(5) state, national, and international governmental organizations grasping to understand the technology and predict its potential impact on monetary policy. While some assert that bitcoin is a novelty that is entirely independent
(10) of the traditional banking system and beyond the reach, for example, of the United States Federal Reserve System, i.e., the central bank of the United States, others argue that bitcoin's potential for nearly instantaneous geometric
(15) expansion could seriously threaten a nation's financial security.

Number of Arguments: _____

Argument Line References: _____

_____

_____

_____

_____

_____

_____

_____

_____

_____

Concept Drill

VIEWSTAMP Analysis: Argument Identification Drill Answer Key—page 111

Passage #1:

Incentivization has recently become a hotly debated topic. On one side of the debate are theorists who believe that the use of incentives is fraught with dangers, including unintended
(5) side effects that could lead to the distortion of our social values and goals. On the other side of the debate are pragmatists who insist that, while such dangers exist and are legitimate concerns, there is no other feasible way to
(10) induce needed social changes.

Lines 2-6: Theorists. The Theorists believe that the use of incentives is troubling and dangerous.

Lines 6-10: Pragmatists. This group agrees with the Theorists that dangers exist, but argues that incentivization is necessary to bring about required social changes.

VIEWSTAMP Analysis: Argument Identification Drill Answer Key

Passage #2:

The Universal Declaration was a needed list
of fundamental human rights drawn up in 1946
after consultation with leading politicians and
philosophers from around the world. While the
(5)   responses from those thinkers were surprisingly
consistent, putting those human rights into practice
was controversial. An early criticism came from
cultural relativists, who argued that the concept
of rights derived from western individualism, and
(10) was thus a form of western cultural imperialism.
These criticisms were unwarranted, however. As
the critics of the cultural relativists noted, each
culture does not contain a wholly separate set of
values, but rather sets of values that at times
(15) intertwine, and many of the values that the
cultural relativists attributed solely to western
thinking were also present within non-western
cultures. Further, critics contended, relativists
ignored the fact that even individual countries
(20) have no single uniform culture, but rather
large numbers of sub-cultures blended together
to create the whole.

Lines 1-7 and Line 11: Author. In Line 1 the author refers to the list as "needed," an opinion. In Line 11, the author rejects the views of the Cultural Relativists.

Lines 7-10: Cultural Relativists. This group argued that rights are a western ideal, and thus establishing a universal statement of rights was culturally imperialistic.

Lines 12-22: Critics. The Critics of the Cultural Relativists noted that, among other things, fundamental rights values already existed in the non-western cultures, which are not uniform anyway.

VIEWSTAMP Analysis: Argument Identification Drill Answer Key

Passage #3:

Neutrinos are subatomic particles, similar to
electrons but lacking an electrical charge. In a
recent scientific controversy, experimental results
indicated that neutrinos were able to travel faster
(5)   than the speed of light, a violation of Einstein's
theory of special relativity. While some researchers
hailed the results as a breakthrough with profound
implications for the future, other researchers
immediately questioned the credibility of the
(10)   reported findings.

3

Lines 5-6: Einstein. This can be a tough argument to identify, because it is inserted so briefly. Einstein asserted the theory of special relativity, and since that theory is violated by the experimental results, Einstein's view would be that according to his theory neutrinos cannot travel faster than the speed of light.

Lines 6-8: Some Researchers. These researchers see the experimental results as having a broad and important effect on society.

Lines 8-10: Other Researchers. These researchers believe the experimental results are possibly false.

VIEWSTAMP Analysis: Argument Identification Drill Answer Key

<u>Passage #4</u>:

The swift emergence of bitcoin (a peer-to-
peer, digital currency that permits electronic
payments between strangers without third-party
intervention) as a form of currency has left

(5) state, national, and international governmental
organizations grasping to understand the
technology and predict its potential impact on
monetary policy. While some assert that bitcoin
is a novelty that is entirely independent

(10) of the traditional banking system and beyond
the reach, for example, of the United States
Federal Reserve System, i.e., the central bank
of the United States, others argue that bitcoin's
potential for nearly instantaneous geometric

(15) expansion could seriously threaten a nation's
financial security.

<u>Lines 8-13: Some</u>. "Some" assert that bitcoin is merely a novelty independent of the Federal Reserve.

<u>Line 13: Others</u>. "Others" argue that bitcoin is a potential threat to national security.

5. Main Point

Identifying ideas at the elemental level is an important ability, and one that will serve you well throughout the GMAT, as well as in business school. However, Reading Comprehension questions sometimes ask you broad questions such as the Main Point of the author's argument. Consequently, you must also see the "big picture" as you read, and develop an ability to track the author's major themes and intents.

This section discusses the "M" in the VIEWSTAMP acronym. The "M" stands for Main Point.

The main point of a passage is the central idea, or ultimate conclusion, that the author is attempting to prove. Although in the majority of passages the main point is stated in the first paragraph, it is not always the case that the main point appears at the very outset. The main point of many passages has appeared in the final sentence of the first paragraph or in the first sentence of the second paragraph, or, at times, in the last paragraph. So, although the main point is often found early in the first paragraph, the test makers have the ability to place the main point anywhere in the passage.

The main point of a passage is the central idea that the author is attempting to prove or relay.

As you read, identify the author's conclusions and track how they link together. What is the author attempting to prove? Are some conclusions used to support others? If so, which is the primary conclusion? Keep in mind that although the main point may be stated succinctly in a sentence or two, all paragraphs of the passage must support the Main Point.

6. Primary Purpose

The Primary Purpose (a concept closely related to Main Point) is the author's central reason for writing the passage, and these questions seem to be a particular focus on the GMAT (the majority of released passages include Primary Purpose questions). If Main Point questions require the "What" of the passage ("What's the point? What is the author driving at?"), then Primary Purpose questions require you to consider the "Why." Why did the author want to write the material in question? Why did the author include this information in support of his or her goals?

This section discusses the "P" in the VIEWSTAMP acronym. The "P" stands for Primary Purpose.

Note that the answers to each Primary Purpose question tend to begin with a verb, so understanding the author's motivation is vital; was the author attempting to describe a work of fiction? ...to explain a process? ...to present a theory? ...perhaps to defend a position?

While Main Point questions and Primary Purpose questions deal with related concepts, many passages are accompanied by questions of both types. On the following pages are several short passages, each followed by both a Main Point and a Primary Purpose question; note the difference in focus between the two different question types as you attempt to form a prephrase for each before considering the answer choices.

VIEWSTAMP Analysis: Main Point/Primary Purpose Identification Drill

Read each of the following paragraphs and try to quickly identify both the main point, and the author's primary purpose in writing each passage. These are considerations that will generally serve you well in reading, and in particular on the Reading Comprehension and Critical Reasoning sections of the GMAT. Each of the reading passages featured in this drill is followed by both a main point, and a primary purpose question. As you approach the questions, and read the subsequent explanations, note the differences between Main Point and Primary Purpose questions, as well as the answer choices that are associated with each. *Answers begin on page 123*

Passage #1:

Socialist realism, the officially approved style of realistic art developed in the Soviet Union during the 1930's, had a relatively simple political objective. As the primary instrument of
(5) state propaganda, it sought to promote the goals of socialism and communism through positive images of rapidly changing villages, grandiose public projects, and well-groomed wholesome youth. Form and content were strictly regulated
(10) by a vast army of cultural bureaucrats, whose only job was to ensure conformity to state doctrine. Accordingly, impressionism and abstraction were quickly abolished, replaced by ostensibly truthful representation of reality in its "revolutionary"
(15) development.

Ultimately, censorship was fated to collaborate in its own undoing. The state correctly perceived the interpretive potential of art to be inherently dangerous, but the effort to contain artistic
(20) ambiguity only amplified the disconnect between reality and fiction. As the Soviet Union's centrally planned economy led to increasingly inefficient resource distribution, the utopian vision of a "revolutionary" world became easy to mock. The
(25) art of socialist realism did provide a refuge from the bleak reality of most ordinary Russians, if only because irony and laughter (unlike bread and butter) were always abundant, and required no food stamps to procure.

1. Which one of the following most accurately states the main point of the passage?

(A) Socialist realism had, as its chief objective, the furtherance of socialist and communist ideology.

(B) Because of censorship, socialist realism never fulfilled its artistic potential.

(C) The art of socialist realism was a welcome distraction from the bleak reality of ordinary Russians.

(D) Conformity to state doctrine led to an ostensibly truthful representation of reality in its revolutionary development.

(E) The proliferation of uniformly positive images of a fictional world impeded, rather than promoted, the political objectives of socialist realism.

2. The primary purpose of the passage as a whole is to

(A) reject an artistic style as a utopian vision.

(B) analyze the disconnect between reality and fiction in the Soviet Union.

(C) explain why an artistic style failed to conform to state doctrine.

(D) examine the extent to which a style of art achieved its political objectives.

(E) describe an instrument of state propaganda.

VIEWSTAMP Analysis: Main Point/Primary Purpose Identification Drill

Passage #2:

Systemic lupus eythematosus (SLE) is an autoimmune disease characterized by the aberrant and chronic stimulation of the innate immune system—our first line of defense against infection.
(5) Under normal circumstances, immune cells are recruited to sites of infection through the production of chemical factors called cytokines. In patients with SLE, cytokines recruit cells to attack normal, healthy tissues without the presence of an
(10) infectious pathogen. This results in the proliferation of antibody-immune complexes that cause inflammation and damage to the kidneys, blood vessels, and skin.

Patients with SLE are often treated with
(15) courses of strong immunosuppressive drugs, such as cytotoxic drugs, antimalarial compounds and glucocorticoids. While glucocorticoid therapy is considered the most effective course of treatment, it is regrettably transient, requiring more aggressive
(20) (and potentially more harmful) treatments such as high-dose methylprednisolone pulse therapy. Discovering why glucocorticoid therapy fails to provide lasting relief has been the subject of numerous recent studies. The main culprit seems
(25) to be the plasmacytoid dendritic cells (pDC)— innate immune cells that circulate in the blood and are found in peripheral lymphoid organs. While pDCs are normally susceptible to treatment with glucocorticoids, they are resistant to such
(30) treatment in patients with SLE. And, since pDCs are responsible for producing the key cytokines involved in SLE pathogenesis, the level of these cytokines does not substantially decrease with treatment, and symptoms quickly relapse. The
(35) precise mechanism by which pDC resistance occurs is still unknown.

1. In the passage the author is primarily concerned with doing which one of the following?

   (A) outlining the mechanisms by which immune cells attack healthy tissues in patients with SLE

   (B) demonstrating the difficulties that must be overcome if a satisfactory cure for SLE is to be found

   (C) describing the pathogenesis of SLE and explaining why the disease is difficult to treat

   (D) showing why one explanation of the difficulties involved in treating SLE falls short in explaining these difficulties.

   (E) evaluating the evidence supporting the explanation as to why SLE is difficult to treat.

2. Which one of the following best states the central idea of the passage?

   (A) Identifying a cure for SLE requires understanding the precise mechanism by which pDC resistance occurs.

   (B) Scientists have made little progress in the treatment of SLE.

   (C) Successful treatment of SLE requires reducing the harmful effects of antibody-immune complexes on healthy tissues.

   (D) In patients with SLE, the risks associated with the currently available courses of treatment outweigh the benefits of such treatments.

   (E) Despite recent advances in our understanding of the immune system, a satisfactory course of treatment for patients with SLE is yet to be found.

VIEWSTAMP Analysis: Main Point/Primary Purpose Identification Drill

Passage #3:

At the turn of the 21st century, some philosophers justifiably wondered exactly how "post" postmodernism actually is, worried that the term—used for an increasingly heterogeneous
(5) assembly of theories and cultural phenomena— may no longer have any meaning at all. There are indeed many differences between the theories of postmodern thinkers such as Baudrillard, Derrida, Lyotard, or Jameson, and many possible ways
(10) of describing and judging the "postmodern" condition of the most advanced Western societies, not to mention their complex relations with other societies in times of postcolonialism and growing globalization. Nevertheless, it is possible to
(15) define—however broadly—the criteria that serve as a common denominator for postmodernism. First and foremost, the postmodern condition cannot be understood without acknowledging the increasing virtualization of our society: the
(20) ubiquity of computers and the Internet has all but blurred the line between fact and fiction, often turning "facts" into mere by-products of "fiction." In academia, postmodernity entails a growing suspicion of such terms as "authenticity," "identity,"
(25) or "essence," believing—correctly—that they are socially constructed categories of human cognition. The primary analytical strategy of postmodern thinkers is that of reading—and deconstructing— the world as a "text" devoid of all-encompassing
(30) grand narratives or stable hierarchical structures. In literature and architecture, the postmodern style transgresses the gap between "high" and "low," "inside" and "outside," purposefully highlighting the constructed nature of any binary formation.
(35) One could say that postmodernism is the reign of the quotation mark. That does not mean, however, that the postmodern world is free of real power or oppression, nor that all ethical concerns have yielded to aesthetic relativism. Such conclusions
(40) are foolish and dangerous in equal measure.

1. The author of the passage is primarily concerned with

   (A) alleviating a philosophical concern by outlining the scope of a key term
   (B) evaluating the cultural relevance of a philosophical movement
   (C) correcting a common misconception about the postmodern world
   (D) questioning the socially constructed nature of certain terms in philosophy and literature
   (E) examining the differences between philosophical theories

2. Which one of the following best states the central idea of the passage?

   (A) Postmodern thinkers approach the world as a "text" devoid of grand narratives or stable hierarchical structures.
   (B) It is reasonable to suspect that the term "postmodern" has lost its original meaning.
   (C) Our understanding of the postmodern condition has been influenced by the ubiquity of computers and the Internet.
   (D) Although postmodernism resists a single definition, it is possible to define the fundamental principles that characterize it.
   (E) Today's philosophers are wrong to question the value of postmodernism, because there are many ways of describing the "postmodern" condition.

VIEWSTAMP Analysis: Main Point/Primary Purpose Identification Drill Answer Key—page 120

Passage #1: Analysis

Question #1: The correct answer choice is (E)

This question asks us to identify the main point of the passage. To do so, it is imperative to understand the structure of the passage as a whole: It opens with a description of the central objectives of socialist realism, and elaborates on the importance of censorship in aligning them to those of the state. The second paragraph changes direction: censorship led to its own undoing. The rest of the paragraph supports this statement by explaining how it occurred, making the first sentence of the second paragraph the main point of the passage.

Answer choice (A) is incorrect, because it does not represent a summary of the passage. The author does not try to *convince* us that socialist realism sought to further socialist and communist ideology; the fact that it did is merely stated as a fact in the first paragraph.

Answer choice (B) is incorrect, because the artistic potential of socialist realism is not under discussion.

Answer choice (C) is incorrect, because it is not the main point of the passage. While socialist realism did provide a refuge from the bleak reality of ordinary Russians, the rest of the passage does not seek to support this claim.

Answer choice (D) is incorrect, because the effects of censorship on artistic representation is not the main point of the passage. Furthermore, as the discussion in the second paragraph shows, censorship led to a *fictitious* representation of reality, which compromised its primary objectives.

Answer choice (E) is the correct answer choice, as it most closely parallels the idea that by censoring artistic expression, the state amplified the disconnect between reality and fiction, which ultimately compromised the objectives of socialist realism.

VIEWSTAMP Analysis: Main Point/Primary Purpose Identification Drill Answer Key

Question #2: The correct answer choice is (D)

Unlike a Main Point question, which requires us to summarize what the author *said*, the Main Purpose question asks us to describe what the author *did*. The two questions are naturally related; however, the Main Purpose question tends to have a broader scope, and the correct answer choice need not be overly specific. Any answer choice that cannot be proven with the information contained in the passage will be incorrect.

Answer choice (A) is incorrect, because it is not the author who rejects the art of socialist realism as a utopian vision: if anything, the Russian people did. "Rejecting" an artistic style implies some sort of judgment, which is not the primary purpose of the passage.

Answer choice (B) is incorrect. The author mentions that there was a disconnect between reality and fiction in the Soviet Union, but the primary purpose of the passage is not to analyze this fact.

Answer choice (C) is attractive, but incorrect. The art of socialist realism failed to achieve its political objectives; its conformity to state doctrine was never under question.

Answer choice (D) is the correct answer choice. The first paragraph outlines the political objectives of socialist realism, while the second paragraph explains why these objectives were not ultimately achieved. In the broadest of terms, the passage as a whole examines the *extent* to which a style of art achieved its political objectives.

Answer choice (E) is incorrect, because it only describes the function of the first paragraph, not of the passage as a whole.

VIEWSTAMP Analysis: Main Point/Primary Purpose Identification Drill Answer Key

Passage #2: Analysis

Question #1: The correct answer choice is (C)

The answer to this Main Purpose question is directly tied to the function of each paragraph: the first one describes the pathology of SLE, while the second one explains why glucocorticoid therapy fails to provide lasting relief. The correct answer choice will ideally contain elements of both ideas.

Answer choice (A) is incorrect, because it only describes the function of the first paragraph, not of the passage as a whole.

Answer choice (B) is incorrect, because the main question in this passage is why is SLE difficult to *treat*, not cure. Furthermore, even if the issue of pDC resistance represents a difficulty that must be overcome in order to find a cure for SLE, this answer choice does not address the function of the first paragraph.

Answer choice (C) is the correct answer choice because it summarizes the function of each paragraph, as well as of the passage as a whole.

Answer choice (D) is incorrect, because the author does not seek to invalidate or challenge the explanation involving pDC.

Answer choice (E) is incorrect, because the author merely introduces the hypothesis that pDC resistance might explain why glucocorticoid therapy fails to provide lasting relief in SLE patients. No evidence supporting this hypothesis has been evaluated.

VIEWSTAMP Analysis: Main Point/Primary Purpose Identification Drill Answer Key

Question #2: The correct answer choice is (E)

Whereas the Main Purpose question tests your abstract understanding of passage structure and function, the Main Point question is more argument-driven: to answer it correctly, you need to summarize a position, i.e. an argument. Since the first paragraph contains no elements of argumentation, the main point is likely to be found in the second paragraph.

Answer choice (A) is incorrect. Understanding how pDC resistance occurs is probably helpful, but by no means a necessary condition for identifying a cure for SLE. This answer choice falls outside the scope of the passage, and does not summarize its main point. Also, note that this answer choice refers to elements taken from the last sentence of the passage—a sure sign of a decoy answer to a Main Point question. Since most students assume that the main point would be found towards the end of the passage, test makers often create incorrect answer choices that exploit this assumption.

Answer choice (B) is attractive, but incorrect. Just because the most effective treatment for SLE is far from perfect does not mean that scientists have made little progress in the treatment of SLE. In fact, the second paragraph outlines the results of numerous studies, which seem to have discovered the reason why glucocorticoid therapy fails to provide lasting relief. This is clearly evidence of progress, even if a successful course of therapy is yet to be found. This answer choice suggests too pessimistic of a viewpoint.

Answer choice (C) is also attractive, but incorrect. Given that SLE is characterized by the proliferation of antibody-immune complexes that cause damage to the kidneys, blood vessels, and skin, we can infer that any successful course of treatment requires reducing these harmful effects. However, just because a given statement is true does not mean that it is also the main point of the passage: not every inference is a conclusion.

Answer choice (D) is incorrect, because the passage does not provide sufficient information to help us determine whether the risks of high-dose methylprednisolone pulse therapy outweigh the benefits. All we know is that this type of therapy is more aggressive—and potentially harmful—than glucocorticoid therapy. Even if it were true, this answer choice would still be incorrect, as it fails to summarize the passage as a whole.

Answer choice (E) is the correct answer choice. The first paragraph merely describes the origination of SLE, which is why the main point of the passage is likely to be found in the second paragraph. And indeed, the central focus of that paragraph is to explain why even the most effective currently available treatment fails to provide lasting relief. In other words, a successful treatment for patients with SLE is yet to be found.

VIEWSTAMP Analysis: Main Point/Primary Purpose Identification Drill Answer Key

Passage #3: Analysis

Question #1: The correct answer choice is (A)

The answer to this Main Purpose question is directly tied to the organization of the passage: the author begins by outlining a (justifiable) philosophical concern regarding postmodernism, and then attempts to alleviate it by defining the criteria common to all postmodern theories.

Answer choice (A) is the correct answer choice. By defining the criteria that serve as a common denominator for postmodernism (lines 13-15), the author outlines the scope of a key term ("postmodernism") in order to alleviate the philosophers' concern described in lines 1-6.

Answer choice (B) is incorrect, because the cultural relevance of postmodernism is not under debate.

Answer choice (C) is attractive, but incorrect. While it is true that the author attempts to alleviate a concern regarding postmodernism, this is not the same as "correcting a common misconception." To compare the philosophers' concern to a "misconception" would be somewhat misleading, because the author views their concern as "justifiably" (line 2). Furthermore, the philosophers' misconception—if any—concerns postmodernism as a movement, not the "postmodern world."

Answer choice (D) is incorrect, because it describes the purpose of the postmodern philosophers, not the author's purpose.

Answer choice (E) is incorrect. The author mentions that there are "many differences" between the theories of certain postmodern thinkers (lines 6-8), but the purpose of the passage as a whole is not to examine these differences. On the contrary—the goal is to show that certain criteria are common to all postmodern theories (lines 13-15).

VIEWSTAMP Analysis: Main Point/ Primary Purpose Identification Drill Answer Key

Question #2: The correct answer choice is (D)

Whereas the Main Purpose question tests your abstract understanding of passage structure and function, the Main Point question is more argument-driven: to answer it correctly, you need to summarize the author's main argument. That can be found in lines 13-15: "Nevertheless, it is possible to define—however broadly—the criteria that serve as a common denominator for postmodernism." This is in direct response to the philosophers' concern outlined earlier, and is also supported by the rest of the passage.

Answer choice (A) is incorrect. It is true that postmodern thinkers approach the world as a "text" devoid of grand narratives or stable hierarchical structures (lines 24-28), this observation merely supports the notion that there are criteria common to all postmodern theories.

Answer choice (B) is incorrect. While the author regards the philosophers' concern outlined in lines 1-6 as justifiable (i.e. reasonable), the mere fact is that it has nothing to do with the main point of the passage.

Answer choice (C) is incorrect. Just because we cannot understand the postmodern condition without acknowledging the increasing virtualization of our society (lines 15-20) does not mean that our understanding of the postmodern condition has been *influenced* by the ubiquity of computers and the Internet. The two ideas are close enough, but are not quite the same. Furthermore, even if true, this is not the main point of the passage, because the evidence presented does not seek to substantiate the connection between computers and the postmodern condition.

Answer choice (D) is the correct answer choice, as it reflects closely the prephrase described above.

Answer choice (E) is incorrect, because there is no reason to suspect that today's philosophers question the *value* of postmodernism. They only question its meaning.

Chapter Four:
Passage Elements
and Formations

Chapter Four: Passage Elements and Formations

Chapter Preview

This chapter will cover sources of passage difficulty and examine the elements and formations in passages which tend to generate questions. That is, we will look at what makes passages hard and what passage elements the test makers most commonly ask about. In this sense, this chapter continues the discussion already in progress: the preceding chapter introduced the "big picture" elements that you must always track, whereas here we will present the more detailed elements that you should note. In the next chapter we will discuss individual question types.

Sources of Difficulty: The Test Makers' Arsenal

There are a number of ways the makers of the test can increase the level of difficulty of any given passage, but before we examine the specific elements they employ, reviewing the general methods that can be used to increase difficulty is helpful.

The following four items are the primary ways the test makers alter your perception of passage difficulty:

Challenging Topic or Terminology

In some passages, the choice of topic makes the passage seem more difficult to test takers. For example, many students fear the appearance of a science-related passage on the GMAT. As we will discuss later, you should not be afraid or unduly worried by science passages (or any passage, for that matter). That said, an unfamiliar or complex topic can make a passage harder, but only incrementally so because the test makers must explain the main concepts of the passage, regardless of the topic. Thus, there may be a few moments of anxiety while you are forced to adjust to an unknown topic, but they should be fleeting since the test makers will always give you the information needed to answer the questions. So this is more of a psychological challenge than one of outright difficulty.

The use of complicated terminology usually concerns students as well. Reading a passage that contains words or ideas that you do not recognize is intimidating and often confusing. You should not be alarmed by unknown concepts, however, mainly because the test makers must *always* define any term or concept not in common public usage.

Ideally by test day you should be comfortable dealing with the unfamiliar subject matter that might appear in Reading Comprehension passages, and remember, since the GMAT is a computer based test, familiarity with the presentation of the passages and questions will be vital on test day.

When you encounter unknown words, they will generally fall into one of two categories: new terms related to the concept under discussion or unknown vocabulary words. In the case of terms directly related to the topic at hand (such as *Monetarism* or *Meteor Streams*), the test makers will explain the term or concept for you in the text, sometimes briefly using synonyms, other times in greater detail. Unknown vocabulary words can be more challenging, but you can use context clues from the surrounding text to help determine the meaning of words you do not recognize. We will briefly discuss this point again later in this chapter.

Challenging Writing Style

The test makers carefully choose whether a passage will have a clear, easy-to-read writing style or a more dense, convoluted construction. Obviously, writing style has a tremendous effect on passage difficulty because even the easiest of concepts can become hard to understand if the presentation is intentionally complex.

In the first few lines of a passage, it is difficult to tell whether the writing style will be challenging. If you do encounter a passage that has a very difficult-to-read style, use some of the tips in the next section to focus on the elements most likely to be tested.

Multiple Viewpoints

In the preceding chapter we discussed the importance of tracking passage viewpoints while reading, and readdress them here because a common and easy way for the test makers to increase difficulty is to add *more* viewpoints. Tracking viewpoints in a passage with only one or two viewpoints is easy; tracking viewpoints in a passage with three or more viewpoints is considerably more challenging. The more viewpoints present, the easier it is for readers to confuse them, or forget who said what. This is especially true because when more viewpoints are present, the test makers typically insert extensive compare-and-contrast sections, which makes separating and mastering each view more difficult.

As you develop the ability to see through the topic and focus on the writing style, you will notice that many passages are not as complex as their topics might suggest.

4

THE POWERSCORE GMAT READING COMPREHENSION BIBLE

Difficult Questions/Answers

The difficulty of a passage set is also affected by the nature of its questions. For example, if the questions are unusual in nature, or, more frequently, if the answers are difficult to separate from one another as right or wrong, then the passage set itself will be difficult or time-consuming. Thus, even an easily-understood passage can turn challenging once you start answering its questions. Later we will discuss question types in detail, and provide you with an effective approach for attacking any question you face.

On the GMAT it's important that you know how to attack any Reading Comprehension question as efficiently as possible, since the Computer Adaptive Test doesn't allow you to skip a question and return to it later.

Passage Elements That Generate Questions

As you read, there are certain specific, consistent passage elements that should jump out at you, primarily because history has reflected the test makers' tendency to use these elements as the basis of questions. That means recognizing these moments when you first encounter them can allow you to predict with confidence what matters most in the passage and what questions are likely to follow it!

For purposes of clarity in this overview, we will divide these elements into two groups: viewpoint-specific elements and text-based elements.

Viewpoint-Specific Elements

Analysis of viewpoints is one of the major approaches we use in attacking the passages, and in the previous chapter we discussed this approach in depth. Separating viewpoints allows you to divide the passage into logical, trackable components, and helps you to more easily understand the passage and to disentangle the many disparate ideas presented. Viewpoints also play a central role in the main themes of the passage, so naturally they serve as the source of many of the questions asked by the test makers. For example, questions about the main point, authorities cited by the author, or the perspective of any of the players in the passage are all related to viewpoints, and thus tracking viewpoints not only makes understanding the passage itself easier, it automatically assists you in answering a *significant* portion of the questions. Thus, while reading you must always focus on identifying each viewpoint in the passage.

When considering viewpoints, be aware that one of the test makers' favorite tricks is to use competing perspectives, a tactic that involves presenting two or more viewpoints on the same subject, with each view containing slightly different elements (while also offering moments of overlap and similarity).

Here is an example:

Topic: Nuclear power

Viewpoint 1:   Nuclear power plants are efficient generators of energy, but they present serious long-term environmental concerns because of the problems associated with storing radioactive waste in the form of spent fuel.

Viewpoint 2:   Nuclear power is the most efficient way to produce energy, and the waste problems associated with them, while significant, are lesser than those associated with more traditional energy production methods, such as those involving coal.

In the paragraphs above, the differences and similarities in viewpoints are easy to identify, even with some less obvious subtleties included ("efficient generators of energy" vs "most efficient way to produce energy," and "serious long-term environmental concerns" vs "waste problems...while significant, are lesser," to name two). But imagine for a moment that the two views are woven together in a passage, and some extraneous information is also interspersed. When you finally attack the questions a few minutes later, it would be very easy to have forgotten the exact similarities and differences, especially in the presence of additional viewpoints.

Since competing perspectives can be quite tricky to follow—it is easy to confuse or misremember different views in the context of entire passages—it should come as no surprise that questions about these elements closely test whether you understand the *exact* differences between the various viewpoints on offer. So precision is paramount!

Because viewpoint analysis was a main feature in the last chapter we will move on for the moment, but in all of the passages we explore in later chapters this element will be a cornerstone of our analysis.

Text-based Elements

In one sense, all questions are based on the text. In using the name "text-based," we're referring to elements that appear directly in the text as an identifiable part—definitions, lists, compare/contrast sections, and specific dates, for example—and not the broader and somewhat more abstract elements such as main point, author's purpose, or passage structure. Under this definition, text-based questions will often be smaller pieces, sometimes just a single word, other times a short section of the text. In this sense, these are the "nuts and bolts" components that you should be aware of when reading.

These are the elements we will discuss (not in order of importance):

1. Initial Information/Closing Information

2. Dates and Numbers

3. Definitions

4. Examples

5. Difficult words or phrases

6. Enumerations/Lists

7. Text Questions

Note these elements as you encounter them in the passages; you are likely to see them again in the questions.

4

Please note that the itemized list above is *not* a checklist to use when attacking passages. You simply can't read while also looking for a seven-part, numbered list. Instead, you must ingrain an understanding of these elements into your Reading Comprehension world view, and then simply take notice of them when they appear. This requires practice, but it is easily achievable with a little work. Approaching passages in this fashion allows you to read broadly for the VIEWSTAMP elements while simultaneously noting the ideas above when they appear. To reiterate an analogy introduced previously, you are like an air traffic controller looking at a radar screen: you only worry about these elements when they appear, and you only react to them when you have to do so.

Let's talk about each item in more detail.

1. Initial Information/Closing Information

The information presented in the first five lines of a passage—especially fine details—is often forgotten by students. This occurs because at the very beginning of a passage you are focused on figuring out the topic and the author's general position, and thus seemingly minor details are hard to retain.

Similarly, the information presented in the last five lines is often forgotten because the average student is eager to jump to the questions and thus skims over the material at the very end of the passage.

The test makers are well aware of these tendencies, so they occasionally question you on your knowledge of information seen at the very beginning or end of the passage. To combat this, make sure to check these areas if you are having difficulty answering a question, especially when you seem to have no idea where in the passage the answer comes from (again, this would most likely occur with detail or fact-based questions).

2. Dates and Numbers

When a GMAT author references more than one date or era, creating a simple timeline can be an effective way to maintain relative perspective, whether the comparison spans days or centuries.

Dates often provide useful markers within a passage, allowing you "before" and "after" points to return to when searching for answers. While in some passages the use of dates is incidental, in other passages a clear chronology is created, and then some of the questions will test your ability to understand the timeline.

The general rule is that the more dates you see in a passage, particularly if they are given in regular intervals or serve as identifiers of progress or change, the more important it is that you make note of them.

Numbers are usually less important than dates, but when numbers are used in a comparative sense, or as part of an explanation, the test makers will sometimes check your comprehension of their meaning.

3. Definitions

Identifying definitions serves two purposes: in those cases where you do not understand the term or concept it helps you to clarify the idea, and even when you do understand the concept the test makers will frequently test you on your understanding of the definition, so noting its location is extremely useful.

The typical definition is presented in the immediate vicinity of the word or concept it represents, like so:

> In England the burden of history weighs heavily on common law, the unwritten code of time-honored laws derived largely from English judicial custom and precedent.

In the text above, the clause after the comma provides the definition for the term *common law*. Of course, some definitions are much shorter, such as this sentence which includes the one-word definition of *maize*:

> Every culture that has adopted the cultivation of maize—also known as corn—has been radically changed by it.

Regardless of the length of a definition, you should make sure that you are comfortable with the term being defined. If you encounter an idea or term that you think should be defined but do not see a definition in the immediate vicinity, then the definition will probably be presented relatively soon (explicitly or through context clues), and the test makers are simply trying to trick you with a "trap of separation," which we will discuss later in this chapter.

Whenever you see an unfamiliar term or concept defined, be sure to take note; if the test makers have provided a clear definition or description, they generally expect you to be able to locate the reference.

4. Examples

GMAT authors often use examples to explain or underscore or even attempt to prove the points they are making. Logically, these examples serve as concrete (often real-world) premises that support the broader conclusion of the author. Functionally, they help you to understand the typically more abstract point that the author is making, and so they can be quite helpful especially when you are having difficulty understanding an argument.

Examples are not the main conclusion or point of the author; the point being supported or explained by the example is the author's central belief.

Examples can be short and specific to a single point, or they can be substantial and involved and appear throughout the passage. Always remember, though, that the example is not the main conclusion or point of the author; generally, examples are provided to *support or explain* the main conclusion.

The words "for example" are the most common way that examples are introduced, but the following phrases all have been used:

> For example
> For instance
> A case in point is
> As shown by
> As demonstrated by

Whenever you see these terms, immediately note what point is being illustrated. Consider this:

> In science, serendipity often plays a crucial role in discoveries. For instance, Teflon was discovered by a scientist attempting to find a new gas for use in refrigeration.

Above, the author introduces a concept (that good luck often plays a crucial role in new discoveries), and immediately exemplifies that belief with the introductory phrase "for instance" and the specific case of Teflon.

5. Difficult Words or Phrases

"Circumpolar vortex" describes the high-altitude westerly winds that circle the Northern hemisphere at the middle latitudes.

To "vituperate" is to berate or address harshly.

As mentioned earlier, challenging words or phrases are items that you should note while reading, but you should not become overly distressed if you do not immediately know what the terms mean. Terms outside the common public domain of knowledge (such as *circumpolar vortex*) are always explained, and unknown vocabulary words (such as *vituperate*) can often be defined by the context of usage. Acronyms, too, are always explained.

The key thing to remember is that even if you do not understand a word or idea, you will still understand virtually all other words and ideas in the passage, and so the potential downside of not knowing one element is very small. If you cannot make sense of something reasonably quickly, simply move on and see if clarity is made possible via some subsequent portion of text.

6. Lists and Enumerations

A number of passages feature sections where the author presents a view by providing a list of points that support or explain the position, or that are possible outcomes of a course of action. When these lists occur, you are almost always tested on your understanding of some or all of the items on the list. In fact, of the seven items discussed in this section, Lists and Enumerations are generally the most reliable question producer: when a passage contains a list of two or more items, chances are nearly 100% that at least one question will be asked in reference to it.

Lists and enumerations are typically the most reliable source of questions, so it is imperative that you recognize and track these elements!

The listed items do not appear as bullet points. Rather, they tend to appear using constructions similar to one of the following:

> "First...Second...Third..."
> "First...Second...In addition..."
> "First...Second...Third...Last..."
> "(1)...(2)..."
> "Initially...And...Further..."
> "One possibility is...Another possibility is...A final possibility..."

The lists usually contain one of two types of items: a list of reasons (premises) that explain why an action was taken or why a circumstance came into being, or a list of examples that relate to the point at hand. But note that any type of enumerated grouping is possible, and a likely source for the questions that follow.

A list of premises may appear as follows:

> The move towards political systems less dependent on monarchical structures came about for several reasons. First, the monetary and military abuses of the royalty placed several governments in severe financial hardship and created a strong undercurrent of discontent and resentment among the populace. Second, the uncertainty over personal human and property rights caused select elements within the upper class to become convinced that a more concrete and accountable political system was necessary, one insulated from the vagaries of royalty. And finally, problems with succession created a political environment fraught with uncertainty and turmoil.

A list of examples might appear as follows:

> Developing nations have used a number of ingenious methods
> to increase energy production—and therefore gross economic
> capacity—while at the same time maintaining a commitment
> to sustaining the environment. Microfinanced solar projects
> in India, Brazil, and Vietnam have all yielded power systems
> able to sustain towns and villages in remote areas, all without a
> material impact on local resources. A wind farm in Morocco is a
> successful collaboration between three commercial firms and the
> government, and now outputs 50 megawatts. In Tibet, where there
> are no significant or obtainable fossil fuel resources, the Nagqu
> geothermal energy field provides 300 kilowatts of power in more
> cost-effective fashion than could any fossil fuel generators.

In the example above, the listed items are not numbered or introduced
as list items, but a list of examples connected to specific countries is
presented nonetheless. When reading, you must be prepared to encounter
lists of items that are not clearly marked as such in the text. Any time
an author presents a series of examples (or a series of *anything*, for that
matter), you should recognize it and expect to refer back to it when you
begin answering the questions.

7. Text Questions

*Text questions
can be explicitly
or implicitly
presented in the
passage.*

When an author poses a question in the passage, in most instances the
author goes on to immediately answer it. Thus, tracking the presence of
text questions is critical because it provides you with an outline for where
the passage will go next. And, because these questions are often central
to the theme of the passage, there is usually a post-passage question that
centers on the answer to the question the author posed.

Most often, text questions are raised in the traditional, explicit manner,
with a question mark, as follows:

> So, what was the ultimate impact of the court's ruling on property rights for the
> Aleutian Islanders?

However, questions can be posed without the traditional question mark:

> And thus, researchers concluded that some other explanation was needed to
> account for the difference in temperatures.

The sentence above implies that there is a question regarding the
temperature difference, and this implicit question is likely to then be
answered in the text.

Two Broad Reasoning Structures ▇▇

Causal reasoning and conditional reasoning appear frequently in the Critical Reasoning questions of the GMAT, but less so with the Reading Comprehension passages. Still, recognizing each reasoning type when it appears is extremely helpful because it provides a framework for understanding the arguments being made.

Let's briefly review causal and conditional reasoning:

Causal Reasoning

Cause and effect reasoning asserts or denies that one thing causes another, or that one thing is caused by another. The cause is the event that makes the other occur; the effect is the event that follows from the cause. By definition, the cause must occur before the effect, and the cause is the "activator" or "ignitor" in the relationship. The effect always happens at some point in time after the cause.

Causality in Reading Comprehension usually is discussed in the context of why certain events occurred. The terms that typically introduce causality—such as *caused by*, *reason for*, *led to*, or *product of*—are still used, but then the author often goes on to discuss the reasons behind the occurrence in depth.

Causality, when it appears in Reading Comprehension, is not normally viewed as flawed reasoning, and GMAT authors usually make an effort to explain the reasoning behind their causal assertions.

Conditional Reasoning

Conditional reasoning is the broad name given to logical relationships composed of sufficient and necessary conditions. Any conditional relationship consists of at least one sufficient condition and at least one necessary condition. A sufficient condition is an event or circumstance whose occurrence indicates that a necessary condition must also occur. A necessary condition is an event or circumstance whose occurrence is required in order for a sufficient condition to occur. In other words, if a sufficient condition occurs, you automatically know that the necessary condition also occurs. If a necessary condition occurs, then it is possible but not certain that the sufficient condition will occur. However, if a necessary condition *fails* to occur, you then know that the sufficient condition cannot occur either.

Conditional relationships in Reading Comprehension passages tend to be unobtrusive, usually occurring as a sideline point to a larger argument. For example, a passage might discuss monetary policy, and in the course of doing so make a conditional assertion such as, "The only way to decrease monetary volatility is to tightly control the supply of money." In this sense, conditionality is usually not the focus or Main Point of a passage, but instead it is a type of reasoning that occurs while discussing or supporting other points.

Of the two types of reasoning, causal reasoning appears more frequently than conditional reasoning in the Reading Comprehension passages. This difference is due to the fact that many passages attempt to address why certain events occurred, and in doing so they naturally fall into causal explanations.

When either of the two reasoning types appears, it is usually discussed in more expansive terms, and the casual or conditional argument is broad and seldom based on single words or sentences. For example, consider the following paragraph:

> While prescriptions for medications are at an all time high, hyperactivity in children appears to be attributable in many cases to diet. Excessive ingestion of processed sugars, for example, has been linked to various disorders. In a recent study of children diagnosed with hyperactivity, many subjects displayed a more positive response to sugar restriction than to traditionally prescribed medication.

In the first sentence, a cause-and-effect relationship is asserted, and then the remainder of the paragraph builds the case for the assertion. Of course, causal or conditional reasoning assertions need not be limited to a single paragraph; entire passages can be built around a single causal or conditional idea.

Pitfalls to Avoid

While there are many concrete elements to track when reading a passage, there are also a number of text formations and configurations you should recognize. These constructions are often used by the test makers to create confusion, so in this sense they function as possible "traps" for the unwary test taker. The following section reviews the most frequently appearing traps, and examines each in detail.

Traps of Similarities and Distinctions™

These sections of text discuss in detail items that have both similarities and differences. By comparing and contrasting the items in a continuous block of text, the test makers create the possibility of confusion (by comparison, if the discussion of the concepts was separated into discrete sections, the information would be easier to manage).

You should not become bogged down in trying to memorize every detail. Instead, take down a simple notation about a given section or paragraph, so that if you are asked about the details you can quickly return to the passage and sort out the specifics.

Compare-and-contrast sections appear frequently in Reading Comp passages, and you should expect to see one or more on your exam.

If a list of comparisons and contrasts starts to get complicated, a simple note ("paragraph two: mills compared") allows you to keep that section in perspective and move on to the rest of the passage.

Trap of Separation™

One favorite trick of the test makers is to take a long discussion of a particular topic and break it up by inserting within it a section of text about a related but distinct topic, effectively creating a separation effect: the main idea bisected by similar but different (and possibly distracting) content in the middle. Then in the questions, the test makers require you to follow and understand the bigger-picture discussion, testing your ability to track the interrupted main concept despite its beginning and end being divided by many lines (or entire paragraphs) in the passage.

In some especially insidious instances, the question stems will specifically refer you to just one of the places where the concept is discussed (for example, "In lines 12-14, the author..."), but this will not be the place in the passage that contains the information needed to answer the question. This trap, known as the Trap of Question Misdirection, can be very difficult to handle because most questions that specifically refer you to a place in the passage are indeed referring you to the area where the information needed to answer the question resides.

The Trap of Question Misdirection occurs when the test makers use a specific line reference in the question stem to direct you to a place in the passage where the correct answer will not be found.

One reason this trick works is that there is a natural tendency on the part of readers to assume that pieces of information that are related should be in close proximity. The logical and linear writing style used in newspapers and textbooks tends to reinforce this belief, thus many students regrettably approach the GMAT with these misguided expectations. However, as we have already discussed, the test makers want to present passages that test your ability to comprehend difficult, nonlinear material, and so they use certain methods to create greater complexity in the passages.

Of course, just as information that is separated can be related, information that is in close proximity does not have to be connected, as discussed next.

Trap of Proximity™

Just because two ideas are presented in close physical proximity to one another within a passage does not mean that they are related. As mentioned in the prior section, the expectation of most readers is that information that is physically close together will be related. This does not have to be the case, and the makers of the GMAT will set up situations to test your ability to make that distinction.

Trap of Inserted Alternate Viewpoint ™

Another ploy the test makers favor is to discuss a particular viewpoint, and in the middle of that discussion insert a new viewpoint. This technique is used to test your ability to track different perspectives and to know who said what.

Traps of Chronology™

Traps of chronology relate to the placement and order of items within the passage, and the tendency of many readers to believe that when one item is presented before another, then the first item occurred first or caused the second item. These two traps are called the Trap of Order and the Trap of Cause:

Trap of Order

Some students make the mistake of believing that because an item is discussed before another item, the first item likely predated the second item. Unless explicitly stated or inherently obvious, this does not have to be the case.

Trap of Cause

Other students make the mistake of assuming that when one item is discussed before another item, then the first item must have caused the second item. This assumption is unwarranted. The easiest way to discern the author's intentions is to carefully examine the language used by the writer because causal relationships almost always feature one or more of the words that indicate causality (such as *caused by*, *produced by*, *determined*, etc.).

The simple truth is that the order of presentation of the items in the passage does not indicate any temporal or causal relationship between those items.

Previously we discussed how passages on any topic could be easy or difficult. Passage difficulty is more a function of writing style, the number of viewpoints, and the exact concepts under discussion than of the general topic of the passage. That said, the test makers will occasionally use the topic to catch test takers off-guard. This technique of theirs works because when the typical student begins reading a passage, the topic often frames their expectations. For example, science passages are thought to be challenging whereas passages about humanities are less feared. The test makers are well aware of these ingrained expectations, and they at times play a sort of "bait and switch" game with students, especially by making a passage initially look hard or easy and then radically changing the level of difficulty after the first few lines or first paragraph.

The point to take from this discussion is that you should not assume that a passage will be easy or hard solely from its topic, and certainly not from reading just the first line or paragraph. The test makers love to play with the expectations of test takers, and one of their favorite tricks is to turn those expectations on their head.

Final Chapter Note

In review, the approach we advocate is a multi-level one. While reading, you should constantly track the major VIEWSTAMP elements discussed in the previous chapter: the various groups and viewpoints discussed within the passage, the tone or attitude of each group or individual, the argument made by each group or individual, the main point of the passage, the author's primary purpose, and the structure and organization of the passage and the organization of ideas.

At the same time, you must also keep an eye on the more singular features that appear throughout the text; items such as examples and definitions, itemized lists, and forms of reasoning, to name a few.

While this approach may sound complicated, with practice it becomes second nature, and soon you will find that you are able to answer many questions very quickly and with more confidence.

On the following pages is a drill that will test your ability to recognize the elements discussed in this chapter, and in the next chapter we move on to discuss the questions and answer choices that follow the reading passages.

Passage Elements Recognition Drill

This drill is intended to help you quickly recognize some of the elements that test makers can use to increase the difficulty of any given passage. After each passage, be sure to note elements from the "Test Makers' Arsenal" discussed earlier in this chapter, and compare your notes with the brief answer key discussions that follow. *Answers begin on page 155*

Example:

Polychlorinated biphenyls (PCBs), which were once widely used in coolants and insulators, were banned by Congress because of the severe danger they presented to the public. Epidemiological
(5) studies of the effects of PCBs on humans revealed potential carcinogenicity and significant long-term persistence in the environment. Non-carcinogenic effects include damage to the immune system, reproductive system, nervous system, and
(10) endocrine system.

Difficult Words
Causality

The passage refers to a number of challenging words, including polychlorinated biphenyls, epidemiological, carcinogenicity, and non-carcinogenic. There are also multiple elements of causality present, from the effects of PCBs on humans to the reason why Congress banned PCBs.

Passage Elements Recognition Drill

Passage #1:

Mozart composed his first musical piece in 1761,
at age 5. The next year he and his sister performed
at the court of Maximilian III, and much of his
youth was spent travelling throughout Europe
(5)   and performing. By 1773, Mozart had gained a
number of admirers in his hometown of Salzburg,
and secured a position as court musician to Count
Colloredo. However, financial concerns and artistic
limitations caused Mozart to resign the Salzburg
(10)   court position in 1777.

Analysis: _____

_____

_____

_____

_____

Passage #2:

Antiquities law addresses the ownership, sale,
and protection of cultural items of value. While
these laws are clear in their protective intent, they
remain, to some extent, open to interpretation,
(5)   and consequently, in some cases the public good
is not protected as intended. What priorities, then,
should a jurist consider when overseeing a case
that involves antiquities?

Analysis: _____

_____

_____

_____

_____

Passage Elements Recognition Drill

Passage #3:

About 5,000 years ago, the Harappan civilization
sprawled over nearly 400,000 square miles (1
million square kilometers) on the plains of the
Indus River in modern-day India and Pakistan,
(5)   and contained 10 percent of the world's population.
Only recently have scientists determined why
this civilization disappeared, and the answer is
climate change. As weather patterns shifted, the
monsoons that fed the Indus River plain began to
(10)   move eastward, and many of the rivers coursing
through the region began to dry up. The result was
a population shift that stripped the Harappans of
economic resources as well as a substantial portion
of the workforce, leading to the collapse of the
(15)   civilization.

Analysis: _____
_____
_____
_____
_____

4

Passage #4:

Neurodiversity is a recent movement that seeks
to establish civil rights for those with non-typical
neurological profiles. A case in point is autism,
which was long thought to be the result of
(5)   nurture factors such as parenting. Neurodiversity
proponents seek to affirm that autism is not a
malady, and, as such, does not need to be cured—
instead, it needs to be better understood.

Analysis: _____
_____
_____
_____
_____

Passage Elements Recognition Drill

Passage #5:

When considering the rate of expansion of the
universe, astrophysical theorists had agreed
that the universe's growth must be slowing
due to gravity. However, observations from the
(5)   Hubble Telescope showed that the universe is
actually expanding more rapidly today than in
the past. What, then, would account for this
surprising observation? One explanation was
that Einstein's theory of gravity was incorrect,
(10)   and that a new theory was needed. A second
explanation suggested that an earlier theory of
Einstein's containing a cosmological constant
could provide the explanation. A final
explanation focused on an unseen energy field
(15)   within space, energy that could account for the
expansion of the universe. However, all three
theories agreed that some form of energy was
present in space.

Analysis: _____

_____

_____

_____

_____

Passage Elements Recognition Drill

Passage #6:

(5)

(10)

(15)

(20)

Recently, the International Court of Justice in The Hague ruled that Japan breached international law when it captured and killed thousands of certain types of whales and issued permits for the killing of other types in an area designated as the Southern Ocean Whale Sanctuary. The ruling, identified by many court observers as unprecedented in its unequivocal rebuke and injunction of whaling activities by a sovereign nation, was lauded by environmentalists. However, many Japanese fisherman, who urged their government to fight the ruling, believe that their whaling is a traditional cultural activity that should be respected. Yet one observer of Japanese politics noted that the banned whaling activities were no longer financially viable, requiring government subsidies anticipated to soon reach $50 million per year, and that this need for subsidies explains the Japanese government's almost immediate decision to abide by the Court's judgment.

Analysis: _____

_____

_____

_____

_____

4

Passage Elements Recognition Drill

Passage #7:

Physicists studying super-heavy atomic nuclei
conducted experiments in which they bombarded
a thin layer of americium, an artificial radioactive
metal created when plutonium atoms absorb
(5)   neutrons during nuclear reactions, with calcium
ions. This collision produced a new element
that has 115 protons at its center. If approved
by an international committee of physicists
and chemists, this new element will be placed
(10)   on the periodic table with the atomic number
115. Temporarily named "Ununpentium," this
artificial element would be the latest super-heavy
element to be created through accelerator based
experimentation. Of the elements found naturally
(15)   occurring on Earth, the heaviest is Uranium,
which has 92 protons in its nucleus, although the
heaviest stable element, meaning an element that
does not decay, is Lead, which has 82 protons in
its nucleus.

4

Analysis: _____

_____

_____

_____

_____

Passage Elements Recognition Drill

Passage #8:

Immediately after pleadings are filed, or at some other time during the pendency of the suit, a trial court may appoint a Guardian ad Litem (GAL) to represent a child in matters of custody and
(5) visitation. GALs are appointed under the theory that the child's parents, embroiled in difficult litigation, may put their own needs above those of the child when making strategic and tactical decisions related to the contest. The decision
(10) regarding whether and when to appoint a GAL for a child is almost universally a matter within the plenary discretion of the trial court, and that decision is given considerable deference by the appellate courts. This wide-ranging
(15) discretion has produced great disparity in how trial judges appoint and use GALs. Some judges appoint them by default, even when the parties are sophisticated and represented by counsel, a situation in which GALs are commonly
(20) considered to be unnecessary. Other judges will appoint a GAL only upon formal motion by a party, and even then only when a party has demonstrated a particularized need for the child to have independent counsel. A new survey
(25) indicates that this disparity in appointment results in substantial practical implications for family law practitioners.

Analysis: _____

_____

_____

_____

_____

Passage Elements Recognition Drill

Passage #9:

Fearing the emergence of a new, pandemic zoonotic disease—a contagious disease transmitted from animals to humans and caused by bacteria, viruses, parasites and fungi carried
(5) by animals and insects—scientists recently created a new pathogen (i.e., a bacterium, virus, or other microorganism that can cause disease) that is 97 percent similar to the 1918 Spanish Flu, which is thought to have originated in birds
(10) and which killed approximately 50 million people. The scientists constructed the new virus by cobbling together wild bird flu fragments. To make the pathogen easier to spread from one animal to another, the scientists mutated
(15) it, making it airborne. Some have labeled the project "insane," stressing the tremendous danger involved in intentionally creating a virus that could potentially kill millions of people if released into the general population, either
(20) accidentally or as a terrorist act. Moreover, they argue that the threat of such a virus emerging naturally from the animal population is too low to justify the risk posed by the research. The researchers, however, defend their work by
(25) pointing to the possibility that a disease similar to the Spanish Flu could spontaneously emerge without warning from the animal population. By creating such a pathogen in a secure, laboratory environment, they argue, health officials can
(30) better prepare to detect and treat a naturally occurring outbreak.

Analysis: _____

_____

_____

_____

_____

Passage Elements Recognition Drill

Passage #10:

In an era of corporate downsizing, large law firms have renewed their insistence that law schools focus less on academia and more on the production of the "practice-ready lawyer."
(5) However, some law professors argue that their institutions should reject what they view as a misguided and short-sighted attempt by the firms to shift their training expenses to the law schools. While the law firms urge law schools to
(10) offer more clinics, externships, and practitioner-specific courses, these professors argue that such an approach is impractical. The first hurdle is in even identifying the proper standard for determining what a practice-ready lawyer is. If
(15) the standard is minimal competence, they argue, then the state-level bar examination already ensures that level of preparedness. Next is the issue of specialization. Are law students now expected to determine a field of practice prior
(20) to graduation, the professors ask? If they do not, then the scope of the private legal market is too broad for the law schools to be able to provide significant practical experience in even the major sub-categories of legal work. Finally,
(25) the professors point out that much of what makes legal practice unique is the confluence of institutional structures, power dynamics, economic incentives, and complex ethical obligations that is impossible to replicate in the law school setting.

4

Analysis: _____

_____

_____

_____

_____

Passage Elements Recognition Drill Answer Key—page 146

Note that this drill seeks to assist you in identifying the passage elements and formations present in written statements. Writing down one or two descriptor words can assist you in concisely identifying these elements for this drill. This is *not* a suggestion that you should write down the names of the specific elements while reading or during the GMAT.

Passage #1:

Mozart composed his first musical piece in 1761, at age 5. The next year he and his sister performed at the court of Maximilian III, and much of his youth was spent travelling throughout Europe
(5)   and performing. By 1773, Mozart had gained a number of admirers in his hometown of Salzburg, and secured a position as court musician to Count Colloredo. However, financial concerns and artistic limitations caused Mozart to resign the Salzburg
(10) court position in 1777.

Dates and Numbers

The passage provides three dates, as well as a subject's age, which together form a time line within the passage. GMAT passages that feature dates and numbers often reference the time line in the questions in order to see if you followed the narrative.

4

Passage #2:

Antiquities law addresses the ownership, sale, and protection of cultural items of value. While these laws are clear in their protective intent, they remain, to some extent, open to interpretation,
(5)   and consequently, in some cases the public good is not protected as intended. What priorities, then, should a jurist consider when overseeing a case that involves antiquities?

Text Question

The passage closes with a classic text question. Antiquities law is also explained, but this is not a definition in the classic sense.

Concept Drill Answer Key

Passage Elements Recognition Drill Answer Key

<u>Passage #3</u>:

About 5,000 years ago, the Harappan civilization sprawled over nearly 400,000 square miles (1 million square kilometers) on the plains of the Indus River in modern-day India and Pakistan,
(5) and contained 10 percent of the world's population. Only recently have scientists determined why this civilization disappeared, and the answer is climate change. As weather patterns shifted, the monsoons that fed the Indus River plain began to
(10) move eastward, and many of the rivers coursing through the region began to dry up. The result was a population shift that stripped the Harappans of economic resources as well as a substantial portion of the workforce, leading to the collapse of the
(15) civilization.

Dates and Numbers
Causality

The passage opens with references to dates, land occupation size, and population size. However, the most notable feature is the series of causal statements that seek to explain why the Harappan civilization disappeared. While many GMAT passages contain causal statements, this section is notable because it details a series of causal relationships, creating a chain of causation that explains what led to the civilization's disappearance.

<u>Passage #4</u>:

Neurodiversity is a recent movement that seeks to establish civil rights for those with non-typical neurological profiles. A case in point is autism, which was long thought to be the result of
(5) nurture factors such as parenting. Neurodiversity proponents seek to affirm that autism is not a malady, and, as such, does not need to be cured— instead, it needs to be better understood.

Definition
Example

The passage begins by defining the term "neurodiversity," and later provides an example ("A case in point..."). Note that this passage indicates that a possible cause (parenting factors) had been previously hypothesized and subsequently dismissed.

Passage Elements Recognition Drill Answer Key

Passage #5:

When considering the rate of expansion of the universe, astrophysical theorists had agreed that the universe's growth must be slowing due to gravity. However, observations from the
(5) Hubble Telescope showed that the universe is actually expanding more rapidly today than in the past. What, then, would account for this surprising observation? One explanation was that Einstein's theory of gravity was incorrect,
(10) and that a new theory was needed. A second explanation suggested that an earlier theory of Einstein's containing a cosmological constant could provide the explanation. A final explanation focused on an unseen energy field
(15) within space, energy that could account for the expansion of the universe. However, all three theories agreed that some form of energy was present in space.

Text Question
List
Causality

The passage centers around a discussion of why the universe is expanding faster than previously believed. A text question is used to ask why this is the case, and then a list of three theories is presented. All three theories assert that some form of energy is the cause of the expansion.

Passage Elements Recognition Drill Answer Key

Passage #6:

Recently, the International Court of Justice
in The Hague ruled that Japan breached
international law when it captured and killed
thousands of certain types of whales and
(5) issued permits for the killing of other types
in an area designated as the Southern Ocean
Whale Sanctuary. The ruling, identified by
many court observers as unprecedented in its
unequivocal rebuke and injunction of whaling
(10) activities by a sovereign nation, was lauded by
environmentalists. However, many Japanese
fisherman, who urged their government to
fight the ruling, believe that their whaling is
a traditional cultural activity that should be
(15) respected. Yet one observer of Japanese politics
noted that the banned whaling activities were no
longer financially viable, requiring government
subsidies anticipated to soon reach $50 million
per year, and that this need for subsidies explains
(20) the Japanese government's almost immediate
decision to abide by the Court's judgment.

The subject matter in this passage excerpt is not difficult. However, there are five viewpoints presented in four sentences, a circumstance in which the viewpoints become very difficult to track. This is known as the Trap of Inserted Alternate Viewpoints. By breaking down the passage, we can make it easier to identify the viewpoints presented:

1. The International Court of Justice ruled that Japan's whale hunting and regulatory activities in a protected area of the ocean violated international law.

2. Many court observers say the Court's ruling was unprecedented because it was unequivocal in its finding against the Japanese government.

3. Environmentalists agree that the Court's ruling was proper.

4. Many Japanese fisherman think the Court's ruling was inappropriate, because whaling is a traditional cultural activity that should be respected.

5. One observer of Japanese politics believes the Japanese government did not fight the Court's ruling because the whaling activities were not financially viable and would require $50 million in subsidies.

Passage Elements Recognition Drill Answer Key

<u>Passage #7</u>:

(5)

(10)

(15)

Physicists studying super-heavy atomic nuclei conducted experiments in which they bombarded a thin layer of americium, an artificial radioactive metal created when plutonium atoms absorb neutrons during nuclear reactions, with calcium ions. This collision produced a new element that has 115 protons at its center. If approved by an international committee of physicists and chemists, this new element will be placed on the periodic table with the atomic number 115. Temporarily named "Ununpentium," this artificial element would be the latest super-heavy element to be created through accelerator based experimentation. Of the elements found naturally occurring on Earth, the heaviest is Uranium, which has 92 protons in its nucleus, although the heaviest stable element, meaning an element that does not decay, is Lead, which has 82 protons in its nucleus.

The difficulty in this passage comes from its scientific theme and the use of unfamiliar terms and concepts. Many students get bogged down in such jargon, and waste valuable time by failing to focus on the VIEWSTAMP items. Also, the numbers in this excerpt are organized in a way that could be confusing. Instead of discussing the numbers of protons in either ascending or descending order, the passage jumbles the order. While this instance of the <u>Trap of Order</u> seems slight, it can interrupt your progress through the passage by disturbing the natural sense of order most readers would anticipate. The concepts involved in this passage are straightforward:

Physicists have created a new artificial element with 115 protons in its nucleus, which is pending official recognition and has temporarily been named "Ununpentium." This is a super-heavy element. The heaviest unstable, naturally occurring element is Uranium, which has 92 protons in its nucleus. The heaviest stable, naturally occurring element is Lead, which has 82 protons in its nucleus.

Passage Elements Recognition Drill Answer Key

Passage #8:

Immediately after pleadings are filed, or at some other time during the pendency of the suit, a trial court may appoint a Guardian ad Litem (GAL) to represent a child in matters of custody and
(5) visitation. GALs are appointed under the theory that the child's parents, embroiled in difficult litigation, may put their own needs above those of the child when making strategic and tactical decisions related to the contest. The decision
(10) regarding whether and when to appoint a GAL for a child is almost universally a matter within the plenary discretion of the trial court, and that decision is given considerable deference by the appellate courts. This wide-ranging
(15) discretion has produced great disparity in how trial judges appoint and use GALs. Some judges appoint them by default, even when the parties are sophisticated and represented by counsel, a situation in which GALs are commonly
(20) considered to be unnecessary. Other judges will appoint a GAL only upon formal motion by a party, and even then only when a party has demonstrated a particularized need for the child to have independent counsel. A new survey
(25) indicates that this disparity in appointment results in substantial practical implications for family law practitioners.

Some may find this passage difficult because of its stilted tone and word choice. This writing style is designed to slow and distract the reader. When you are forced to wade through unnecessarily complicated wording, you are able to devote fewer mental resources to actually understanding the argument being made. Once you move past the stylistic complications, the ideas contained in the passage are not difficult:

A Guardian ad Litem (GAL) is an attorney who may be appointed to represent the interests of a child whose parents are litigating the custody and visitation of the child, and who may therefore put their own interests before those of the child. The trial court has a great deal of discretion in deciding whether to appoint a GAL. Some judges always appoint a GAL, even when it is not clear that one is necessary, while other judges almost never appoint a GAL. A new survey indicates that this difference in how judges appoint GALs impacts how lawyers involved in these types of cases do their work.

Passage Elements Recognition Drill Answer Key

Passage #9:

(5)

(10)

(15)

(20)

(25)

(30)

Fearing the emergence of a new, pandemic zoonotic disease—a contagious disease transmitted from animals to humans and caused by bacteria, viruses, parasites and fungi carried by animals and insects—scientists recently created a new pathogen (i.e., a bacterium, virus, or other microorganism that can cause disease) that is 97 percent similar to the 1918 Spanish Flu, which is thought to have originated in birds and which killed approximately 50 million people. The scientists constructed the new virus by cobbling together wild bird flu fragments. To make the pathogen easier to spread from one animal to another, the scientists mutated it, making it airborne. Some have labeled the project "insane," stressing the tremendous danger involved in intentionally creating a virus that could potentially kill millions of people if released into the general population, either accidentally or as a terrorist act. Moreover, they argue that the threat of such a virus emerging naturally from the animal population is too low to justify the risk posed by the research. The researchers, however, defend their work by pointing to the possibility that a disease similar to the Spanish Flu could spontaneously emerge without warning from the animal population. By creating such a pathogen in a secure, laboratory environment, they argue, health officials can better prepare to detect and treat a naturally occurring outbreak.

The difficulty in this passage comes from the scientific subject matter and challenging terminology, like "zoonotic," "pandemic," and "pathogen." However, most of the difficulty is confined to the opening sentence. In addition to the unusual terminology, the first sentence has a complicated sentence structure designed to bog you down. For many students, encountering a sentence such as this at the beginning of a passage means an early defeat, because they let the dense opening demoralize them. However, the proper perspective can help you realize the purpose of this opening sentence and move on to the rest of the passage, which is remarkably simpler to understand. While a passage may have difficult sections, remember that the GMAT is not a knowledge-based test, and the difficult terminology or subject matter is included to camouflage what often turns out to be fairly straightforward argumentation. In this case, the passage contains only two subject perspectives, that of the researchers and that of the critics. We can summarize the passage quite simply:

Researchers have developed a potentially lethal virus in order to learn how to better detect and treat unexpected outbreaks of diseases that originate in animals but are transmitted into humans. Critics, however, believe that the researchers' work is very dangerous and that the risk of unexpected outbreaks is too low to justify the risk posed by the research itself.

Passage Elements Recognition Drill Answer Key

Passage #10:

In an era of corporate downsizing, large law
firms have renewed their insistence that law
schools focus less on academia and more on
the production of the "practice-ready lawyer."
(5)   However, some law professors argue that their
institutions should reject what they view as a
misguided and short-sighted attempt by the
firms to shift their training expenses to the law
schools. While the law firms urge law schools to
(10)   offer more clinics, externships, and practitioner-
specific courses, these professors argue that
such an approach is impractical. The first hurdle
is in even identifying the proper standard for
determining what a practice-ready lawyer is. If
(15)   the standard is minimal competence, they argue,
then the state-level bar examination already
ensures that level of preparedness. Next is the
issue of specialization. Are law students now
expected to determine a field of practice prior
(20)   to graduation, the professors ask? If they do
not, then the scope of the private legal market
is too broad for the law schools to be able to
provide significant practical experience in even
the major sub-categories of legal work. Finally,
(25)   the professors point out that much of what
makes legal practice unique is the confluence
of institutional structures, power dynamics,
economic incentives, and complex ethical
obligations that is impossible to replicate in the
law school setting.

The convoluted structure of this passage makes the passage difficult to read. Adding to the
confusion is the repeated reference to law schools, as distinct from law professors, for which no
viewpoint has actually been expressed. In preparing yourself to answer questions based on this
passage, the best approach is to separate the concerns of the law firms and the law professors,
and to summarize the concerns of each, rather than retaining in your memory the various items
from each of the lists.

Here, we can say that the law firms, motivated by business concerns, want legal education to be
more practical and less academic, so that the law student emerges as a "practice-ready lawyer."
The law professors, on the other hand, think it is impractical to do as the law firms ask, because
the standards are ill defined, the areas of specialization are too diverse, and the unique aspects of
legal practice cannot be reproduced in the law school setting.

Chapter Five:
The Questions and
Answer Choices

Chapter Five: The Questions and Answer Choices

The Questions

Each Reading Comprehension passage on the GMAT is accompanied by a group of questions, which can cover a wide range of tasks, and will variously ask you to:

- describe the main point and/or primary purpose of the passage

- describe the structure and organization of the passage

- identify the viewpoint of the author or the viewpoint of subjects discussed within the passage

- identify details of the passage or statements proven by the passage

- describe the meaning, function, or purpose of words or phrases in the passage

- strengthen, weaken, or parallel elements of the passage

- augment or expand the passage

Analyzing the Question Stem

At first glance, Reading Comprehension passages appear to have a multitude of different types of question stems. The test makers create this impression by varying the words used in each question stem. As we will see shortly, even though they use different words, many of these question stems are identical in terms of what you are asked to do.

In order to easily handle the different questions, we categorize the question stems that appear on the GMAT. Fortunately, every question stem can be defined as a certain type, and the more familiar you are with the question types, the faster you can respond when faced with individual questions. Thus, one of your tasks is to learn each question type and become familiar with the characteristics that define each type. We will help you accomplish this goal by including a variety of question type identification drills and by examining each type of question in detail.

> The makers of the GMAT warn: "If you have some familiarity with the material presented in a passage, do not let this knowledge influence your choice of answers to the questions. Answer all questions on the basis of what is stated or implied in the passage itself."

5

All Reading Comprehension question stems provide some insight into where in the passage you should begin your search for the correct answer. This element is called "location," and you should always establish location as you read each question stem.

Location can be divided into three categories—Specific Reference, Concept Reference, and Global Reference:

Specific Reference (SR). These question stems refer you to a specific line, paragraph, or sentence. (On the actual test, referenced words and phrases will be highlighted, but in this book we will use the format used in the Official Guide, in which references are made by line). Other questions will refer to relevant portions by paragraph. For example:

> "The author of the passage uses the phrase 'rational expectations' on line 39 primarily in order to"

> "Which one of the following best defines the word 'pragmatic' as it is used in the second paragraph of the passage?"

Although the correct information in a Specific Reference question is not always found in the exact lines referenced, those line references are always an excellent starting point for your analysis.

To attack Specific Reference questions that refer to an exact word, line or sentence, always return to the passage and start reading three to five lines above the reference, or from the most logical nearby starting point such as the start of a paragraph. To attack Specific Reference questions that refer to a paragraph, return to the passage and consider the paragraph in question. We will discuss this approach in more detail when we begin dissecting individual passages.

Make sure to read each question stem very carefully. Some stems direct you to focus on certain areas of the passage and if you miss these clues, the problem becomes much more difficult.

To attack Specific Reference questions, return to the passage and start reading three to five lines above the reference, or from the most logical nearby starting point such as the start of a paragraph.

5

Concept Reference (CR). Some questions refer you to ideas or themes within the passage that are not identified by a specific line or paragraph reference, but that are identifiable because the ideas are clearly enunciated or expressed within one or two areas of the passage. When reading questions that contain concept references, you should typically know where to search in the passage for the relevant information even though no line reference is given. Examples include:

"The passage suggests which one of the following about the behavior of elk in conflict situations?"

"The author's discussion of telephone answering machines serves primarily to..."

"The passage indicates that prior to the use of carbon dating, at least some historians believed which one of the following?"

In each of the above instances, although no specific location reference is given, an engaged student would know where in the passage to begin searching for the correct answer, and he or she would then return to the passage and take a moment to review the relevant information.

Global Reference (GR). Global Reference questions ask about the passage as a whole, or they fail to identify a defined area or isolated concept within the question stem. For example:

"Which one of the following most accurately expresses the main point of the passage?"

"The primary purpose of the passage is to..."

"Information in the passage most strongly supports which one of the following statements?"

Although they might at first seem intimidating, many Global questions can be answered from your initial reading of the passage. For example, you know that you are always seeking to identify the main point of the passage as you read, so the presence of a Main Point question should not alarm you or cause you any undue work. On the other hand, Global questions that ask you to prove statements drawn from the passage can be time-consuming because they typically require you to return to the passage and cross-check each answer choice.

Note that not every question stem that refers to a concept is a Concept Reference question. For example, if an entire passage is about the poet Rita Dove, and the question stem asks about the views of Rita Dove, that question would be classified as Global. We will discuss this classification in more detail when we examine individual questions.

Throughout this book, all questions are first classified as one of these three types. There are also additional indicators designating question type, etc.

As we classify Reading Comprehension questions, location will always appear as the first element of the classification. Thus, every question classification in this book will begin with the shorthand reference of SR, CR, or GR.

Throughout this section we will indicate how frequently each type of question appears. Assessing just the Location element, this is the frequency of appearance in the tests that have been released by GMAC.

Frequency of SR Questions: About 20% overall

Frequency of CR Questions: About 65% overall

Frequency of GR Questions: About 15% overall

Location Designation Drill

Each of the following items contains a sample Reading Comprehension question stem. In the space provided, categorize each stem into one of the three Location designations: Specific Reference (SR), Concept Reference (CR), and Global Reference (GR). While we realize that you have not yet worked directly with each question type, by considering the designations you will now have an advantage as you attack future questions. *Answers on page 170*

1. Question Stem: "Which one of the following most accurately describes the organization of the material presented in the passage?"

    Location Designation: _____

2. Question Stem: "The third paragraph of the passage provides the most support for which one of the following inferences?"

    Location Designation: _____

3. Question Stem: "The discussion of Muniz' first theory is intended to perform which of the following functions in the passage?"

    Location Designation: _____

4. Question Stem: "The author mentions the number of species (lines 20-23) primarily in order to support which of the following claims?"

    Location Designation: _____

5. Question Stem: "Which of the following is mentioned in the passage as an important characteristic of each of the three theories discussed in the passage? "

    Location Designation: _____

6. Question Stem: "Which one of the following titles most completely and accurately describes the contents of the passage?"

    Location Designation: _____

5

Location Designation Drill Answer Key—page 169

The typical student misses a few questions in this drill. Do not worry about how many you miss; the point of this drill is to acquaint you with the idea of Location as it is presented in different question stems. As you see more examples of each type of question, your ability to correctly identify the Location element will improve.

1. Location Type: Global Reference

Because this stem asks about the "organization of the material presented in the passage," it references the passage as a whole and is thus best described as a Global Reference question.

2. Location Type: Specific Reference

This stem specifically references the "third paragraph of the passage," and so this is a Specific Reference question.

3. Location Type: Concept Reference

This question stem does not refer to a specific line or paragraph, so it cannot be a Specific Reference question. The reference to a particular theory is enough to suggest that this is more specific than a Global Reference question, so this example can be classified a Concept Reference question.

4. Location Type: Specific Reference

This stem specifically references the "lines 20-23," and therefore this is a Specific Reference question.

5. Location Type: Concept Reference

This question stem does not refer to a specific line or paragraph, so it cannot be a Specific Reference question. However, the question also does not refer to the passage in general, and the idea mentioned in the stem is specific enough to suggest that this is a Concept Reference question.

6. Location Type: Global Reference

This stem discusses the "contents of the passage," and is thus best described as a Global Reference question.

Reading Comprehension Question Types

After establishing Location, the next element you must identify when reading question stems is the type of question that you face. The questions which accompany the Reading Comprehension passages are similar to the Critical Reasoning questions, and virtually all question stems that appear in the Reading Comprehension passages of the GMAT can be classified into one of the following types:

Many of the question types discussed in the Critical Reasoning Bible are also covered here.

1. Must Be True/Most Supported
2. Main Point
3. Purpose/Primary Purpose
4. Strengthen
5. Weaken
6. Parallel Reasoning
7. Cannot Be True
8. Evaluate the Argument

Note that some of the other Critical Reasoning question types, such as Justify the Conclusion and Resolve the Paradox, *could* appear with a Reading Comprehension passage, but they appear so infrequently that focusing on those question types would not be worthwhile in this context.

You must correctly analyze and classify every question stem because the question stem ultimately determines the nature of the correct answer choice. A mistake in analyzing the question stem almost invariably leads to a missed question. Properly identifying the question stem type will allow you to proceed quickly and with confidence, and in some cases it will help you determine the correct answer before you read any of the five answer choices.

Remember, the GMAT presents questions one at a time, and you should be able to quickly recognize a question's type quickly so that you know how to attack most effectively.

Occasionally, students ask if we refer to the question types by number or by name. We always refer to the questions by name, as that is an easier and more efficient approach. Numerical question type classification systems force you to add two unnecessary levels of abstraction to your thinking process. For example, consider a question that asks you to "weaken" the argument. In a numerical question classification system, you must first recognize that the question asks you to weaken the argument, then you must classify that question into a numerical category (say, Type 4), and then you must translate Type 4 to mean "Weaken." Literally, numerical classification systems force you to perform an abstract, circular translation of the meaning of the question, and the translation process is both time-consuming and valueless.

We now turn to a brief discussion of each of the primary Reading Comprehension question types:

1. Must Be True/Most Supported

    This category is simply known as "Must Be True." Must Be True questions ask you to identify the answer choice that is best proven by the information in the passage. Question stem examples:

    > "Which of the following can be inferred about the study discussed in the first paragraph?"

    > "The passage provides support for which of the following statements?"

    Must Be True questions are the dominant category within the Reading Comprehension passages. This should not be surprising, considering that Reading Comprehension is about trying to understand a lengthy passage of text. The best way to test your comprehension of this information is to ask a series of questions aimed at determining whether you properly interpreted the facts that you read, and can make accurate assessments both of and from them.

    Many of the Must Be True questions that accompany the Reading Comprehension passages ask you to perform a more specific action, such as to identify the author's viewpoint or the function of a word or phrase. In the next section we will examine these attributes in more detail as we discuss each type of Must Be True question.

2. Main Point/Main Idea

    Main Point questions are a variant of Must Be True questions. As you might expect, a Main Point question asks you to find the primary focus of the passage. Question stem examples:

    > "The main point made by the passage is that"

    > "Which of the following most accurately expresses the main idea of the passage?"

    Although Main Point questions appear less frequently on the GMAT than Primary Purpose questions, recognizing the main idea will be an important part of any passage analysis, regardless of the specific question types that happen to follow.

3. Purpose/Primary Purpose

Primary Purpose questions, another variant of Must Be
True questions, accompany almost every GMAT Reading
Comprehension Passage, and require you to understand what the
author hoped to achieve in writing the passage. Question stem
example:

> "The primary purpose of the passage is to"

> "The passage is primarily concerned with"

Local Purpose (or Function) questions require you to understand
the role of a given word, phrase, paragraph, or idea presented in the
passage. Question stem example:

> "The author mentions the length of the rainy season in order to"

4. Strengthen

These questions ask you to select the answer choice that provides
support for the author's argument or strengthens it in some way.
Question stem example:

> "Which of the following, if true, would most strengthen the hypothesis
> discussed at the beginning of the passage?"

5. Weaken

Weaken questions ask you to attack or undermine the author's
argument. Question stem example:

> "Which of the following, if true, would most weaken the argument present-
> ed in the third paragraph of the passage?"

Considered together, Strengthen and Weaken questions appear far
less frequently than Must Be True questions.

6. Parallel Reasoning

Parallel Reasoning questions ask you to identify the answer choice that contains reasoning most similar in structure to the reasoning presented in the passage. Question stem example:

"Which one of the following arguments is most similar in its pattern of reasoning to the argument above?"

Like Strengthen and Weaken Questions, Parallel Reasoning questions appear less frequently than Must Be True questions.

7. Cannot Be True

Cannot Be True questions ask you to identify the answer choice that cannot be true or is most weakened based on the information in the passage. Question stem example:

"If the statements above are true, which one of the following CANNOT be true?"

8. Evaluate the Argument

Evaluate the Argument questions ask you to identify the piece of information that would be most useful in assessing a given argument. Question stem example:

"The answer to which one of the following questions would contribute most to an evaluation of the argument?"

Other question elements will also be discussed, most notably question variants (such as Author's Perspective questions) and overlays (such as Principle questions). Those will be covered later in this chapter.

Rephrasing Question Stems

As you may have noticed in examining the question stem examples presented for each type, not all stems are phrased in the form of a question. Clearly the test makers are quite fond of variety, but this goes beyond a simple preference for diverse constructions: students often have greater difficulty completing a sentence than answering a direct question!

So we encourage you to get in the habit of rephrasing—translating partial-statement stems into their equivalent question forms—so that you are always responding to a precise *inquiry* rather than a more abstract unfinished sentence. Many readers perform this step naturally, but if you find yourself struggling to properly anticipate the nature of right and wrong answers following question stems lacking a question, formalizing this approach will likely help.

Question Classification Review

At this point we have established that every question which accompanies a Reading Comprehension passage has two elements: Location and Question Type. When questions are classified in this book, those two elements are always listed in order, as follows:

Location, Question Type

Here are several sample question classifications featuring both elements:

SR, Must
(Location: Specific Reference, Type: Must Be True)

CR, Strengthen
(Location: Concept Reference, Type: Strengthen)

GR, MP
(Location: Global Reference, Type: Main Point)

SR, Parallel
(Location: Specific Reference, Type: Parallel Reasoning)

The following pages contain a drill designed to strengthen your ability to correctly classify questions by both location designation and question type.

Identify the Question Stem Drill

Each of the following items contains a sample question stem. In the space provided, categorize each stem into one of the three Location designations: Specific Reference (SR), Concept Reference (CR), and Global Reference (GR), and then categorize each stem into one of the six main Reading Comprehension Question Types: Must Be True, Main Point, Strengthen, Weaken, Parallel Reasoning, Cannot be True, or Evaluate the Argument. While we realize that you have not yet worked directly with each question type, by considering the designations now you will have an advantage as you attack future questions. *Answers begin on page 178*

1. Question Stem: "Which one of the following, if true, would lend the most support to the view of most 20th century critics?"

   Classification: _____

2. Question Stem: "The author would most likely disagree with which one of the following statements?"

   Classification: _____

3. Question Stem: "Which one of the following most accurately describes the author's purpose in referring to literature of the past as being 'unfairly burdened'" (line 51) in some cases?"

   Classification: _____

4. Question Stem: "Which one of the following most accurately expresses the main point of the passage?"

   Classification: _____

5. Question Stem: "Which one of the following, if true, would most call into question the author's assertion in the last sentence of the passage?"

   Classification: _____

6. Question Stem: "In discussing the tangential details of events, the passage contrasts their original significance in the courtroom (lines 52-59). This contrast is most closely analogous to which one of the following?"

   Classification: _____

Identify the Question Stem Drill

7. Question Stem: "Which one of the following most accurately describes the organization of the passage?"

    Classification: _____

8. Question Stem: "Which one of the following, if true, most weakens the author's criticism of the assumption that parasitic interactions generally evolve toward symbiosis?"

    Classification: _____

9. Question Stem: "The author of the passage would be most likely to agree with which one of the following statements?"

    Classification: _____

10. Question Stem: "Which one of the following would be most helpful in determining the validity of the theory presented in the second paragraph of the passage?"

    Classification: _____

11. Question Stem: "Which one of the following, if true, offers the most support for Rose's hypothesis?"

    Classification: _____

12. Question Stem: "According to the passage, the elimination of which one of the following obstacles enabled scientists to identify the evolutionary origins of the platypus?"

    Classification: _____

13. Question Stem: "Which one of the following is most similar to the relationship described in the passage between the new methods of the industry and pre-twentieth-century methods?"

    Classification: _____

14. Question Stem: "The third paragraph of the passage most strongly supports which one of the following inferences?"

    Classification: _____

5

Identify the Question Stem Drill Answer Key—page 176

The typical student misses about half of the questions in this drill. Do not worry about how many you miss; the point of this drill is to acquaint you with the different question stems. As you see more examples of each type of question, your ability to correctly identify each stem will improve.

1. CR, Strengthen

Location: Here we are asked to find the answer choice that would support a particular view referenced from the passage, so this is a <u>Concept Reference</u> question.

Type: The presence of the phrase "Which of the following, if true," generally introduces either a Strengthen or a Weaken question. In this case, since the correct answer will support the referenced view, this is clearly a <u>Strengthen</u> question.

2. GR, Cannot

Location: This example provides no direction, conceptual or otherwise, as to location in the passage. It is therefore a <u>Global Reference</u> question.

Type: This question requires you to find the answer choice with which the author would disagree. Because the correct answer choice will be inconsistent with the author's attitude, this question stem can be classified as a <u>Cannot Be True</u> question (that is, "according to the author, which of the following cannot be true?").

3. SR, Must

Location: This example provides the exact location of the referenced quote, so this is a <u>Specific Reference</u> question.

Type: The correct answer must pass the Fact Test; in this case it must provide an accurate description of the referenced quote's purpose in the passage. Therefore this question stem falls under the <u>Must Be True</u> category.

4. GR, Main Point

Location: This common question stem refers to the passage as a whole and is therefore a <u>Global Reference</u> question.

Type: Since this question stem asks for the main point of the passage, this is a clear example of a <u>Main Point</u> question. The correct answer choice will be the one which most accurately and completely reflects the central focus of the passage.

Identify the Question Stem Drill Answer Key

5. SR, Weaken

Location: Although no line reference is provided in this example, the reader is directed specifically to the last sentence of the passage, so this is a <u>Specific Reference</u> question.

Type: A question stem that begins with "Which of the following, if true" is nearly certain to be a Strengthen or Weaken question. In this case, the information in the correct answer will call the referenced assertion into question, so this should be classified as a <u>Weaken</u> question.

6. SR, Parallel

Location: Since an exact line reference is provided, this is a <u>Specific Reference</u> question.

Type: Here the reader is asked to find the answer choice which is most closely analogous to the referenced discussion, which makes this a <u>Parallel</u> question. The correct answer choice will reflect a contrast similar to that discussed in the passage.

7. GR, Must

Location: Since this question stem deals with the entire passage, this is a <u>Global Reference</u> question.

Type: This question requires that the reader understand the overall structure of the given passage, and the correct answer choice must reflect that structure. This is a <u>Must Be True</u> question.

8. CR, Weaken

Location: Although this question does not provide a line reference, it refers to a very specific assumption on the author's part. It is thus a <u>Concept Reference</u> question.

Type: This is one of the more readily recognizable question types, since the word "weaken" is in the question stem; this is a standard <u>Weaken</u> question which in this case requires that the correct answer choice reduce the credibility of the author's referenced criticism.

9. GR, Must

Location: This question deals with the passage as a whole, so this is a <u>Global Reference</u> question.

Type: This common question requires that the reader understand the author's perspective. The correct answer choice must reflect the author's attitude, and pass the Fact Test, so this is a <u>Must Be True</u> question.

5

Identify the Question Stem Drill Answer Key

10. SR, Evaluate

Location: The paragraph reference at the end of this question stem identifies this example as a <u>Specific Reference</u> question.

Type: Since this question asks for the information that would help with an evaluation, it is an Evaluate the Argument question.

11. GR, Strengthen

Location: Without reading the passage, it might be difficult to assess the scope of this question's reference (although you should immediately recognize that this is <u>not</u> a Specific Reference question). If the passage is largely focused on the referenced hypothesis, this is a <u>Global Reference</u> question.

Type: Since the correct answer choice will somehow support the referenced hypothesis, this is a <u>Strengthen</u> question.

12. CR, Must

Location: This question stem requires the reader to identify a particular obstacle but does not provide its specific location in the passage, so this is a <u>Concept Reference</u> question.

Type: In this case, the correct answer choice will come directly from information provided in the passage, so this is a <u>Must Be True</u> question.

13. CR, Parallel

Location: This question refers to a specific relationship but offers no line references, thus it is a <u>Concept Reference</u> question.

Type: The question stem asks you to find an answer that is "most similar to the relationship" in the passage, and thus this is a <u>Parallel</u> question.

14. SR, Must

Location: Specification of "the third paragraph" makes this a <u>Specific Reference</u> question.

Type: Although this question stem uses the word "supports," the correct answer choice will be the one which, based on the passage, <u>Must Be True</u>.

Reading Comprehension Question Types Examined in Detail ██████

Must Be True/Most Supported Questions ████████████

Must Be True questions appear far more frequently than any other question type. Thus, to perform well with Reading Comprehension passages, you must dominate Must Be True. In this section we will examine the theory behind Must Be True questions, and then explore a variety of specific Must Be True subtypes. In each instance we will provide helpful tips and strategies to attack the type and subtype.

Must Be True questions require you to select an answer choice that is proven by the information presented in the passage. The correct answer choice can be a paraphrase of part of the passage or it can be a logical consequence of one or more parts of the passage. However, when selecting an answer, you must have proof from the passage that supports it. As mentioned, this is called the Fact Test™:

> The correct answer to a Must Be True question can always be proven by referring to the facts stated in the passage.

The test makers will try to entice you with incorrect answer choices that could possibly occur or are likely to occur, but are not *certain* to occur. You must avoid those answers and instead select the choice that is most clearly supported by what you read. Similarly, do not bring in information from outside the passage (aside from commonsense assumptions); all of the information necessary to answer the question is included in the text.

Must Be True questions are considered the foundation of Reading Comp because the skills required to answer Must Be True are also required for every other question type: read text, and understand the facts that logically follow. To Weaken or Strengthen an argument, for example, you first need to correctly ascertain its details and what reasonable conclusions can be drawn; this allows you to recognize any invalid conclusions on the part of the author, and then to attack or resolve those potential mistakes, respectively. And the same goes for every other type of question.

Because every question type relies on the fact-finding skills used to answer Must Be True questions, your performance with Must Be True dictates your overall Reading Comprehension score. For this reason, you must master this question category now! The pages that follow will provide the tools necessary to do so.

The majority of questions accompanying the Reading Comprehension passages are Must Be True.

5

Attacking Must Be True Questions

Your approach to Must Be True questions will, in part, be determined by the Location element specified in each question stem. That is, your approach to an SR, Must question will necessarily be different from your approach to a GR, Must question. Here we examine how the difference in Location affects how you attack Must Be True questions.

Specific Reference

As mentioned in the Location section:

> To attack Specific Reference questions that refer to an exact line number or sentence, always return to the passage and start reading three to five lines above the reference, or from the most logical nearby starting point such as the start of a paragraph.

The prevalence of Must Be True questions is incredibly beneficial to you as a test taker because the answer to every Must question resides directly in the text of each passage.

As we will see when discussing specific passages and questions, the "three to five line" recommendation is open-ended because what you are seeking is the most logical starting point for your reading, and that starting point is typically the prior complete sentence or two.

For Specific Reference questions that refer to a paragraph, return to the passage and consider the paragraph in question.

Concept Reference

With Concept Reference Must Be True questions, you must return to the areas in the passage mentioned in the question stem and quickly review the information. These questions are more vague than Specific Reference questions and so you must rely on your passage diagramming or memory to return to the correct area.

Global Reference

Global Must Be True questions are usually Main Point, Purpose, or Organization questions, and you will typically not need to refer back to the passage prior to attacking the answer choices because you should already know the answer from your reading. Remember, if you seek to identify the critical VIEWSTAMP elements of each passage, you will automatically know the answer to every Global Must Be True question. Thus, you would only need to refer back to the passage to eliminate or confirm individual answer choices.

Must Be True Question Subtypes ████

Although many of the questions which follow the Reading Comprehension passages are straightforward Must Be True questions, many questions are subtypes of the Must Be True category. Fundamentally, these subtypes are approached in exactly the same manner as regular Must Be True questions. That is, the Fact Test applies and you must still be able to justify your answer with evidence from the passage. However, some of these subtypes ask for very specific information, and thus an awareness of each subtype is essential.

Main Point/Main Idea

Main Point questions may be the question type most familiar to test takers. Many standardized tests that you have already encountered, such as the SAT and ACT, contain questions that ask you to ascertain main points, where you summarize the central focus of a passage. Even in daily conversation you will hear, "What are you driving at?," or, "What's your point?" Main Point questions, as you might suspect from the name, simply ask you to summarize an author's chief conclusion for the whole passage.

The answer you select must follow from the information in the passage, but be careful: even if an answer choice must be *true* according to the passage, if it fails to capture the author's *main* argument, it cannot be correct. This is the central truth of Main Point questions: Like all Must Be True question variants, the correct answer must pass the Fact Test, but with the additional criterion that the correct answer choice must capture the author's central point.

As discussed previously, one key to identifying an author's main point is to remember that, although it may be stated succinctly in a sentence or two, all paragraphs of the passage may be required to determine the author's primary message. Thus, the *main* point of the passage will rarely reflect the function of just a single paragraph. To best assess the situation, apply the viewpoint identification approach and argument identification methods discussed previously. These two VIEWSTAMP items will direct you toward the Main Point during your reading of the passage. Thereafter, you will be in excellent position to answer any Main Point question.

The Main Point question stem format is remarkably consistent, requiring you in each case to identify the conclusion or point of the argument, as in the following examples:

> "Which one of the following most accurately expresses the main point of the passage?"

> "Which one of the following statements best expresses the main idea of the passage?"

Two types of *incorrect* answers frequently appear in Main Point questions:

1. Answers that are true but do not encapsulate the author's point.

2. Answers that repeat portions of the passage but not the Main Point.

Each answer type is attractive because they are true based on what you have read. However, neither summarizes the author's main point and therefore both are incorrect. Fortunately, these traps are also easily recognized and avoided, as we will discuss shortly.

Primary Purpose/Local Purpose (P)

Global Purpose questions are almost always phrased using the words "primary purpose" and ask for the author's main purpose or goal in writing the passage. These questions ask you to describe why the author wrote the passage, and the correct answer is often an abstract version of the main point (and if not, at the very least the answer to a Primary Purpose question will agree with the Main Point).

> "The primary purpose of the passage is to"

> "In the passage, the author seeks primarily to"

At the Specific Reference and Concept Reference level, Purpose questions ask why the author referred to a particular word, phrase, or idea. To determine the reasons behind the author's use of words or ideas, refer to the context around the reference, using context clues and your knowledge of the viewpoints and structure of the passage. Here are several example question stems:

> "The author of the passage uses the phrase "the flux within Hawaiian society" (line 33) primarily in order to"

> "The author's discussion of people's positive moral duty to care for one another (lines 44-49) functions primarily to"

> "The author's discussion of telephone answering machines serves primarily to"

> "Which one of the following best states the function of the third paragraph of the passage?"

Remember, on the actual GMAT you will see references to highlighted portions of text rather than references by line number.

A complete understanding of any passage requires that you identify the author's primary purpose for writing the passage, even when a passage does not include a Primary Purpose question.

5

Perspective Questions

This categorization contains questions about two of the VIEWSTAMP elements: viewpoints and tone. These two elements are very closely related, and we combine them in our question classification using the term "perspective" to capture the idea behind both elements.

Perspective questions can be divided into two categories: questions that ask about the author's views and tone, and questions that ask about the views and tone of one of the other groups discussed in the passage. These two types are discussed below.

Author's Perspective Questions (AP)

Author's Perspective questions ask you to select the answer choice that best reflects the author's views on a subject or the author's attitude toward a subject. Because identifying the position of the author is a critical part of your strategy when reading, normally these questions should be relatively painless:

> "The author of the passage would most likely agree with which one of the following statements?"

> "It can be inferred that the author of the passage believes which one of the following about the history of modern jurisprudence?"

> "It can be reasonably inferred from the passage that the author's attitude is most favorable toward which one of the following?"

Understanding the author's viewpoint is an integral part of mastering any passage.

Subject Perspective Questions (SP)

In this question type, we use the term "subject" to refer to a person or group who is discussed in the passage. Subject Perspective questions, then, ask you to select the answer choice that best reflects the views or attitude of one of the other groups in the passage. Because identifying all views is a critical part of your strategy when reading, you should be well-prepared for these questions.

> "Given the information in the passage, which one of the following is Lum most likely to believe?"

> "It can be inferred that Peter Goodrich would be most likely to agree with which one of the following statements concerning common law?"

These questions are considered Must Be True subtypes because the correct answer follows directly from the statements in the passage.

Organization Questions (O)

These questions usually appear in reference to either a specific paragraph or to the passage as a whole, and refer less frequently to specific lines.

At the line level, you are normally asked to identify the way in which pairs of lines relate to each other:

> "The logical relationship of lines 8-13 of the passage to lines 23-25 and 49-53 of the passage is most accurately described as"

At a specific paragraph level, you will either be asked to identify the structure of the paragraph, or to identify how one paragraph relates to another paragraph. Question examples include the following:

> "Which one of the following most accurately describes the relationship between the second paragraph and the final paragraph?"

> "Which one of the following most accurately describes the organization of the material presented in the second and third paragraphs of the passage?"

At the Global level, these questions ask you to describe the overall structure of the passage. For example:

> "Which one of the following best describes the organization of the passage?"

> "Which one of the following most accurately describes the organization of the material presented in the passage?"

> "Which one of the following sequences most accurately and completely corresponds to the presentation of the material in the passage?"

In both the Specific and Global versions, these questions are similar to the Method of Reasoning questions in Critical Reasoning, but they are generally broader. Given that you must track structure as you read, these questions should be fairly straightforward exercises in matching answer choices to what you already know occurred in the passage.

Recognition of passage structure can be particularly important on computer based tests such as the GMAT, since you will not have the option of actually notating the passage.

Although questions which specifically reference Passage Organization make up only a small percentage of questions in this section, a strong grasp of the structure of a passage will allow you to attack Concept Reference and Specific Reference questions far more efficiently.

Expansion Questions (E)

Expansion questions require you to extrapolate ideas from the passage to determine one of three elements: where the passage was drawn from or how it could be titled, what sentence or idea could come before the passage, and what sentence or idea could follow the passage. The following examples show the range of phrasing in these questions:

> "Which one of the following would be most suitable as a title for this passage if it were to appear as an editorial piece?"

> "Which one of the following titles most completely summarizes the contents of the passage?"

> "If this passage had been excerpted from a longer text, which one of the following predictions about the near future of U.S. literature would be most likely to appear in that text?"

> "Which one of the following sentences would most logically begin a paragraph immediately following the end of the passage?"

> "Which one of the following is the most logical continuation of the last paragraph of the passage?"

> "Which one of the following sentences could most logically be appended to the end of the last paragraph of the passage?"

Questions about the title or source of the passage typically reflect the Main Point or Primary Purpose of the passage. Questions asking you to identify pre- or post-passage sentences, however, are usually immediately dependent upon the two or three sentences at the beginning or end of the passage, and then more generally dependent upon the passage as a whole. These questions are not particularly common but can be difficult because they ask you to infer the flow and direction of the passage from a somewhat limited set of clues.

In fact, broadly speaking, any questions that require you to infer an answer from the text rather than pull an answer directly from it—whether an Author's or Subject's Perspective (AP or SP), or an Expansion question (E) discussed above—are commonly felt to be the most challenging questions in a Reading Comprehension passage set.

Correct Answers in Must Be True Questions

Let us take a moment to discuss two types of answers that will always be correct in a Must Be True question and any Must Be True subtype (except for Main Point questions).

1. Paraphrased Answers

   Paraphrased Answers are answers that restate a portion of the passage in different terms. Because the language is not exactly the same as in the passage, Paraphrased Answers can be easy to miss. Paraphrased Answers are designed to test your ability to discern the author's exact meaning. Sometimes the answer can appear to be almost too obvious since it is drawn directly from the passage.

2. Combination Answers

   Answers that are the sum of two or more passage statements: any answer choice that would result from combining two or more statements in the passage will be correct.

Should you encounter either of the above as an answer choice in a non-Main Point, Must Be True question, select the answer with confidence.

Incorrect Answers in Must Be True Questions

There are several types of answers that appear in Must Be True questions that are incorrect. These answers appear frequently enough that we have provided a review of the major types below. Each answer category below is designed to attract you to an incorrect answer choice. As we begin to look at actual passages and questions in the next chapter, we will examine instances of these types of answers.

1. Could Be True or Likely to Be True Answers

Because the criteria in the question stem require you to find an answer choice that Must Be True, answers that merely could be true or are even likely to be true are incorrect. These answers are attractive because there is nothing demonstrably wrong with them (for example, they do not contain statements that are counter to the passage). Regardless, like all incorrect answers, these answers fail the Fact Test. Remember, you must select an answer choice that must occur based on what you have read.

This category of "incorrect answer" is very broad, and some of the types mentioned below will fall under this general idea but place an emphasis on a specific aspect of the answer.

2. Exaggerated Answers

Exaggerated Answers take information from the passage and then stretch that information to make a broader statement that is not supported by the passage. In that sense, this form of answer is a variation of a Could Be True answer since the exaggeration is possible, but not proven based on the information.

Here is an example:

> If the passage states, "*Some* software vendors recently implemented more rigorous licensing procedures."

> An incorrect answer would exaggerate one or more of the elements: "*Most* software vendors recently implemented more rigorous licensing procedures." In this example, *some* is exaggerated to *most*. While it could be true that most software vendors made the change, the passage does not prove that it must be true. This type of answer is often paraphrased, creating a deadly combination where the language is similar enough to be attractive but different enough to be incorrect.

Here is another example:

> If the passage states, "Recent advances in the field of molecular biology make it *likely* that many school textbooks will be rewritten."

> The exaggerated and paraphrased version would be: "Many school textbooks about molecular biology will be re-written." In this example, *likely* has been dropped, and this omission exaggerates the certainty of the change. The paraphrase also is problematic because the passage referenced school textbooks whereas the paraphrased answer refers to school textbooks *about molecular biology*.

5

3. "New" Information Answers

Because correct Must Be True answers must be based on information in the passage or the direct result of combining statements in the passage, be wary of answers that present so-called new information—that is, information not mentioned explicitly in the passage or information that would not fall under the umbrella of a statement made in the passage. For example, if a passage discusses the economic policies of Japan, be careful with an answer that mentions U.S. economic policy. Look closely at the passage—does the information about Japanese economic policy apply to the U.S., or are the test makers trying to get you to fall for an answer that sounds logical but is not directly supported?

4. The Shell Game

Shell Game answers can occur in all GMAT question types, not only in Must Be True questions.

The GMAT makers have a variety of psychological tricks they use to entice test takers to select an answer choice. One of their favorites is one we call the Shell Game: an idea or concept is raised in the passage, and then a very similar idea appears in the answer choice, but the idea is changed just enough to be incorrect but still attractive. This trick is called the Shell Game because it abstractly resembles those street corner gambling games where a person hides a small object underneath one of three shells, and then scrambles them on a flat surface while a bettor tries to guess which shell the object is under (similar to three-card Monte). The object of a Shell Game is to trick the bettor into guessing incorrectly by mixing up the shells so quickly and deceptively that the bettor mistakenly selects the wrong shell. The intent of the GMAT makers is the same.

5. The Opposite Answer

As the name suggests, the Opposite Answer provides an answer that is completely opposite of the stated facts of the passage. Opposite Answers are very attractive to students who are reading too quickly or carelessly.

5

6. The Reverse Answer

Here is a simplified example of how a Reverse Answer works, using italics to indicate the reversed parts:

Reverse Answers can occur in any type of question.

> The passage might state, "*Many* people have *some* type of security system in their home."

> An incorrect answer then reverses the elements: "*Some* people have *many* types of security systems in their home."

The Reverse Answer is attractive because it contains familiar elements from the passage, but the reversed statement is incorrect because it rearranges those elements to create a new, unsupported statement.

7. The Wrong View

Wrong View answers frequently appear in Perspective questions. For example, the question will ask you to identify a statement that agrees with the author's view, but then place one or more answers that would agree with the view of another group in the passage. You can avoid these answers by carefully tracking viewpoints as discussed earlier.

8. Hidden References

In some Specific Reference questions, you will be sent to a certain location in the passage but the information needed to answer the question will reside elsewhere in the passage, in a section that also touches on the issue in the Specific Reference. This can be difficult to handle if the information is a large number of lines away.

Non-Must Be True Question Types ▪

In this section we examine all other Reading Comprehension question types. As mentioned earlier, these questions appear with far less frequency than Must Be True questions.

Strengthen Questions ▬▬▬▬▬▬▬

Strengthen questions ask you to identify the answer choice that best supports a section of the passage or a particular view from the passage. The correct answer choice does not necessarily prove the argument beyond a shadow of a doubt, nor is the correct answer choice necessarily an assumption of the argument. The correct answer choice simply helps the argument in some way.

Following are examples of Strengthen question stems:

"Which one of the following would, if true, most strengthen the author's position regarding the practical applicability of the theory presented in the passage?"

"Which one of the following would, if true, most strengthen the claim made by the author in the last sentence of the passage (lines 20-26)?"

"Which one of the following, if true, would lend the most support to the claims of critics discussed in lines 9-17?"

5

How to Strengthen an Argument

Use the following strategies to effectively strengthen arguments:

1. Identify what you are trying to strengthen!

   Before you can examine the answer choices, you must know what it is that you must strengthen. When evaluating an answer, ask yourself, "Would this answer choice assist the position in question in some way?" If so, you have the correct answer.

2. Personalize the argument.

   Personalizing allows you to see the argument from a very involved perspective and helps you assess the strength of each answer.

3. Look for weaknesses in the argument.

   This may seem like a strange recommendation since your task is to strengthen the argument, but a weak spot in an argument is tailor-made for an answer that eliminates that weakness. If you see a weakness or flaw in the argument, look for an answer that eliminates the weakness. In other words, close any gap or hole in the argument.

   Many Strengthen questions require students to find the missing link between a premise and the conclusion. These missing links are assumptions made by the author or by the party in question, and bringing an assumption to light strengthens the argument because it validates part of the author's thinking.

4. Remember that the correct answer can strengthen the argument just a little or a lot. This variation is what makes these questions difficult.

5

Three Incorrect Answer Traps

Some of the wrong answer types from the Must Be True section do not apply to Strengthen and Weaken questions. For example, the New Information answer is usually wrong in a Must Be True question, but not in a Strengthen or Weaken question because new information is acceptable in the answer choices.

The following types of wrong answer traps frequently appear in Strengthen questions:

1. Opposite Answers. These answers do the exact opposite of what is needed—they weaken the position in question. Because of their direct relation to the argument they are tempting, despite the fact that they result in consequences opposite of those intended.

2. Shell Game Answers. Remember, a Shell Game occurs when an idea or concept is raised in the passage and then a very similar idea appears in the answer choice, but the idea is changed just enough to be incorrect but still attractive. In Strengthen questions, the Shell Game is usually used to support a conclusion or position that is similar to, but slightly different from, the one presented in the passage.

3. Out of Scope Answers. These answers simply miss the point of the argument and support issues that are either unrelated to the argument or tangential to the argument.

These three incorrect answer traps are not the only forms that an attractive wrong answer may take, but they appear frequently enough that you should be familiar with each form.

Because the same types of wrong answer traps appear in Strengthen as in Weaken questions, the three items above apply to both this section and the following section on Weaken questions.

Weaken Questions ▰▰▰▰▰▰

Weaken questions require you to select the answer choice that undermines a position as decisively as possible. In this sense, Weaken questions are the polar opposite of Strengthen questions.

Note that the makers of the GMAT can use a variety of words to indicate that your task is to weaken the argument:

> weaken
> attack
> undermine
> refute
> argue against
> call into question
> cast doubt
> challenge
> damage
> counter

You do not need to find an answer that disproves or destroys the author's position. Instead, simply find an answer that hurts the argument.

Here are two Weaken question stem examples:

> "Which one of the following, if true, would most weaken the author's argument against harsh punishment for all infractions?"

> "Which one of the following, if true, would most seriously challenge the position of the biologists mentioned in line 19?"

Weaken question stems tell you to accept the answer choices as true, so you cannot throw out an answer because it doesn't seem possible.

5

When approaching Weaken questions, always remember to:

1. Isolate and assess the position you are attacking. Only by understanding the structure of the position can you gain the perspective necessary to attack that position.

2. Know the details of what was said in the passage.

3. Accept the answer choices as given, even if they include "new" information. Unlike Must Be True questions, Weaken answer choices can bring into consideration information outside of or tangential to the passage. Just because a fact or idea is not mentioned in the passage is not grounds for dismissing an answer choice. Your task is to determine which answer choice best attacks the position.

By focusing on the points above, you will maximize your chances of success on Weaken questions.

Parallel Reasoning Questions ■

Parallel Reasoning questions ask you to identify the answer choice that contains reasoning most similar in structure to the reasoning in a section of the passage. Because each answer choice is a wholly new argument, these questions force you to evaluate five arguments in one question, and as such they can be quite time consuming (a fact known to and exploited by the test makers).

The typical Reading Comprehension Parallel Reasoning question asks you to parallel the structure of a section or paragraph, and thus you usually need only understand the basic outline of what occurred in the section. Then, select the answer choice that contains the same structure. If you find yourself choosing between two or more answer choices, then simply compare some of the other elements in the passage—intent of the author or group, force and use of premises, the relationship of the premises to a conclusion, and the soundness of the argument.

Question stem examples:

> "Which one of the following is most analogous to the literary achievements that the author attributes to Maillet?"

> "As described in the passage, re-creating an accident with a computer-generated display is most similar to which one of the following?"

> "Based on the passage, the relationship between strengthening current copyright access to a Web document is most analogous to the relationship between"

5

Cannot Be True Questions

Cannot Be True questions occur infrequently with Reading Comprehension passages. Nonetheless, a familiarity with the principles behind these questions is helpful.

In Cannot Be True questions your task is to identify the answer choice that cannot be true or is most weakened by the information in the passage. Thus, instead of using the information in the passage to prove that one of the answer choices must be true, you must instead prove that one of the answer choices cannot occur, or that it disagrees with the information in the passage.

In the abstract, Cannot Be True questions can be viewed in two ways:

1. Polar Opposite Must Be True Questions

   Cannot Be True questions are the polar opposite of Must Be True questions: rather than prove an answer choice, you disprove an answer choice.

2. Reverse Weaken Questions

   Cannot Be True questions are like reverse Weaken questions: use the information in the passage to attack one of the answers.

Question types that appear infrequently, such as Cannot Be True, tend to consume more time because students are not used to seeing those types of questions.

Both question descriptions are similar, and neither sounds very difficult. In practice, however, Cannot Be True questions are tricky because the concept of an answer choice being possibly true and therefore wrong is counter intuitive. This type of question appears very infrequently, but the test makers are savvy and they know Cannot questions can catch test takers off-guard and consume more time than the average question. When you encounter a Cannot Be True question, you must mentally prepare yourself to eliminate answers that could be true or that are possible, and select the one answer choice that cannot be true or that is impossible.

Cannot Be True questions can be worded in a variety of ways, but the gist of the question type is to show that an answer cannot logically follow, as in these examples:

> "Which one of the following, if true, is LEAST consistent with Riechart's theory about fighting behavior in spiders?"

> "Given the information in the passage, the author is LEAST likely to believe which one of the following?"

When the word "least" and "except" are used in question stems, they are capitalized.

Evaluate the Argument Questions ▇▇

Evaluate the Argument questions ask you to consider a question, statistic, or piece of information that would best help determine the logical validity of the argument presented in the passage. In other words, you must select the answer choice that helps decide whether the argument is good or bad.

To better understand this question type, imagine that you are examining an argument and you have to ask one question that—depending on the answer to the question—will reveal whether the argument is strong or weak. By this definition, there must be a flaw in each argument, and your question, if posed correctly, can reveal that flaw or eliminate the flaw. Please note that you are not being asked to prove with finality whether the argument is good or bad—rather, you must simply ask the question that will best help analyze the validity of the argument. For this reason, Evaluate the Argument questions can be seen as a combination of a Strengthen question and a Weaken question: if you ask the best question, depending on the answer to the question the argument could be seen as strong or weak.

Evaluate the Argument question stems almost always use the word "evaluate" or a synonym such as "judge" or "assess," but the intent is always identical: the question stem asks you to identify the piece of information that would be most helpful in assessing the argument.

Question stem examples:

> "The answer to which one of the following questions would contribute most to an evaluation of the argument?"

> "Which one of the following would be most important to know in evaluating the hypothesis in the passage?"

> "Which one of the following would it be most relevant to investigate in evaluating the conclusion of George's argument?"

Evaluate the Argument questions appear infrequently on the GMAT, but the uniqueness of the question type forces students to take a moment to adjust when they do appear. Some question types, such as Must Be True and Primary Purpose, recur so frequently that students become used to seeing them and are comfortable with the process of selecting an answer. When a question type appears rarely, test takers are often thrown off-balance and lose time and energy reacting to the question. The makers of the GMAT are well aware of this, and this is the reason they intersperse different question types in each section (again, imagine how much easier the GMAT would be if the Verbal section were composed of 25 Must Be True questions). One reason we study each type of question is to help you become as comfortable as possible with the questions you will encounter on the test, making your reaction time as fast as possible.

The Variance Test™

Solving Evaluate questions can be difficult. The nature of the answer choices allow for separate interpretations, and deciding on a single answer can be challenging. In order to determine the correct answer choice on an Evaluate the Argument question, apply the Variance Test™.

The Variance Test consists of supplying two polar opposite responses to the question posed *in the answer choice* and then analyzing how the varying responses affect the conclusion in the passage. If different responses produce different effects on the conclusion, then the answer choice is correct. If different responses do not produce different effects, then the answer choice is incorrect. For example, if an Evaluate the Argument answer choice states "What is the percentage of people who live near a nuclear plant?" look to test the two most extreme possibilities: first test the response "0%" for its effect on the conclusion and then test the response "100%" for its effect on the conclusion. If the answer choice is correct, one of the percentages should strengthen the argument and one of the percentages should weaken the argument. If the answer choice is incorrect, neither response will have an effect on the argument.

Of course, the answer choice does not have to be about percentages for the technique to work; the Variance Test will work regardless of the nature of the answer choice. Here are some more example answer choices and Variance Test responses:

> If an answer choice asks "Is the pattern permanent?" first test "Yes" as a response and then test "No" as a response (remember, you *must* test opposite answers). If the answer choice is correct, one response should strengthen the argument and one response should weaken the argument. If the answer choice is incorrect, neither response will have an effect on the argument.

> If an answer choice asks "Are corporate or environmental interests more important?" first test "Corporate interests are more important" as a response and then test "Environmental interests are more important" as a response. If the answer choice is correct, one response should strengthen the argument and one response should weaken the argument. If the answer choice is incorrect, neither response will have an effect on the argument.

The Variance Test is a very powerful tool for attacking Evaluate the Argument questions. Because of the unique structure of Evaluate questions, the Variance Test can only be used with these questions and the test does not apply to any other question type.

5

Question Modifiers and Overlays ▮▮▮

Certain words that appear in question stems can have a powerful impact on the nature of the answer choice you are seeking. The most important of these words are discussed below.

"Most" and "Best" in Question Stems

Many question stems contain the qualifiers "most" or "best." For example, a typical question stem will state, "Which one of the following most accurately expresses the main point of the passage?" or "Which one of the following best expresses the main idea of the passage?" Astute test takers realize that the presence of "most" or "best" opens up a Pandora's box of sorts: by including "most" or "best," there is a possibility that other answer choices will also meet the criteria of the question stem (Main Point, Strengthen, Parallel, etc.), albeit to a lesser extent. In other words, if a question stem says "most weakens," the possibility is that every answer choice weakens the argument and you would be in the unenviable task of having to choose the best of a bunch of good answer choices. *Fortunately, this is not how it works.* Even though "most" or "best" will appear in a number of stems, you can rest assured that only one answer choice will meet the criteria. So, if you see a "most weakens" question stem, only one of the answers will weaken the argument. So, then, why does "most" or "best" appear in so many question stems? Because in order to maintain test integrity the test makers need to make sure their credited answer choice is as airtight and defensible as possible. Imagine what would occur if a question stem, let us say a Weaken question, did not include a "most" or "best" qualifier: any answer choice that weakened the argument, even if only very slightly, could then be argued to meet the criteria of the question stem. A situation like this would make constructing the test exceedingly difficult because any given problem might have multiple correct answer choices. To eliminate this predicament, the test makers insert "most" or "best" into the question stem, and then they can always claim there is one and only one correct answer choice.

Of course, every once in a while two answer choices achieve the desired goal; in those cases you simply choose the better of the two answers. Normally, the difference between the two answers is significant enough for you to make a clear distinction as to which one is superior.

5

"Except" and "Least" in Question Stems

The word "except" has a dramatic impact when it appears in a question stem. Because "except" means "other than," when "except" is placed in a question it negates the logical quality of the answer choice you seek. Literally, it turns the intent of the question stem upside down. For example, if a question asks you what must be true, the one correct answer must be true and the other four answers are not necessarily true. If "except" is added to the question stem, as in "Each of the following must be true EXCEPT," the stem is turned around and instead of the correct answer having the characteristic of must be true, the four incorrect answers must be true and the one correct answer is not necessarily true.

Many students, upon encountering "except" in a question stem, make the mistake of assuming that the "except" charges you with seeking the polar opposite. For example, if a question stem asks you to weaken a statement, some students believe that a "Weaken EXCEPT" question stem actually asks you to strengthen the statement. This is incorrect. Although weaken and strengthen are polar opposites, because except means "other than," when a "Weaken EXCEPT" question stem appears, you are asked to find any answer choice other than Weaken. While this could include a strengthening answer choice, it could also include an answer choice that has no effect on the statement. Thus, in a "Weaken EXCEPT" question, the four incorrect answers Weaken the statement and the one correct answer does not weaken the statement (could strengthen or have no effect). Here is another example:

"Which one of the following, if true, strengthens the argument above?"

> One correct answer: Strengthen
> Four incorrect answers: Do not Strengthen

"Each of the following, if true, strengthens the argument above EXCEPT:"

> One correct answer: Does not Strengthen
> Four incorrect answers: Strengthen

As you can see from the example, the presence of except has a profound impact upon the meaning of the question stem. Because "except" has this powerful effect, it always appears in all capital letters whenever it is used in a GMAT question stem.

"Except" is used more frequently in GMAT Reading Comprehension question stems than "least."

The true effect of "except" is to logically negate the question stem.

5

The word "least" has a similar effect to "except" when it appears in a question stem. Although "least" and "except" do not generally have the same meaning, when "least" appears in a question stem you should treat it *exactly the same* as "except." Note: this advice holds true only when this word appears in the question stem! If you see the word "least" elsewhere on the GMAT, consider it to have its usual meaning of "in the lowest or smallest degree."

Because "least," like "except," has such a strong impact on the meaning of a question stem, the test makers kindly place "least" in all capital letters when it appears in a question stem.

In the answer keys to this book, we will designate questions that contain "except" or "least" by placing an "X" at the end of the question stem classification. For example, a "Must Be True EXCEPT" question stem would be classified as "MustX." A "Parallel EXCEPT" question stem would be classified as "ParallelX" and so on. The only exception to this rule will be a question that states, "Each of the following could be true EXCEPT." Those questions will be designated "Cannot Be True."

Principle Questions

Principle questions (PR) are not a separate question type but are instead an "overlay" that appears in a variety of question types. For example, there are Must Be True Principle questions (Must-PR), Strengthen Principle questions (Strengthen-PR), and Cannot Be True Principle questions (Cannot-PR), among others. In a question stem, the key indicator that the Principle concept is present is the word "principle." Here are two examples:

The word "proposition" or "precept" can be used in place of "principle."

"Which one of the following principles can be most clearly said to underlie the author's arguments in the third paragraph?"

"Given the information in the passage, the author can most reasonably be said to use which one of the following principles to refute the advocates' claim that computer conferences can function as communities (line 15)?"

A principle is a broad rule that specifies what actions or judgments are correct in certain situations. For example, "Some companies are profitable" is not a principle because no rule is involved and no judgment can be drawn from the statement. "All companies should strive to be profitable" is a principle, and one that can be applied to any company.

The degree of generality of principles can vary considerably, and some are much narrower than others. For example, "Children at Smith Elementary School must wear uniforms" is a principle restricted to children attending Smith. The principle does not apply to a child attending a different school. On the other hand, the principle "Any person of voting age has an obligation to vote" applies to a large number of people regardless of background, education, wealth, etc.

Because a principle is by definition a broad rule (usually conditional in nature), the presence of the Principle indicator serves to broaden the scope of the question. The question becomes more abstract, and you must analyze the problem to identify the underlying relationships. Functionally, you must take a broad, global proposition and apply it in a specific manner, either to the answer choices (as in a Must or Parallel question) or to the passage (as in a Strengthen or Weaken question).

All-that-Apply Questions

Occasionally the GMAT will include Reading Comprehension questions that require you to consider three option, listed as "I," "II," and "III," from which you must determine all of the options which accurately respond to the question. Here is an example:

> Which of the following factors is required for the development of dissociative personality disorder?
>
> I.   Parental conflict
> II. Different parental treatment of siblings, if siblings are present
> III. Early childhood trauma
>
> (A) I only
> (B) II only
> (C) I and II only
> (D) I and III only
> (E) I, II, and III

Although they appear relatively rarely in the GMAT sample tests that have been released, you should be prepared for such questions, which require that you choose *all* of the choices that are accurate according to the passage, and *only* those that are confirmed by the statements presented.

Question Type Variety

One of the aims of the test makers is to keep you off-balance. An unsettled, flustered test taker is prone to make mistakes. By mixing up the types of questions you face as well as the location you must search in order to find the proper information, the makers of the test can keep you from getting into a rhythm. Imagine how much easier the Reading Comprehension passages would be if you faced four consecutive Must Be True questions with each passage. For this reason, you will always see a range of questions within each section, and you will rarely see the same exact question type twice in a row.

Since this situation is guaranteed to occur on your GMAT, before the test begins prepare yourself mentally for the quick shifting of mental gears that is required to move from question to question.

5

Location, Type, and Sub-type Drill

The following is another collection of sample Reading Comprehension questions. In the space provided, categorize each stem into one of the three Location designations: Specific Reference (SR), Concept Reference (CR), and Global Reference (GR), and then categorize each stem into one of the six main Reading Comprehension Question Types: Must Be True, Main Point, Strengthen, Weaken, Parallel Reasoning, Cannot Be True, or Evaluate the Argument. In addition, include any relevant sub-type designations as discussed in this chapter: Purpose (P), Organization (O), Author's Perspective (AP), Subject Perspective (SP), Passage Expansion (E), Except (X), or Principle (PR). *Answers begin on page 208*

1. Question Stem: "It can be reasonably inferred from the passage that the author's attitude is most favorable toward which one of the following?"

   Question Type: _____

2. Question Stem: "Which one of the following views can most reasonably be attributed to the experts cited in line 39?"

   Question Type: _____

3. Question Stem: "As described in the passage, NASA's approach to solving the dark matter problem is most analogous to which of the following?"

   Question Type: _____

4. Question Stem: "Based on information in the passage, it can be inferred that which one of the following sentences could most logically be added to the passage as a concluding sentence?"

   Question Type: _____

5. Question Stem: "Which one of the following, if true, would most weaken the author's argument against harsh punishment for debtors?"

   Question Type: _____

Location, Type, and Sub-type Drill

6. Question Stem: "Which one of the following, if true, would lend the most credence to the author's argument in the second paragraph of the passage?"

   Question Type: _____

7. Question Stem: "Which one of the following best states the main idea of the passage?"

   Question Type: _____

8. Question Stem: "Which one of the following most accurately describes the organization of the passage?"

   Question Type: _____

9. Question Stem: "The passage provides information that answers each of the following questions EXCEPT:"

   Question Type: _____

10. Question Stem: "The author's primary purpose in the passage is"

    Question Type: _____

11. Question Stem: "The logical relationship of lines 7-9 of the passage to lines 23-25 of the passage is most accurately described as"

    Question Type: _____

12. Question Stem: "Which one of the following, if true, would most cast doubt on the author's interpretation of the study involving the family discussed on line 17?"

    Question Type: _____

13. Question Stem: "The passage contains information sufficient to justify inferring which one of the following?"

    Question Type: _____

Location, Type, and Sub-type Drill

14. Question Stem: "The author's attitude toward Zeno's development of a new hypothesis about atomic processes can most aptly be described as"

Question Type: _____

15. Question Stem: "Which one of the following institutions would NOT be covered by the multi-tier classification system proposed by Jacobs?"

Question Type: _____

16. Question Stem: "Which one of the following most closely expresses the author's intended meaning in using the term "unabashedly" (line 14)?"

Question Type: _____

17. Question Stem: "The author's attitude toward the studies mentioned in lines 14 - 23 is most likely"

Question Type: _____

18. Question Stem: "Based on the passage, the author would probably hold that which one of the following principles is fundamental to long-term reduction of recidivism rates?"

Question Type: _____

19. Question Stem: "Which one of the following most accurately describes the organization of the material presented in the first and second paragraphs of the passage?"

Question Type: _____

20. Question Stem: "In discussing the tangential details of events, the passage contrasts their original significance to witnesses with their possible significance in the courtroom (lines 52-59). That contrast is most closely analogous to which one of the following?"

Question Type: _____

5

Location, Type, and Sub-type Drill Answer Key—page 205

The typical student misses at least half of the questions in this drill. Do not worry about how many you miss; the point of this drill is to acquaint you with the different question stems. As you see more examples of each type of question, your ability to correctly identify each stem will improve.

1. GR, Must, AP

Location: This question stem provides no reference points, so this is a Global Reference Question.

Type: The correct answer to this question must reflect the author's attitude as described in the passage, and it must pass the Fact Test. This is a Must Be True question.

Sub-type: Since the question deals with the author's attitude, this is an Author's Perspective question.

2. SR, Must, SP

Location: This question stem provides a line reference, so this is a Specific Reference question.

Type: The correct answer must be consistent with the passage's description of the referenced experts, so this is a Must Be True question.

Sub-Type: Here we are asked about the views of experts cited in the passage, so we must understand their perspective to find the answer to this Subject Perspective question.

3. CR, Parallel

Location: This question stem refers to a particular approach discussed somewhere in the passage, so this is a Concept Reference question.

Type: Here we are asked to parallel the referenced approach, so this is a Parallel Reasoning question (as with most questions that contain the word "analogous").

4. SR, Must, E

Location: This question stem specifies the location by asking for a logical concluding sentence.

Type: The correct answer to this question must provide a logical conclusion, which can be determined based on information from the passage, so this is a Must Be True question.

Sub-type: This question requires that a logical conclusion be added to the end of the passage, which makes this a Passage Expansion question.

Location, Type, and Sub-type Drill Answer Key

5. CR, Weaken

Location: This question deals with a particular argument made by the author, so this is a Concept Reference question (if the entire passage were focused on this one argument, this would then be a Global Reference question).

Type: Since this question asks for the answer choice which will weaken the author's argument, this is of course a Weaken question.

6. SR, Strengthen

Location: The line reference makes this a Specific Reference question.

Type: In this case we are asked to "lend credence" to an argument (otherwise known as "strengthening"). This is a Strengthen question.

7. GR, MP

Location: This question stem regards the passage as a whole, so this is a Global Reference Question.

Type: Since this question asks for the central focus of the passage, this is a Main Point question.

8. GR, Must, O

Location: As this question provides no specific reference points, it is a Global Reference question.

Type: The answer to this question stem will come directly from information in the passage, so this is a Must Be True question.

Sub-Type: This is a clear example of an Organization question, which requires that you have an understanding of the overall structure of the passage.

9. GR, MustX

Location: This question references the passage in its entirety, so this is a Global Reference question.

Type: The information needed to answer this question comes directly from the passage, so this is a Must Be True question.

Sub-Type: This is an Except question, so the four incorrect answers in this case will be those choices that can be answered with information provided in the passage. The correct answer choice will be the one that cannot be answered by the passage.

Location, Type, and Sub-type Drill Answer Key

10. GR, Must, P

Location: This common question stem refers to the passage as a whole, and is therefore a Global Reference question.

Type: The answer to this question will be based on information from the passage (and should be prephrased). This is a Must Be True question.

Sup-Type: Since this question asks for the author's main purpose, this is a Purpose question.

11. SR, Must, O

Location: This question refers us specifically to various locations in the passage, so this is a Specific Reference question.

Type: The answer comes from information from the passage, making this a Must Be True question.

Sub-Type: Because this question requires that you understand the structure of the passage, as well as the relationship between various sections of the passage, this is an Organization question.

12. SR, Weaken

Location: The reference to line 17 makes this a Specific Reference question.

Type: When we see a question begin with "Which of the following, if true," we can generally expect either a Strengthen or a Weaken question. In this case, because the correct answer will "cast doubt," this is a Weaken question.

13. GR, Must

Location: This stem gets no more specific than "The passage," so this is a Global Reference question.

Type: Although the wording in this case is somewhat convoluted, if an answer choice must be a "sufficiently justified inference," then it Must Be True.

14. CR, Must, AP

Location: This question stem refers to a particular hypothesis, which makes this a Concept Reference question.

Type: A proper description of the author's attitude will come directly from information in the passage (and therefore should certainly be prephrased), so this is a Must Be True question.

Sub-type: This question requires an understanding of the author's attitude, so it is an Author's Perspective question.

Location, Type, and Sub-type Drill Answer Key

15. CR, Cannot

Location: This question stem deals with a proposed classification system. If this system were the focus of the passage as a whole, this would be a Global Reference question. In the actual passage, however, that is not the case, making this a Concept Reference question.

Type: Since the correct answer choice cannot be covered by the proposed classification, this is a Cannot question.

16. SR, Must, P

Location: This question refers us to line 14, which makes this a Specific Reference question.

Type: The answer to this question should be prephrased, as it will come directly from information offered in the passage. It is a Must Be True question.

Sub-Type: Since this question stem requires that we consider the intended meaning of the given term, it is a Function/Purpose question.

17. SR, Must, AP

Location: This question stem specifies that the study is mentioned in lines 14-23, so this is a Specific Reference question.

Type: This question regards information about the author which comes directly from the passage, and the answer must pass the Fact Test. This is a Must Be True question.

Sub-type: This example requires an understanding of the author's attitude, so it is an Author's Perspective question.

18. GR, Must, AP, PR

Location: If this question deals with a passage which focuses on recidivism rates, then this is a Global Reference question. If recidivism only makes up a part of the discussion, this would be a Concept Reference question.

Type: The answer to this question will come from the information offered in the passage, so this is a Must Be True question.

Sub-type: Since this question regards the author's attitude, it is an Author's Perspective question, and because the answer will involve fundamental principles, it is also a Principle question.

5

Location, Type, and Sub-type Drill Answer Key

19. SR, Must, O

Location: This question refers to a specific portion of the passage, so it is a Specific Reference question.

Type: The answer to this Must Be True question will come from information provided in the passage, and should be prephrased.

Sub-Type: This question stem requires an understanding of the structure of the passage, as it is a Passage Organization question.

20. SR, Parallel

Location: Since this question refers to lines 52-59, it is a Specific Reference question.

Type: This question requires that we find an "analogous contrast," which basically means that we have to find a parallel scenario. This is a Parallel Reasoning question.

Prephrasing Answers

Most students tend to simply read the question stem and then move on to the answer choices without further thought. This is disadvantageous because these students run a greater risk of being tempted by the expertly constructed incorrect answer choices. One of the most effective techniques for quickly finding correct answer choices and avoiding incorrect answer choices is prephrasing. Prephrasing an answer involves quickly speculating on what you expect the correct answer will be based on the information in the passage.

Although every answer you prephrase may not be correct, there is great value in considering for a moment what elements could appear in the correct answer choice. Students who regularly prephrase find that they are more readily able to eliminate incorrect answer choices, and of course, many times their prephrased answer is correct. In part, prephrasing puts you in an attacking mindset: if you look ahead and consider a possible answer choice, you are forced to involve yourself in the problem. This process helps keep you alert and in touch with the elements of the problem.

Keep in mind that prephrasing is directly related to attacking the passage; typically, students who closely analyze the critical elements of the passage can more easily prephrase an answer.

Further, note that while the answers to many questions can be prephrased, not all answers can be prephrased. A question that asks, "Which one of the following most accurately states the main point of the passage?" should immediately bring an answer to mind. On the other hand, if a question asks, "To which one of the following questions does the passage most clearly provide an answer?" you cannot prephrase an answer, because you are not given sufficient information to pre-form an opinion. Yes, you will have some general knowledge based on your reading, but because the test makers can choose any angle from the passage, you will probably not come up with a strong prephrase to this question. This should not be a concern—prephrase when you can, and if you cannot, move ahead.

Because of the GMAT's time constraints, some students are afraid to pause between reading the questions and assessing the answers. Always prephrase when possible! Prephrasing is far more efficient, and makes you less susceptible to the test makers' cleverly worded incorrect answer choices.

All high-scoring test takers are active and aggressive. Passive test takers tend to be less involved in the exam and therefore more prone to error.

5

The Answer Choices

All GMAT Reading Comprehension questions have five answer choice options and each question has only one correct, or "credited," response. As with other sections, the correct answer in a Reading Comprehension question must meet the Uniqueness Rule of Answer Choices™, which states that "Every correct answer has a unique logical quality that meets the criteria in the question stem. Every incorrect answer has the opposite logical quality." The correctness of the answer choices themselves conforms to this rule: there is one correct answer choice; the other four answer choices are the opposite of correct, or incorrect. Consider the following specific examples:

1. Logical Quality of the Correct Answer: Must Be True

   Logical Quality of the Four Incorrect Answers:

   > The opposite of Must Be True = Not Necessarily True (could be not necessarily the case or never the case)

2. Logical Quality of the Correct Answer: Strengthen

   Logical Quality of the Four Incorrect Answers:

   > The opposite of Strengthen = Not Strengthen (could be neutral or weaken)

3. Logical Quality of the Correct Answer: Weaken

   Logical Quality of the Four Incorrect Answers:

   > The opposite of Weaken = Not Weaken (could be neutral or strengthen)

There may be times when you would not read all five answer choices. For example, suppose you only have two minutes left in the section and you determine that answer choice (B) is clearly correct. In that case, you would choose answer choice (B) and then move on to the next question.

Even though there is only one correct answer choice and this answer choice is unique, you still are faced with a difficult task when attempting to determine the correct answer. The test makers have the advantage of time and language on their side. Because identifying the correct answer at first glance can be quite hard, you must always read all five of the answer choices. Students who fail to read all five answer choices open themselves up to missing questions without ever having read the correct answer. There are many classic examples of the test makers' placing highly attractive wrong answer choices just before the correct answer. If you are going to make the time investment of analyzing the passage and the question stem, you should also make the wise investment of considering each answer choice.

5

As you read through each answer choice, sort them into Contenders and Losers. If an answer choice appears somewhat attractive, interesting, or even confusing, keep it as a contender and quickly move on to the next answer choice. You do not want to spend time debating the merits of an answer choice only to find that the next answer choice is superior. However, if an answer choice immediately strikes you as incorrect, classify it as a loser and move on. Once you have evaluated all five answer choices, return to the answer choices that strike you as most likely to be correct and decide which one is correct.

The Contender/Loser separation process is exceedingly important, primarily because it saves time. Again consider two students—1 and 2— who each approach the same question, one of whom uses the Contender/Loser approach and the other who does not. Answer choice (D) is correct:

Student 1 (using Contender/Loser)

As you practice narrowing down answer choices, do your work on a separate noteboard with grids, as discussed in the introduction, because that's what you will be doing when you take the actual test.

> Answer choice A: considers this answer for 10 seconds, keeps it as a Contender.
>
> Answer choice B: considers this answer for 5 seconds, eliminates it as a Loser.
>
> Answer choice C: considers this answer for 10 seconds, eliminates it as a Loser.
>
> Answer choice D: considers this answer for 15 seconds, keeps it as a Contender, and mentally notes that this answer is preferable to (A).
>
> Answer choice E: considers this answer for 10 seconds, would normally keep as a contender, but determines answer choice (D) is superior.

After a quick review, Student 1 selects answer choice (D) and moves to the next question. Total time spent on the answer choices: 50 seconds (irrespective of the time spent on the passage).

Student 2 (considering each answer choice in its entirety)

Answer choice A: considers this answer for 10 seconds, is not sure if the answer is correct or incorrect. Returns to stimulus and spends another 15 seconds proving the answer is wrong.

Answer choice B: considers this answer for 5 seconds, eliminates it.

Answer choice C: considers this answer for 10 seconds, eliminates it.

Answer choice D: considers this answer for 15 seconds, notes this is the best answer.

Answer choice E: considers this answer for 10 seconds, but determines answer choice (D) is superior.

After a quick review, Student 2 selects answer choice (D) and moves to the next question. Total time spent on the answer choices: 65 seconds.

Comparison: both students answer the problem correctly, but Student 2 takes 15 more seconds to answer the question than Student 1.

Again, we might note that the time difference in this example is small (15 seconds). We should keep in mind that the extra 15 seconds is for just one problem.

Imagine if that same thing occurred on every single Reading Comprehension problem in the section: that extra 15 seconds per question would translate to a loss of 3 minutes when multiplied across 12 questions in a section! And that lost time would mean that Student 2 would get to two or three fewer questions, minimum, than Student 1, just in this one section. This example underscores an essential GMAT truth: Little things make a big difference, and every single second counts. If you can save even five seconds by employing a certain method, then do so!

Occasionally, students will read and eliminate all five of the answer choices. If this occurs, return to the passage and re-evaluate what you have read. Remember—the information needed to answer the question always resides in the passage, either implicitly or explicitly. If none of the answers are attractive, then you must have missed something key in the passage.

Tricks of the Trade ▰▰▰▰▰▰▰

The individuals who construct standardized tests are called *psychometricians*. Although this job title sounds ominous (almost villainous), breaking this word into its two parts reveals a great deal about the nature of the test makers. Although we could make a number of jokes about the *psycho* part, this portion of the word refers to psychology; the *metrician* portion relates to metrics or measurement. Thus, the purpose of these individuals is to create a test that measures you in a precise, psychological way.

As part of this process, the makers of the GMAT carefully analyze reams of data from every test administered in order to assess the tendencies of test takers. As Arthur Conan Doyle observed through his character Sherlock Holmes, "You can, for example, never foretell what any one man will do, but you can say with precision what an average number will be up to." By studying the actions of all past test takers, the makers of the exam can reliably predict where you will be most likely to make errors. Throughout this book we will reference those pitfalls as they relate to specific questions and passage types.

For the moment, we would like to highlight one mental trap you must avoid at all times in any GMAT section: the tendency to dwell on past problems. Many students fall prey to "answering" a problem, and then continuing to think about it as they start the next problem. Obviously, this is distracting and creates an environment where missing the next problem is more likely. When you finish a problem, you must immediately put it out of your mind and move to the next problem with 100% focus. If you let your mind wander back to previous problems, you make yourself far more vulnerable to psychological influence and answer choice traps.

5

Final Chapter Note ▰▰▰▰▰▰▰

This concludes our general discussion of Reading Comprehension passages. In the next chapter we will briefly review ideas previously discussed, and then we will use those techniques to work through complete passages and question sets. If, in the future, you find yourself unclear about some of these ideas, please return to the earlier chapters and revisit those concepts.

If you feel as if you are still hazy on some of the ideas discussed so far, do not worry. When discussing the theory that underlies all questions and approaches, the points can sometimes be a bit abstract and dry. In the next chapter we will focus more on the application of these ideas to common Reading Comprehension questions, which often helps a heretofore confusing idea become clear.

Chapter Six:
Putting It All Together

Chapter Six: Putting It All Together

Chapter Preview ■■■■■■■■

Up to this point we have focused on the methods needed to analyze the passages, and in doing so we have isolated individual sections of text that relate directly to each discussion. Now it is time to combine all of the strategies you have learned and analyze some complete passage sets. Accordingly, this chapter contains two sections:

1. A review of the basic elements of our approach to Reading Comprehension passages.

2. Two practice Reading Comprehension passages, with detailed analyses of the passage text and each question.

Reading Approach Review ■■■■■■■■

The following section provides a brief review of the reading approaches discussed in the previous chapters.

VIEWSTAMP

After you have ascertained the topic, as you move deeper into the passage you must carefully track the key VIEWSTAMP elements:

1. Viewpoint Identification and Analysis

A viewpoint is the position or approach taken by a person or group. On the GMAT, Reading Comprehension passages may contain one viewpoint, or might reflect two (or more) different perspectives. These viewpoints can be the author's or those of groups discussed by the author.

As you read, you must identify each viewpoint that is presented in the passage. This is a fairly straightforward process—whenever a new group or individual viewpoint is discussed, simply note the presence of that group.

6

2. Passage Structure

You will most likely need to return to the passage when responding to some of the questions. In order to maximize the efficiency of the process of returning to the passage, identifying the underlying logical structure of the passage as you read can be quite helpful in quickly locating important information once you begin to answer the questions.

3. Tone of the Author

As you track various passage elements remember to take notes on a separate noteboard as you will be doing when you take the GMAT CAT.

The author's attitude is revealed through the author's choice of words. To make a determination of attitude, you must carefully examine the words used by the author. In most passages, GMAT authors tend not to be extreme in their opinions, generally attempting to offer reasoned arguments in support of their position, arguments that will sway the average reader (note also that tone is representative of the passage as a whole, and not just of a single section).

4. Passage Argumentation

Identifying viewpoints and tone is critical to getting a generalized feel for how a passage unfolds. Understanding the arguments will help you understand the details of the passage, so take note of arguments asserted by the author or the person or people discussed in the passage.

5. The Main Point of the Passage

The main point of a passage is the central idea, or ultimate conclusion, that the author is attempting to prove. As you read, identify the author's conclusions, and track how they link together. What is the ultimate aim of the author's statements? What is he or she attempting to prove? Are some conclusions used to support others? If so, which is the primary conclusion? Keep in mind that although the main point may be stated succinctly in a sentence or two, all paragraphs of the passage must support the main point.

6. The Primary Purpose of the Passage

The Primary Purpose is the author's central reason for writing the passage. These questions require you to consider the "Why." Why did the author want to write the passage? Note that the answers to each Primary Purpose question tend to begin with a verb, so understanding the author's motivation is vital.

Sources of Difficulty in GMAT Passages

There are four general ways the makers of the test can increase the difficulty of any given passage:

1. Challenging Topic or Terminology

2. Challenging Writing Style

3. Multiple Viewpoints

4. Difficult Questions/Answers

Remember, some students consider the format of the GMAT a source of difficulty in itself, A thorough familiarity with the presentation of the computer-based test can be vital to ensure a strong performance on test day.

Passage Elements That Generate Questions

As you read, there are certain specific, consistent passage elements that should jump out at you, primarily because history has reflected the test makers' tendency to use these elements as the basis of questions. For purposes of clarity, we will divide these elements into two types:

Viewpoint-Specific Elements

1. Track all viewpoints

2. Be wary of competing perspectives

Text-based Questions

Text-based elements will often be smaller pieces, sometimes just a single word, but sometimes short sections of the text. In this sense, these are the "nuts and bolts" elements that you should be aware of when reading:

1. Initial Information/Closing Information

2. Dates and Numbers

3. Definitions

4. Examples

5. Difficult Words or Phrases

6. Enumerations/Lists

7. Text Questions

Two Broad Reasoning Structures

Causal reasoning and conditional reasoning appear frequently in the Critical Reasoning questions on the GMAT, but less so with the Reading Comprehension passages.

Causal Reasoning

Cause and effect reasoning asserts or denies that one thing causes another, or that one thing is caused by another. The cause is the event that makes the other occur; the effect is the event that follows from the cause. By definition, the cause must occur before the effect, and the cause is the "activator" or "ignitor" in the relationship. The effect always happens at some point in time after the cause.

Causality in Reading Comprehension usually is discussed in the context of why certain events occurred. The terms that typically introduce causality—such as *caused by*, *reason for*, *led to*, or *product of*—are still used, but then the author often goes on to discuss the reasons behind the occurrence in depth.

Conditional Reasoning

Conditional reasoning is the broad name given to logical relationships composed of sufficient and necessary conditions. Any conditional relationship consists of at least one sufficient condition and at least one necessary condition.

Conditional relationships in Reading Comprehension passages tend to be unobtrusive, usually occurring as a sideline point to a larger argument.

Of the two types of reasoning, causal reasoning appears more frequently than conditional reasoning in Reading Comprehension passages.

6

Pitfalls to Avoid

There are a number of text formations and configurations you should recognize. These constructions are often used by the test makers to create confusion, so in this sense they function as possible "traps" for the unwary test taker.

Traps of Similarities and Distinctions

This trap occurs when, in a continuous section of text, an author discusses in detail items that have both similarities and differences. By comparing and contrasting the items in close proximity, the test makers create a greater likelihood for confusion.

Trap of Separation

One favorite trick of the test makers is to take a long discussion of a particular topic and break it up by inserting within it a section of text about a related but distinct topic, effectively creating a separation effect: the main idea bisected by similar but different (and possibly distracting) content in the middle. Then questions will test your ability to track the interrupted main concept despite its beginning and end being divided by many lines (or entire paragraphs) in the passage.

The Trap of Question Misdirection

This trap occurs when the test makers use a specific line reference in the question stem to direct you to a place in the passage where the correct answer will not be found.

Trap of Proximity

Just because two ideas are placed in physical proximity in a passage does not mean that they are related. Similarly, items widely separated in the passage are not necessarily unrelated.

Trap of Inserted Alternate Viewpoint

Another ploy the test makers favor is to present several different viewpoints in a single passage, even a single paragraph, forcing readers to track both the topical information and the various perspectives.

6

Traps of Chronology

Traps of chronology relate to the placement and order of items within the passage, and the tendency of many readers to believe that when one item is presented before another, then the first item occurred first or caused the second. These two traps are called the Trap of Order and the Trap of Cause, respectively:

Trap of Order

Some students make the mistake of believing that because an event or situation is discussed before another event, the first event likely predated the second. Unless explicitly stated or inherently obvious, this does not have to be the case.

Trap of Cause

Some students also mistakenly assume that when one scenario is discussed before another, then the first item must have caused the second item. This assumption is unwarranted. The easiest way to discern the author's intention is to carefully examine the language used because causal relationships almost always feature one or more of the words that indicate causality (such as *caused by*, *produced by*, *determined*, *led to*, *resulted in*, etc).

The simple truth is that the order of presentation of the items in the passage does not indicate any temporal or causal relationship between them.

Passage Topic Traps

Passage difficulty is more a function of writing style, the number of viewpoints, and the exact concepts under discussion than of the general topic of the passage. That said, the test makers will occasionally use the topic to catch test takers off-guard. This technique of theirs works because when the typical student begins reading a passage, the topic often frames their expectations. The test makers are well aware of these ingrained expectations, and they at times play a sort of "bait and switch" game with students, especially by making a passage initially look hard or easy and then radically changing the level of difficulty after the first few lines or first paragraph.

6

GMAT Reading Comprehension Questions

Each Reading Comprehension passage on the GMAT is accompanied by a group of questions, which can cover a wide range of tasks, and will variously ask you to:

- describe the main point or primary purpose of the passage

- describe the structure and organization of the passage

- identify the viewpoint of the author or the viewpoint of subjects discussed within the passage

- identify details provided in or proven by the passage

- describe the meaning, function, or purpose of words or phrases in the passage

- strengthen, weaken, or parallel elements of the passage

- augment or expand the passage

All Reading Comprehension question stems provide some insight into where in the passage you should begin your search for the correct answer. This element is called "location," and you should always establish location as you read each question stem. Location can be divided into three categories—Specific Reference, Concept Reference, and Global Reference.

6

Reading Comprehension Question Types

Must Be True/Most Supported/Properly Inferred

This category is simply known as "Must Be True." Must Be True questions ask you to identify the answer choice that is best proven by the information in the passage.

Main Point

Main Point questions are a variant of Must Be True questions. As you might expect, a Main Point question asks you to find the main conclusion of the passage.

Purpose/Primary Purpose

Primary Purpose questions, which accompany almost every GMAT Reading Comprehension passage, require you to understand what the author hoped to achieve in writing the passage.

Strengthen

These questions ask you to select the answer choice that provides support for the author's argument or strengthens it in some way.

Weaken

Weaken questions ask you to attack or undermine the author's argument.

Parallel Reasoning

Parallel Reasoning questions ask you to identify the answer choice that contains reasoning most similar in structure to the reasoning presented in the passage.

Cannot Be True

Cannot Be True questions ask you to identify the answer choice that disagrees with, or is most weakened based on, the information in the passage.

Evaluate the Argument

Evaluate the Argument questions ask you to select a question, statistic, or piece of information that would best help determine the logical validity of the argument presented in the passage.

6

Prephrasing Answers

One of the most effective techniques for quickly finding correct answer choices and avoiding incorrect answer choices is prephrasing. Prephrasing an answer involves quickly speculating on what you expect the correct answer will be based on the information in the passage. Students who regularly prephrase find that they are more readily able to eliminate incorrect answer choices, and of course, many times their prephrased answer is correct. This process helps keep you alert and in touch with the elements of the problem; typically, students who closely analyze the critical elements of the passage can more easily prephrase an answer.

Prephrasing can be particularly important on the GMAT Computer Adaptive Test because the ability to quickly locate the correct answer choice obviates the need to create a grid and narrow down the contenders.

6

Two Sample Passages Analyzed

On the following pages two practice GMAT passages are presented, followed by a complete analysis of each passage. <u>One important note</u>: remember that maintaining a positive attitude is critical! Approach the passages with energy and enthusiasm and you will see your performance improve.

Sample Passage I

"Dissociative identity disorder," or multiple personality disorder, is a rare psychological disorder in which an individual exhibits entirely different personalities and behaviors. Although the
(5) exact psychological mechanism that creates multiple personalities is not known, psychiatrists have agreed that a severe emotional trauma must occur prior to age seven, the age at which a child's mind matures into a unified identity. In addition to
(10) this trauma, certain familial elements must be present. First, the parents of the child must be in conflict, essentially playing opposing, warring roles in the child's life. Typically, this is manifested by one parent abusing the child and the other parent
(15) denying or ignoring the abuse. Second, if siblings are present, they must be treated differently (and generally better) by the parents than the dissociated child. This difference in treatment is critical since it shows the dissociated child that he or she is
(20) "different" and undeserving of love and other emotional valuation. If all children in a family are treated in a similar fashion, then multiple personality disorder will not tend to occur. The above elements, while necessary for the rise of
(25) multiple personalities, do not guarantee that a child will develop multiple personalities.

1. The passage provides information to answer all of the following questions EXCEPT:

   (A) Are siblings necessary for the creation of multiple personality disorder?
   (B) Will a trauma in a young child's life guarantee the onset of multiple personality disorder?
   (C) How does a child establish multiple personalities?
   (D) What are some of the necessary preconditions for multiple personality disorder?
   (E) How common is the occurrence of multiple personality disorder in the population?

2. Which of the following individuals would be the most likely candidate for development of multiple personality disorder?

   (A) A fifteen-year-old female runaway with two abusive parents and two poorly-treated siblings.
   (B) A nine-year-old male with divorced parents and three well-treated sisters.
   (C) A five-year-old female who lost both her parents in a car accident.
   (D) A six-year-old male with one abusive parent and two well-treated brothers.
   (E) A seven-year-old female with two abusive parents and no siblings.

3. In the passage, the author is primarily concerned with doing which of the following?

   (A) Describing a psychiatric problem and proposing a solution.
   (B) Presenting information and drawing conclusions from the information.
   (C) Summarizing the current research into a common psychological disorder.
   (D) Citing evidence to support a view.
   (E) · Discussing a phenomenon and several factors required for its development.

4. Which of the following factors is required for the development of dissociative personality disorder?

   I. Parental conflict
   II. Different parental treatment of siblings, if siblings are present
   III. Early childhood trauma

   (A) I only
   (B) II only
   (C) I and II only
   (D) I and III only
   (E) I, II, and III

Sample Passage I—Answer Key

This passage begins with a definition of its topic, "dissociative identity disorder." This term describes the rare case of an individual who displays distinct multiple personalities and behaviors. While the exact cause of the pathology is unknown, the author provides a list of several factors common to those who suffer from this multiple personality disorder:

1. A child must suffer some severe emotional trauma before the age of seven, because this is the age at which a child's mind develops a "unified identity."

2. There must be conflict between the child's parents, typically with one parent who is abusive and the other in denial of, or at least ignoring, this abuse.

3. Finally, if the child has brothers or sisters, the parents' treatment of these siblings must be different from that of the affected child. The author points out that this factor plays an important role, because this different treatment sends the message that the affected child is different, has less value, and is unworthy of love.

One interesting note regarding the factors listed above: Although the author uses the term "first" to introduce the necessity of parental conflict, and uses the term "second" to introduce the requirement of different parental treatment of siblings, these are actually the second and third factors, respectively, required for the development of multiple personality disorder. The first factor, although not presented in list form, is that of severe emotional trauma suffered prior to age seven.

The author closes the paragraph with an important distinction: Although these factors are required for the development of dissociative identity disorder, their presence does not guarantee that the disorder will be developed (in conditional reasoning terms, the presence of these elements is *necessary* to the outcome, but not *sufficient* to guarantee the outcome).

6

Sample Passage I—Answer Key

<u>VIEWSTAMP</u> Analysis:

The sole **Viewpoint** presented in this passage is that of the author, who presents facts but neither provides any opinions nor draws any conclusions regarding the topic.

The **Structure** of this passage is quite simple, since the entire passage is composed of only one paragraph, in which the author introduces the concept of dissociative identity disorder, provides a definition of the disorder, and lists factors required for the development of the disorder.

The **Tone** of the passage is unbiased and academic, as the author provides facts about the disorder without drawing any conclusions or presenting any opinions on the matter.

Since this passage is basically a presentation of facts, there is no real **Argument** present, except perhaps for the assertion that the three factors listed are required if the disorder is to be developed.

The **Main Point** of this passage is that dissociative identity disorder is associated with severe emotional childhood trauma, parents in conflict, and different treatment of siblings (if present), although such experiences do not guarantee that one will develop this disorder.

The author's **Primary Purpose** is to introduce a psychological pathology and list several factors that are associated with, but do not guarantee the onset of the rare personality disorder.

Question #1: GR, MustX. The correct answer choice is (C)

Since this is an Except question, the four incorrect answer choices will present questions which are answered by the information provided within the passage, and the correct answer choice will be the one that presents a question which is unanswered by the information in the passage.

Answer choice (A): The question presented in this answer choice is covered in lines 15-16. The author tells us that if siblings are present, they must be treated differently than the affected child. This wording (specifically, the use of the term "if") implies that siblings need not be present.

Answer choice (B): In lines 23-26, the author points out that the factors listed are necessary to the development of the disorder, but do not guarantee its development. Since this question is answered in the passage, this answer choice is incorrect.

Answer choice (C): This is the correct answer choice, because this question is not answered in the passage. Although the elements listed are common to all those who suffer from the disorder, the author points out in lines 5-6 that the exact mechanism which causes the disorder is unknown.

Answer choice (D): This question is answered by the list of factors presented in lines 6-25, so this answer choice cannot be correct.

Answer choice (E): Since dissociative identity disorder is defined as "rare," this question is answered by the information in the passage, making this answer choice incorrect.

6

Question #2: CR, Must. The correct answer choice is (D)

As discussed earlier in the book, we should prephrase answers whenever possible. In this case, a candidate for multiple personality disorder would likely have suffered early emotional trauma, have parents in conflict, and be treated differently than his or her siblings (if siblings are present).

Answer choice (A): This female would be an unlikely candidate, because there is no clear conflict between the parents (she would be a more likely candidate if one parent ignored or denied the other's abuse), and she also lacks the element of parental treatment which is different from the treatment of her siblings.

Answer choice (B): The information provided in this answer choice is not sufficient to define this male as a likely candidate, because there is no mention of early emotional trauma, abuse, or differential treatment.

Answer choice (C): While this girl seems to have suffered the requisite early emotional trauma, there is no mention of abuse, conflict, or differential treatment, so there is no way to conclude that she is a likely candidate for the disorder.

Answer choice (D): This is the correct answer choice. Although the factors listed do not guarantee that this child will develop dissociative identity disorder, he is clearly the most likely candidate listed, considering the elements present in his case: He is younger than seven, has possibly suffered severe trauma from abuse, has one abusive parent, and is treated differently than his brothers.

Answer choice (E): This case lacks the opposing parental roles necessary for the development of the disorder, so this answer choice is incorrect.

6

Sample Passage I—Answer Key

Question #3: GR, Primary Purpose. The correct answer choice is (E)

The answer to this question should be prephrased as well: The author's primary purpose in this case is to define dissociative identity disorder, and provide a list of elements common to all who suffer from this disorder.

Answer choice (A): Although the author does describe a psychiatric problem, no solution is proposed in the passage.

Answer choice (B): The author is certainly concerned with presenting information about the disorder, but no conclusions are drawn.

Answer choice (C): There is no mention of current research into the disorder, and the author specifically mentions that it is a rare phenomenon.

Answer choice (D): The author does not cite evidence to support any view, choosing instead to merely present facts, so this answer choice is incorrect.

Answer choice (E): This is the correct answer choice, as any solid prephrase would have predicted. The author is primarily concerned with discussing the rare phenomenon of multiple personality disorder, and several factors necessary for development of the disorder.

Question #4: CR, Must. The correct answer choice is (E)

This question is particularly conducive to prephrasing, because all three factors listed below the question are necessary for development of the disorder. Note that factor III (early childhood trauma) is not presented in list form like the others in the passage ("First..." "Second..."), but is nonetheless a requirement for one to become dissociated and develop multiple personalities.

Answer choice (A): This answer choice lists only one of three necessary factors.

Answer choice (B): This answer choice also lists only one element.

Answer choice (C): This answer choice is the most commonly chosen wrong answer, because these are the two factors presented in the passage as "First" and "Second." Since early emotional trauma (before age seven) is necessary, however, this answer choice is incorrect.

Answer choice (D): Factor II is also necessary.

Answer choice (E): This is the correct answer choice, because it is the only answer which includes all three elements necessary for the development of dissociative identity disorder.

Sample Passage II

The next chapter is comprised entirely of practice passages and questions, so for the passage below, you need not answer any accompanying questions. Instead, practice the approaches we've discussed to create a simple translation of the passage. Once you have done so, list the VIEWSTAMP elements of the passage (listed below for review), then compare the analysis in the answer key to your own passage analysis.

The elements of VIEWSTAMP:

1. The various groups and Viewpoints discussed within the passage. (VIEW)
2. The Structure of the passage and the organization of ideas. (S)
3. The Tone or attitude of each group or individual. (T)
4. The Argument made by each group or individual. (A)
5. The Main Purpose of the passage. (M)
6. The Primary Purpose of the passage (P).

James Joyce, the Irish poet considered by many to be among the most influential writers of the modern era, is probably known best as the author of Ulysses, the modernist novel first published in
(5) 1922. To say that Joyce's writings are subject to complex and varied interpretation would be an understatement; the author continues to provide fodder for modern scholarly journals, and countless books and articles by subsequent
(10) authors have been dedicated solely to the assessment of his often enigmatic works. One such work is an obscure collection of short stories known as "Finn's Hotel."

For many years, the tales which comprise
(15) "Finn's Hotel" were believed by most scholars to be nothing more than a series of preliminary sketches the amalgamation of which was eventually to serve as the basis for the author's more famous "Finnegan's Wake." Recently,
(20) however, a Joyce scholar in Ireland has offered a new perspective on the collection. Danis Rose, an independent writer who has been developing his own critical edition of "Finnegan's Wake" for over fifteen years, will soon release a previously
(25) unpublished collection by Joyce (the works involved have been published before, but never as a collection). Rather than early drafts of a later work, says Rose, the collection represents its own anthology of distinct works—one which provides
(30) important insights about the writer's path from Ulysses to Finnegan's Wake.

Rose arrived at his conclusions about the anthology after examining correspondence between Joyce and the poet's patron, Harriet
(35) Shaw Weaver. These letters only recently became available, which explains why the "Finn's Hotel" stories had been mischaracterized for so many years.

6

Sample Passage II—Answer Key

Paragraph One:

This passage begins with an introduction to James Joyce, a writer best known as the author of the modernist novel *Ulysses*. Joyce's writings, we are told, are not easily understood; despite the fact that Joyce was published in the early 20th century, the writer's works are still the subject of varied and complex interpretations among modern scholars. Like many GMAT authors, the writer of this passage begins with a paragraph that is viewpoint neutral—an opinion-free presentation of facts, intended to provide context for the subsequent discussion of the anthology of obscure stories known as *Finn's Hotel*.

Paragraph Two:

The author begins this second paragraph with the perspective of "most scholars," who perceived the stories from *Finn's Hotel* as nothing more than early sketches which were to provide the foundation for Joyce's later, better-known work, *Finnegan's Wake*. At line 19 of the passage, the author begins the presentation of the alternate viewpoint of Danis Rose, a writer who argues that the stories of *Finn's Hotel* are not early drafts of *Finnegan's Wake*. Rose instead asserts that these stories are important in their own right, reflecting the evolution which took place between Joyce's writing of *Ulysses* and that of *Finnegan's Wake*. Structurally, the author opens this paragraph with the perspective of "most scholars," and closes with Rose's rebuttal of that position.

Paragraph Three:

The author begins the final paragraph with the fact that Rose's perspective is based on correspondence between Joyce and his patron, Harriet Shaw Weaver. Until this point in the passage, different viewpoints have been discussed, but the author's opinion has not been presented. Beginning at line 35, the author's perspective finally becomes clear: Because the patron correspondences were previously unavailable, the author asserts, the stories from the Joyce anthology were "mischaracterized" for years. The claim that the *Finn's Hotel* stories had been mischaracterized (presumably by the scholars referenced in the second paragraph) reflects the author's opinion, not empirical fact. This final sentence of the passage clarifies the position of the author, who shares Rose's perspective.

6

Sample Passage II—Answer Key

<u>**VIEWSTAMP**</u> Analysis:

There are three main **Viewpoints** presented in the passage: that of "most scholars," that of Danis Rose, and that of the author. Rose and the author are in agreement, and both oppose the referenced scholars.

The **Structure** of the passage is as follows:

The first paragraph discusses Joyce and some of the poet's works, including *Finn's Hotel*. The second paragraph presents the scholars' perspective on the anthology, and introduces Rose and his alternate viewpoint on the matter. The third paragraph reflects the perspective of the author, who agrees with Rose.

Rose and the scholars are at odds, but the **Tone** of the disagreement does not appear to be acrimonious. For example, critics "believed" and Rose "has offered a new perspective." Those are fairly mild words that simply indicate general disagreement, not particularly strong opposition.

The author appears to disagree with the scholars to a greater degree. In lines 37-38, the author asserts that "the *Finn's Hotel* stories had been mischaracterized for so many years," to indicate that he or she does not share the position of "most scholars."

The "scholars" referenced by the author in line 15 **Argue** that *Finn's Hotel* represents nothing more than early drafts for Joyce's later work, *Finnegan's Wake*.

Rose and the author disagree with the scholars: the author calls the scholars' perspective a "mischaracterization," and Danis asserts that the anthology should be considered a group of distinct works, providing "important insights" about Joyce's progression as a writer.

The author's **Main Point** is that Joyce's "*Finn's Hotel*" is properly characterized as its own unique anthology and is not merely a series of preliminary sketches created for "*Finnegan's Wake*," as previously thought.

The author's **Primary Purpose** is to introduce James Joyce and "*Finn's Hotel*," present a misguided perspective from the past, and join passage subject Danis Rose in asserting that the Joyce anthology stands alone as a collection of distinct works.

6

Overall, this is a nice passage—several viewpoints exist, clear authorial position and attitude are presented, and reasonably clear structure and argumentation exist. Granted, the topic may not be the most exciting, but you can engage yourself by focusing on the disagreement between the parties.

One final note: If you can consistently apply the VIEWSTAMP ideas we have discussed throughout this book, you will be in an excellent position to attack the questions. You now have a powerful arsenal of tools to dissect each problem, and, in many cases, you will discover that you know what the correct answer will say before you even begin reading the five answer choices.

6

Chapter Seven:
Practice Passages

POWERSCORE
TEST PREPARATION

Chapter Seven: Practice Passages

Chapter Notes

This section contains eight individual Reading Comprehension practice passages. As you read, consider the VIEWSTAMP elements discussed in Chapter 3, and create a brief summary of each. As you read the questions that follow each passage remember to try to prephrase an answer to each question before considering the choices provided (also, remember to take any notes on a separate noteboard, because you don't want to become dependent on notating the passage directly). The passages are followed by an answer key which provides a full VIEWSTAMP analysis of each passage and a discussion of each question and answer choice.

Stay focused, be positive, and good luck!

Passage #1

The Vienna Circle, an association of philosophers gathered around the University of Vienna in 1922, pioneered a "positivist" philosophy of science. Their aim was to present a unified vision of the world, where
(5) knowledge can only derive from experience through the application of logical analysis. Not surprisingly, most members of the Vienna Circle eschewed metaphysics, embracing a decidedly empiricist attitude toward the pursuit of scientific truth. Their attitude was shared
(10) by other prominent scientists such as Albert Einstein, whose works were frequently cited in monographs published by members of the Circle. Ironically, by the time the Vienna Circle "discovered" an intellectual bond with Einstein, he had departed from his positivist views
(15) to pursue less optimistic answers to the question of political, philosophical and scientific unity.

1. The main concern of the passage is to

(A) draw parallels between two philosophical movements and explain why a particular scientist embraced one of these movements at the expense of the other.

(B) relate a philosophical movement to a societal cause and contrast the movement's intellectual objectives with those of a prominent scientist.

(C) discuss the origins of a philosophical movement and summarize its effect on the work of a prominent scientist.

(D) contrast two philosophical views and examine their relation to a third view.

(E) summarize the objectives of a philosophical movement and examine their relation to the views of a prominent scientist

7

2. It can be inferred from the passage that Albert Einstein would be most likely to agree with which one of the following statements concerning the "positivist" philosophy of science, pioneered by the Vienna Circle in 1922?

(A) Though theoretically valuable, it erroneously embraced an empiricist attitude toward the pursuit of scientific truth.

(B) Its rejection of metaphysics resulted in a quest for scientific unity that was too optimistic.

(C) Its emphasis on empirical knowledge was laudable, even if the goal of presenting an unified vision of the world was ultimately unrealistic.

(D) Its quest for political, philosophical and scientific unity was detrimental to its pursuit of scientific truth.

(E) Though initially promising, its quest for scientific unity was a failure.

3. This passage suggests which one of the following about metaphysics?

(A) It was a reaction against the positivist philosophy of science.

(B) It failed to present a unified vision of the world.

(C) It did not necessarily seek to derive knowledge through experience alone.

(D) It was initially embraced by prominent scientists such as Einstein.

(E) It was regarded by members of the Vienna Circle as intellectually suspect.

7

Passage #2

Nutritional biologists have long argued that sugar should be classified as a toxin. Indeed, excessive consumption of simple carbohydrates, especially fructose, has been definitively linked to an increased

(5) risk of cardiovascular disease, diabetes, and cancer. However, to classify sugar as a "toxin" would be a misnomer. Almost any otherwise benign nutritional substance can be toxic if ingested in quantities sufficiently large to cause harm. Moreover, our

(10) obsession with sugar is itself harmful, as it detracts from focusing on an equally important part of any balanced diet: sodium.

Just like sugar, excessive consumption of sodium represents a significant health risk, especially for those

(15) suffering from hypertension. Everyone needs some sodium in his or her diet to replace routine losses. But while an adequate and safe intake of sodium for healthy adults is 1,100 to 3,300 milligrams a day, most processed foods exceed the upper limit of that range at

(20) least two-fold. It is likely that excessive sodium intake plays a role in the etiology of hypertension, additionally elevating the risk of stroke, coronary heart disease, and renal disease. Furthermore, since the salt used in the preparation of processed foods is generally refined, its

(25) consumption fails to satisfy the organism's need for other salts and minerals, which induces further craving. The excessive consumption of sodium can therefore enhance caloric overconsumption, and—just like dietary fructose—contribute to weight gain.

(30) Unfortunately, by limiting the intake of sugar, many of today's "fad diets" inadvertently increase the consumption of sodium. This is because diets low in sugar are often tasteless, and salt increases their palatability. Of course, substituting one harmful

(35) additive for an equally harmful one is nothing new: manufacturers were quick to promote "low-fat" foods in the 1980's when fat was viewed as the enemy, but increased the sugar content to keep consumers happy. Good nutrition, just like good health, is best viewed

(40) holistically. A well-balanced diet does not focus on any single nutritional additive in isolation. Instead, it uses natural foods to satisfy the body's need for macronutrients (carbohydrates, proteins, fat) while also taking into account the role of vitamins, minerals and

(45) fiber.

1. The primary purpose of the passage is to

   (A) argue that excessive consumption of sodium is more harmful than is excessive consumption of sugar.
   (B) explain why low-carb diets may induce an undesirable dietary habit.
   (C) call attention to the undesirable effects of sodium intake.
   (D) reject the view that sugar should be classified as a toxin.
   (E) compare and contrast the effects of two harmful nutritional substances.

2. The author mentions the fact that diets low in carbohydrates are often tasteless (line 32) primarily in order to

   (A) distinguish low-carbohydrate diets from low-fat diets
   (B) indicate a way in which low-carbohydrate diets promote unhealthy eating habits
   (C) explain why low-carbohydrate diets often fail to achieve their primary objectives
   (D) illustrate a potential downside unique to low-carbohydrate diets
   (E) suggest why an alternative dietary regimen is superior to low-carbohydrate diets

3. Based on the passage, the author would be most likely to agree with which one of the following statements about sodium intake?

   (A) It is a necessary component of any diet.
   (B) It interferes with the body's ability to absorb nutrients.
   (C) It is just as toxic as sugar.
   (D) It represents a significant health risk.
   (E) In large amounts, it invariably exacerbates hypertension.

4. The author would be most likely to regard low-carbohydrate diets as

   (A) somewhat beneficial, because added sugar has no nutritional value.
   (B) clearly healthful, because they limit the consumption of a potentially toxic substance.
   (C) overly restrictive of an important macronutrient.
   (D) inconsistent with the tenets of a well-balanced diet.
   (E) harmful, because they require an increased consumption of sodium.

5. Which one of the following best describes the function of the second paragraph of the passage?

   (A) It outlines the structure of the author's central argument.
   (B) It provides the rationale for correcting a misconception described in the first paragraph.
   (C) It explains why an outlook suggested in the first paragraph is potentially harmful.
   (D) It presents research that undermines the argument presented in the first paragraph.
   (E) It supports a course of action recommended in the first paragraph.

6. Which one of the following statements would most appropriately continue the discussion at the end of the passage?

   (A) Clearly, food cannot be judged one component at a time.
   (B) Thus, no single dietary regimen is likely to be completely harmless.
   (C) Nor surprisingly, our evolving views on nutrition are reflected in the dietary choices we make.
   (D) Therefore, manufacturers must strive for greater consistency in their dietary recommendations.
   (E) Otherwise, if one waits long enough, almost any food will be reported as healthful.

7

Passage #3

In 1996, the State of Arizona introduced a statute that divests the juvenile court of jurisdiction over juvenile offenders fifteen years of age or older who are accused of first and second degree murder, forcible sexual
(5)   assault, armed robbery or other violent felony offenses. Opponents have rightfully argued that by assigning automatic criminal responsibility to juveniles based solely on their age and the type of offense with which they are charged, many of the extenuating circumstances
(10) that would have previously been considered by a juvenile court judge are now largely irrelevant. In fact, if prosecution finds sufficient grounds for charging a juvenile offender with, say, armed robbery, juvenile court review will be entirely bypassed and the offender
(15) will automatically be tried in criminal court as an adult. The choice of court, therefore, rests entirely in the discretion of the prosecution. Regrettably, courts have been reluctant to question the constitutionality of such discretion, and little hope remains that they would
(20) subject it to judicial review any time soon.

1. The author mentions armed robbery (line 13) primarily in order to

(A) provide an example of a type of offense with which offenders are rarely charged in juvenile court
(B) show how the prosecution can automatically decide a jurisdictional issue involving some juvenile offenders
(C) illustrate a type of offense that the new statute will make more difficult to prosecute
(D) explain why extenuating circumstances must be considered when assigning criminal responsibility to juvenile offenders
(E) emphasize the severity of the offenses that are typically considered only in cases tried in criminal court

2. Which one of the following words employed by the author is most indicative of the author's attitude toward the ability of prosecutors to bypass juvenile court review following the passage of the new statute?

(A) rightfully
(B) hope
(C) regrettably
(D) reluctant
(E) divests

3. The passage suggests which one of the following about a sixteen-year old offender charged with armed robbery in the state of Arizona prior to 1996?

(A) The offender could be prosecuted either in juvenile or in criminal court.
(B) The prosecution did not have sufficient grounds to charge the offender with a more serious crime.
(C) The court would consider all extenuating circumstances relevant to his case.
(D) The prosecution could decide to bypass juvenile court review and try the offender in criminal court.
(E) The choice of courts did not rest entirely in the discretion of the prosecution.

4. The author's main purpose in the passage is to

(A) defend a proposed statutory change against criticism
(B) explain the unforeseen consequences of a legal reform
(C) support a critical evaluation of a statute
(D) criticize the constitutionality of judicial discretion
(E) articulate opposing arguments and propose a reconciliation

7

Passage #4

Many of the most popular diets today, including the so-called "Paleo diet," are premised on the dubious assumption that increased consumption of meat and meat by-products pose minimal health risks to the human
(5) body. Proponents of such diets correctly observe that cholesterol intake does not directly correlate with the concentration of harmful low-density lipoprotein (LDL) cholesterol particles in the blood plasma. Studies show, however, that cholesterol intake exacerbates the negative
(10) effect of saturated fatty acids on LDL concentrations, thus increasing LDL levels indirectly. Furthermore, there is evidence suggesting that the oxidation of low-density lipoproteins in human beings is itself atherogenic, and there appears to be a consistent positive association
(15) between the consumption of saturated animal fats and the oxidation of LDL particles. Although antioxidants and dietary fiber can help prevent oxidative modification of LDL, most diets fail to recommend sufficient amounts of either supplement.

1. In the passage, the author is primarily interested in

   (A)   proposing a solution to a health problem.
   (B)   recommending a particular nutritional plan.
   (C)   discrediting an erroneous belief.
   (D)   evaluating the benefits of a dietary regimen.
   (E)   criticizing the shortcomings of modern diets.

2. Which one of the following most accurately states the main point of the passage?

   (A)   Increased consumption of meat and meat by-products may be harmful to one's health.
   (B)   Cholesterol intake can exacerbate the negative effects of saturated fatty acids on LDL concentrations.
   (C)   Most diets are not as healthful as their proponents are led to believe.
   (D)   Although cholesterol intake is not directly responsible for increasing the concentration of LDL particles in the blood plasma, it can cause such an increase indirectly.
   (E)   The healthiest diets are those that eliminate meat and meat by-products.

7

3. Which one of the following most accurately describes the role played in the argument by the claim that cholesterol intake does not directly correlate with the concentration of harmful low-density lipoprotein (lines 6-8)?

(A) It is a claim on which the argument depends but for which no support is given.

(B) It is used to refute the causal explanation described by the conclusion of the argument.

(C) It summarizes a position that the argument as a whole is directed toward discrediting.

(D) It acknowledges a possible objection to the recommendation put forth in the argument.

(E) It is a proposition for which the argument seeks to advance a causal explanation.

4. Which one of the following, if true, would most strengthen the proponents' argument that increased consumption of meat and meat by-products pose minimal health risks to the human body?

(A) Excessive consumption of salt, often found in meat by-products, is associated with increased risk of cardiovascular disease.

(B) Some animal fat contains large amounts of omega-3 fatty acids, which mitigate the ill effects of increased LDL concentrations.

(C) Of all plant-based diets, those that exclude meat and meat by-products are the most protective against atherosclerosis.

(D) Drugs that lower cholesterol levels can also prevent cardiovascular disease, but carry the risk of adverse side effects.

(E) Antioxidants and dietary fiber are not the only substances that can prevent oxidative modification of LDL.

7

Passage #5

The topic of criminality in Andrew Blanchard's work is a commonly pursued one. Its richness lies as much within the thematic framework of Blanchard's prose as it does within the author's own scandalous
(5) life. Not surprisingly, scholars frequently examine Blanchard's fictional world for clues that could reveal the "real" story of their author. While the verdict of such critiques traverses the entire spectrum of moral judgments, from wholehearted compassion to reluctant
(10) absolution and dismissive condemnation, they all share a certain smugness that prevents them from appreciating the poetic brilliance of their *objet de critique*.

At the less commendable end of this critical spectrum is Mark Newman's 1989 study titled, *Andrew*
(15) *Blanchard: Biography of Deceit*. In his book, Newman undertakes the formidable challenge of correcting and clarifying certain aspects of Blanchard's biography. The study, a detective narrative in its own right, seeks to expose Blanchard not only as a petty thief, but also
(20) as a bad playwright. Newman holds no punches in condemning Blanchard's plays as disturbing, distasteful, even disgusting. He even dislikes the playwright's penchant for meta-theater, arguing that only a highly skilled dramaturge can interweave multiple plays-
(25) within-a-play and still maintain a coherent narrative structure. The implication being, of course, that Blanchard was far from being a skilled dramaturge.

1. The primary purpose of the passage is to

(A) examine Blanchard's fictional world for clues that could reveal his criminal past.
(B) clarify certain aspects of Blanchard's biography.
(C) reject Blanchard's critical reception as unappreciative of his creative genius.
(D) correct a common misconception regarding the work of a famous playwright.
(E) defend a playwright against accusations that may be factually incorrect

2. Which one of the following summarizes the main point of the passage?

(A) By judging Andrew Blanchard's personal life rather than the quality of his work, critics fail to accord him the appreciation he deserves.
(B) Some of the themes that inhabit Andrew Blanchard's fictional world are drawn from his criminal past.
(C) Mark Newman's biography of Andrew Blanchard is well-informed, but the judgments it reaches are overly harsh.
(D) Andrew Blanchard's fictional world provides a valuable insight into his personal life.
(E) Andrew Blanchard's moral failings have prevented him from reaching his true artistic potential.

3. The author most likely uses the phrase "fictional world" (line 6) to refer to

   (A)   a body of work produced by an artist
   (B)   a true belief that something is objectively false
   (C)   an artistic concept
   (D)   a potentially deceptive work
   (E)   a body of work that has no relation to its author's real life

4. It can be inferred from the passage that Mark Newman would be most likely to agree with each one of the following statements about the work of Andrew Blanchard, EXCEPT:

   (A)   It is written by someone with a criminal past.
   (B)   It is not the product of a highly skilled dramaturge.
   (C)   It requires correction and clarification.
   (D)   It can be offensive as well as incoherent.
   (E)   It makes an unsuccessful attempt at meta-theater.

7

Passage #6

In establishing economic policy, policymakers usually rely on preexisting models of development and tend to adopt the dominant development theory of their era. With dominant theories quickly losing credibility
(5) as a result of flaws exposed through their application, alternative theories often take hold. Such intellectual shifts are welcome in academia, but can adversely affect the economic development of developing nations.

Unlike most first-world countries whose economic
(10) policies are subject to scrutiny by democratically-elected government officials and tend to change gradually, developing nations can be easily compelled to accept structural adjustment policies by international regimes such as the World Trade Organization (WTO) and the
(15) International Monetary Fund (IMF). In the early 1980's, for instance, the IMF forced many developing countries to accept neoclassical policies in return for funding. This quickly devalued the states' currency, cut government spending, raised prices, and phrased out agricultural
(20) subsidies. By compelling developing countries to abolish trade protections and participate in free trade regimes, the IMF left those markets vulnerable to exploitation and predation.

1. Which one of the following best describes the organization of the passage?

(A) A predicament is outlined, factors leading up to the predicament are scrutinized, and an example of the predicament is offered.

(B) A phenomenon is described, an implication of the phenomenon is suggested, and an illustration of that implication is offered.

(C) A problem is presented, an example of the problem is provided, and a course of action addressing the problem is suggested.

(D) A generalization is made, evidence supporting the generalization is presented, and a particular instance illustrating the generalization is evaluated.

(E) A particular worldview is explained, its shortcomings are discussed, and an evaluation of these shortcomings is presented.

7

2. Which one of the following best describes the relationship of the second paragraph to the passage as a whole?

    (A)   It predicts a future development.

    (B)   It qualifies an assertion made earlier by the author.

    (C)   It introduces a hypothesis that the author later expands upon.

    (D)   It clarifies a claim made in the preceding paragraph.

    (E)   It presents a counterexample to a general thesis.

7

Passage #7

Biologists have long suspected that vegetal behavior is exceptionally complex, but such hypotheses were impossible to test due to limited technical resources. We assumed that plants are able to
(5) adaptively respond to stimuli, but were unable to test our assumptions. Similarly, we observed that plants can process informational input on humidity and light, but could not analyze the physiological mechanisms allowing them to do so. Until recently, it was impossible
(10) to compare the neural architecture that gives rise to animal cognition to biologically plausible forms of learning in plants. Consequently, no one suspected that plants could anticipate imminent hazards, let alone communicate these hazards through biochemical cues.
(15) Today, with the advent of plant neurobiology, scientists can finally shed light on the incredible complexity that underlies vegetal behavior.

Plant neurobiology studies the complex patterns of behavior of plants through information-processing
(20) systems. Research in plant neurobiology has not only deepened our knowledge of vegetal behavior, but has also prompted a critical reevaluation of "cognition" as an operative term in a variety of seemingly unrelated fields, such as linguistics, philosophy, and anthropology.
(25) Thanks to plant neurobiologists, we now have definitive proof that plants possess cognitive capacities even though they lack the synaptic structures that give rise to animal cognition.

The accelerated pace of discoveries involving
(30) plant intelligence warrants significant institutional commitment, which can only be provided by establishing a Department of Plant Neurobiology at our university. Some of my colleagues worry that this department would have no clear rationale, because
(35) its objectives are in principle achievable by plant physiologists. This is not true. By assembling scientists to study vegetal behavior under one roof, a department dedicated solely to plant neurobiology will be uniquely capable of addressing issues far beyond the scope of
(40) plant physiology. Not before long, we will discover that plants are capable of not only experiencing pain, but also of employing complex cost-benefit analysis to adapt and learn from their mistakes. Our appreciation of vegetal behavior is attainable if, but only if, we
(45) recognize the value of plant neurobiology as an autonomous discipline worthy of institutional support.

1. Which one of the following most accurately expresses the main point of the passage?

   (A) Plant neurobiology has deepened our understanding of the incredible complexity that underlies vegetal behavior.
   (B) Thanks to recent advances in plant neurobiology, our understanding of cognition has evolved.
   (C) Advances in the field of plant intelligence require establishing an autonomous department dedicated to the study of plant neurobiology.
   (D) Plant neurobiology has accelerated the pace of scientific discoveries involving vegetal behavior.
   (E) Plants possess cognitive capacities even though they lack the neural architecture that gives rise to animal cognition.

2. Each one of the following is mentioned in the passage as an example of known vegetal behavior, EXCEPT:

   (A) to process environmental input
   (B) to communicate information
   (C) to experience pain
   (D) to interact through signals
   (E) to use biochemical cues

3. The author observes that plants "lack the neural or synaptic structures that give rise to animal cognition" (lines 27-28) mainly in order to

   (A) indicate a necessary precondition for cognitive function
   (B) differentiate the cognitive abilities of plants from those of animals
   (C) explain why scientists find it difficult to attribute cognitive abilities to plants
   (D) show that certain physiological attributes are no longer sufficient to prove cognitive function
   (E) suggest a way in which our understanding of "cognition" has changed over time

7

4. Which one of the following most accurately describes the relationship between the second paragraph and the final paragraph?

    (A) The second paragraph anticipates the objections raised in the final paragraph.
    (B) The second paragraph helps to justify the course of action recommended in the final paragraph.
    (C) The final paragraph supports the argument made in the second paragraph by clarifying the potential significance of an academic initiative.
    (D) The second paragraph describes a controversial view that the author defends in the final paragraph.
    (E) The final paragraph debates the significance of a biological phenomenon, which is described in the second paragraph.

5. The passage provides information that answers each of the following questions EXCEPT:

    (A) How can research in plant physiology contribute to our future understanding of vegetal behavior?
    (B) Has plant neurobiology altered our conception of cognition?
    (C) What impact has the study of plant neurobiology made on other academic fields?
    (D) How do plant neurobiologists study vegetal behavior?
    (E) What are some of the directions for future research in vegetal behavior?

6. Given its tone and content, from which one of the following was the passage most likely drawn?

    (A) a textbook on plant neurobiology
    (B) a grant application for an experimental study
    (C) an editorial published in a national newspaper
    (D) a strategic initiative proposed by an academic dean
    (E) a study focusing on vegetal behavior

7. Which one of the following is most analogous to the position discussed in lines 33-35?

    (A) A car manufacturer refuses to develop a new type of electric car, because the currently existing hybrid model is environmentally friendly.
    (B) A car manufacturer refuses to develop a new type of electric car, because the cost of research and development is far greater than the potential earnings from the sale of such cars.
    (C) A car manufacturer refuses to develop a new type of electric car, because such cars merely exchange one form of pollution for another, equally destructive form.
    (D) A car manufacturer refuses to develop a new type of electric car, because there is no scientific consensus on the issue of global warming.
    (E) A car manufacturer refuses to develop a new type of electric car, because the infrastructure required to support such cars is not yet available.

7

Passage #8

For business executives, managing the growth of a company at an appropriate rate is a central challenge. For small businesses, the issue is even more critical. An improperly managed small business usually does
(5) not have the necessary cash reserves to overcome mismanagement, and if growth is neither sustained nor managed properly, the existence of the business can be jeopardized.

A number of experts have suggested that a strong
(10) guiding business plan is the key to handling small business growth. A potent and well-formulated plan can lay the foundation for years of rising profitability, and can help a small business prepare for changes in the market. While a strong business plan can help a business
(15) grow, a good plan does not ensure growth. At times, market conditions change so rapidly as to relegate the plan to obsolescence. In other businesses, the plan is not used as intended, or is simply ignored. Evidence from a number of business case studies suggests that a more
(20) important factor in managing growth is the presence of an executive with a clear vision of the business and its market position. If there is also a competent business plan in place, this can assist the executive, but leaders with a strong market vision can easily overcome the lack
(25) of a good business plan.

The truth of this assertion is borne out by the experience of one regional travel agency. Although the company did not have even a basic business plan in place, they had a forceful, involved leader who
(30) understood the dynamics of the marketplace. With the rise of the internet, revenues from the consumer travel market began to wane. Realizing that the market landscape was changing irrevocably, the executive quickly initiated a retrenchment that dropped most
(35) consumer lines of business and instead focused on handling outsourced business travel. By repositioning the company as business travel specialists and increasing quality of service—24-hour service availability, emergency travel specialists, and business concierges—
(40) the company was able increase revenues by over 500% yearly.

1. Which of the following best states the main idea of the passage?

(A) Market repositioning by a travel agency can foster growth and increase revenues.
(B) A strong business plan, while helpful, is not essential to managing business growth.
(C) Ignoring a business plan can be detrimental to the economic well-being of a business.
(D) Improperly managed small businesses can run out of cash reserves.
(E) A strong executive is necessary for business success.

2. According to the passage, which of the following statements about business growth is likely to be true?

(A) The size of the business can affect the importance of growth management.
(B) Experts agree on the importance of a strong business plan to business growth.
(C) A leader with strong business vision will make a business succeed.
(D) Improper management of business growth will kill the business.
(E) Regional travel agencies provide a model for general business growth.

B

A

3. Which of the following best describes the way the last paragraph functions in the context of the passage?

(A) An example is presented to undermine the assertion that a leader with vision can succeed without a business plan.

(B) The elements of a company's success are outlined to prove a point about changing market conditions.

(C) A chain of reasoning is discussed in order to identify assumptions.

(D) A specific example is presented to illustrate a point made in the previous paragraph.

(E) The main conclusion of the passage is stated.

4. The author's attitude toward the view that business plans are essential is best described as

(A) unequivocal agreement
(B) tentative acceptance
(C) mild skepticism
(D) grudging acceptance
(E) studious criticism

7

Passage #1 Analysis: Vienna Circle

The passage discusses the intellectual objectives of the Vienna Circle and relates them to the views of Albert Einstein.

VIEWSTAMP Analysis:

There are two **Viewpoints** suggested in this passage: the Vienna Circle's (lines 3-9) and Albert Einstein's (lines 9-16). The author alludes to the metaphysicists' attitude towards scientific truth in lines 6-9, but does not elaborate on their views.

The **Structure** of the passage is as follows:

Given that the passage consists of a single paragraph, the structural analysis of the passage will be at the sentence level:

Sentence 1:	Introduce the Vienna Circle in its historical context.
Sentence 2:	Outline the principal objectives of the Vienna Circle.
Sentence 3:	Draw a contrast between metaphysics and the attitude of the Vienna Circle toward scientific truth.
Sentence 4:	Trace the common intellectual ground between Albert Einstein and the Vienna Circle.
Sentence 5:	Suggest that Einstein's views and those of the Vienna Circle eventually diverged.

The **Tone** is scholarly and not overly polemic.

The passage presents a set of facts. As such, it contains no **Argumentation**.

The **Main Point** is that the Vienna Circle sought to present a unified vision of the world—a positivist philosophy that was initially shared, but ultimately abandoned, by Albert Einstein.

The **Primary Purpose** of the passage is to introduce a philosophical movement, describe its objectives, and relate them to those of a prominent scientist who initially embraced, but later abandoned them.

Question #1: GR, Primary Purpose. The correct answer choice is (E)

The answer to this Primary Purpose question is prephrased in our VIEWSTAMP analysis above.

Answer choice (A) is incorrect, because the author does not draw parallels between two movements. Metaphysics is only mentioned as a point of contrast, and no meaningful discussion of the parallels between positivism and metaphysics is presented.

Answer choice (B) is incorrect, because positivism is not linked to any particular societal cause.

Answer choice (C) is incorrect, because the origins of positivism are never discussed.

Answer choice (D) is incorrect, because positivism and metaphysics are never compared and contrasted; furthermore, Einstein is only related to positivism, not to metaphysics.

Answer choice (E) is the correct answer choice. The passage begins by summarizing the intellectual objectives of the Vienna Circle (lines 1-9), then relates them to those of Albert Einstein, who initially embraced, but later abandoned them (lines 9-16).

Question #2: CR, Must, SP. The correct answer choice is (C)

This Subject Perspective question tests our understanding of Einstein's views regarding the philosophical tenets of the Vienna Circle.

Answer choice (A) is incorrect, because Einstein shared the philosophers' empiricist attitude toward the pursuit of scientific truth. Nowhere in the passage do we have evidence that Einstein considered such attitude to be "erroneous."

Answer choice (B) is incorrect. While Einstein might perceive the quest for scientific unity as overly optimistic, the positivists' rejection of metaphysics has nothing to do with that. This answer choice assumes a causal relationship for which there is no evidence in the passage.

Answer choice (C) is the correct answer choice. From the discussion in lines 8-10, we know that Einstein shared the Circle's "decidedly empiricist attitude toward the pursuit of scientific truth." Thus, Einstein would probably find their emphasis on empirical knowledge to be "laudable." But, as we learn at the end of the passage, Einstein later "departed from his positivist views to pursue *less* optimistic answers to the question of political, philosophical and scientific unity" (lines 14-16). It is likely, therefore, that he would regard the goal of presenting a unified vision of the world as *too* optimistic (i.e. as "ultimately unrealistic").

Answer choice (D) is incorrect, because Einstein does not perceive the quest for unity to be particularly harmful: it is merely too optimistic.

Answer choice (E) is incorrect, because "failure" is too strong of a word, for which no evidence is presented in the passage.

7

Question #3: CR, Must. The correct answer choice is (C)

This Concept Reference question concerns metaphysics, which is mentioned in line 7.

Answer choice (A) is incorrect, because there is no evidence suggesting that metaphysics was a reaction against positivism. If anything, the relationship seems to be inverted: it is the positivists that rejected metaphysics, not the other way around.

Answer choice (B) is incorrect, as it alludes to Einstein's attitude toward positivism, not metaphysics.

Answer choice (C) is the correct answer choice. In line 7, the author mentions metaphysics as a philosophical movement rejected by the Vienna Circle, who instead embraced a more empiricist attitude toward the pursuit of scientific truth. A central tenet of this worldview was the belief that knowledge can only derive from experience (line 5). We can easily infer that metaphysicists did not share this empiricist attitude, i.e. that they did not necessarily seek to derive knowledge through experience alone.

Answer choice (D) is incorrect, because it is positivism—not metaphysics—that was initially embraced by Einstein (lines 9-12).

Answer choice (E) is attractive, but also incorrect. While the Vienna Circle rejected metaphysics (presumably because the latter's disregard for experiential knowledge), we have little evidence that the Vienna Circle would regard metaphysics as "intellectually suspect." This is too strong of a label, and insufficient evidence is presented to substantiate such a definitive claim.

Passage #2 Analysis: Nutrition and Sodium

Paragraph One:

In the first paragraph, the author concedes that excessive intake of sugar is harmful, but rejects the view that sugar is itself toxic. In fact, the author regards our obsession with sugar as harmful in itself, because it detracts our attention from keeping track of our sodium intake. The last sentence of the first paragraph is critical, as it captures the main point of the passage.

Paragraph Two:

The second paragraph describes the deleterious effects of excessive sodium intake, which explains the position stated in the last sentence of the first paragraph: by focusing exclusively on our sugar intake, we fail to recognize the dangers inherent in consuming too much sodium.

Paragraph Three:

The third paragraph outlines yet another reason why low-carb diets can be harmful: not only do they distract us from monitoring our sodium intake (first paragraph), but they also inadvertently increase our consumption of sodium. The author draws an analogy between low-carb and low-fat diets, suggesting that each diet merely substitutes one harmful additive for an equally harmful one. The passage concludes by outlining an alternative nutritional approach: well-balanced diets that use natural ingredients to satisfy our needs.

VIEWSTAMP Analysis:

There are two **Viewpoints** outlined in this passage: the nutritional biologists' (lines 1-2) and the author's.

The **Structure** of the passage is as follows:

Paragraph 1: Reject the view that sugar is toxic, and shift our attention to the importance of sodium intake.

Paragraph 2: Explain why excessive sodium intake can be harmful.

Paragraph 3: Describe the harmful nature of "fad diets" and suggest an alternative nutritional approach.

The author appears well-informed on the subject of nutrition. While the **Tone** is predominantly descriptive, the author takes a clear stance against "fad diets," which adds a polemic touch to the tone of the passage.

The passage presents one central **Argument**, which is causal. Low-carb diets are potentially harmful, because:

1. they detract our attention from monitoring our sodium intake, and

2. they are often tasteless, which increases the consumption of sodium.

This position assumes that excessive sodium intake is undesirable, an assumption supported by evidence presented in the second paragraph of the passage.

The **Main Point** of the passage is to argue that low-carb diets lead to an increased consumption of sodium, and explain why this is potentially harmful.

Broadly speaking, the **Purpose** of the passage is to argue that a particular dietary trend is potentially harmful, and explain why this is so.

Question #1: GR, Main Point. The correct answer choice is (B)

The answer to this Main Purpose question is prephrased in the VIEWSTAMP analysis above.

Answer choice (A) is attractive, but incorrect. The author clearly seeks to shift the reader's attention from sugar to sodium, arguing that the latter can be just as harmful when taken in excess. However, this answer choice fails the Fact Test, because there is no evidence suggesting that excessive consumption of sodium is *more* harmful than is excessive consumption of sugar. In fact, the author refers to added sodium "equally harmful" (lines 33-34), and believes that our obsession with sugar detracts from focusing on an "equally important part of any balanced diet: sodium" (lines 10-11).

Answer choice (B) is the correct answer choice, because the first and the third paragraphs assert that our obsession with sugar is harmful (lines 9 and 29-31), whereas the second paragraph explains why it is so (it promotes the increased consumption of sodium—an undesirable dietary habit).

Answer choice (C) is incorrect, because it focuses exclusively on the content of the second paragraph, not of the passage as a whole. Furthermore, sodium intake itself is not undesirable; *excessive* sodium intake is.

Answer choice (D) is incorrect. While the author does reject the view that sugar is toxic (lines 5-6), this is not the main purpose of the passage.

Answer choice (E) is incorrect for a number of reasons. First, neither sugar nor sodium are "harmful nutritional substances." They are harmful as additives (line 35) when consumed in excess, but they are "otherwise benign nutritional substance[s]" (line 7). Secondly, although the author does enumerate the harmful effects of consuming too much sugar (line 5) and salt (lines 21-23), the main purpose of the passage is not to compare and contrast these effects.

7

Question #2: SR, Must, P. The correct answer choice is (B)

This question asks us to examine why the author mentions the fact that low-carb diets are often tasteless (line 33). Arriving at a suitable prephrase is key. The author remarks on the tasteless nature of low-carb diets in order to explain why they inadvertently increase the consumption of sodium (lines 30-32), which is unhealthy.

Answer choice (A) is incorrect, because the author does not intend to distinguish low-carb from low-fat diets; on the contrary—she draws an analogy between the two (lines 34-38).

Answer choice (B) is the correct answer choice. Since low-carb diets are tasteless, we try to make them tastier by consuming more salt, and in doing so substitute one harmful additive for another. In other words, the tasteless nature of low-carb diets indicates a way in which such diets promote unhealthy eating habits.

Answer choice (C) is incorrect, because the failure rate of low-carb diets was never discussed.

Answer choice (D) is attractive, but incorrect. While tastelessness is clearly a downside of low-carb diets, there is no evidence that it is *unique* to such diets. Furthermore, the purpose of this paragraph is not to illustrate the downsides of low-carb diets, but rather to explain the particular mechanism by which they promote increased consumption of sodium.

Answer choice (E) is incorrect, because no alternative dietary regimen is recommended.

Question #3: CR, Must. The correct answer choice is (A)

This Must Be True question concerns sodium intake. As always, passage organization is key: sodium intake is discussed primarily in the second paragraph, which can serve as a useful reference point in validating the correct answer choice.

Answer choice (A) is the correct answer choice, because "everyone needs some sodium in his or her diet" (lines 15-16). Clearly, then, sodium intake is a necessary component of any diet.

Answer choice (B) is incorrect, because it describes the harmful effects of *excessive* sodium intake only, not of sodium intake in general.

Answer choice (C) is incorrect, because sodium is just as toxic as sugar only in sufficiently large quantities (line 8).

Answer choice (D) is incorrect, because sodium intake itself does not necessarily represent a health risk. Excessive consumption of sodium does.

Answer choice (E) is incorrect, because it contains an exaggeration ("invariably"). While excessive consumption of sodium is indeed a risk factor for those suffering from hypertension (lines 20-22), we cannot conclusively prove that it *invariably* makes hypertension worse.

7

Question #4: CR, Must. AP. The correct answer choice is (D)

This Author Perspective question tests our understanding of the author's attitude towards low-carb diets. The answer should be prephrased: the author considers them potentially harmful, because they may lead to an increased consumption of sodium (lines 30-31). The attitude is therefore negative, which helps eliminate answer choices (A) and (B). Remember: the general direction of your prephrase is more important than the precision with which you can predict the correct answer choice.

Answer choice (A) is incorrect, because the author does not necessarily regard low-carb diets as beneficial: the third paragraph clearly suggests that the costs of such diets might outweigh the benefits. This answer choice describes the viewpoint of the nutritional biologists mentioned in lines 1-5, which is not the author's viewpoint.

Answer choice (B) is incorrect, because the author has a somewhat negative view of low-carb diets. Although she regards sugar as potentially toxic, she does not necessarily believe that the benefits of low-carb diets outweigh the costs.

Answer choice (C) is incorrect. Although carbohydrates are indeed a macronutrient (lines 41-43), the author never describes low-carb diets as *overly* restrictive of carbohydrates. Remember: the author views excessive consumption of sugar as harmful (first paragraph), and is likely to agree that sugar consumption should be somewhat restricted. Whether low-carb diets are *overly* restrictive of sugar is impossible to determine given the information provided in the passage.

Answer choice (D) is the correct answer choice. The third paragraph contrasts well-balanced diets to those that focus on a single nutritional additive in isolation (lines 39-41). Since low-carb diets exemplify the latter trend, it is reasonable to infer that the author would regard them as inconsistent with the tenets of a well-balanced diet.

Answer choice (E) is attractive, but incorrect. The author clearly sees low-carb diets as harmful, in part because they detract from focusing on sodium (lines 10-11), and also because they lead to an increased consumption of sodium (lines 31-32). There is no evidence, however, that low-carb diets *require* us to consume more sodium. The author's argument is causal, not conditional.

Question #5: SR, Must, P. The correct answer choice is (C)

The answer to this Purpose question is prephrased in the VIEWSTAMP analysis above.

Answer choice (A) is incorrect, because the second paragraph only supports the author's central argument, which is suggested in the first and summarized in the third paragraphs.

Answer choice (B) is attractive, but incorrect. While the first paragraph certainly suggests that classifying sugar as a "toxin" is a misconception, the second paragraph makes no attempt of explaining why this misconception should be corrected, i.e. why sugar should *not* be classified as a toxin. The purpose of the second paragraph is to explain why a different nutritional additive—sodium—can be just as harmful when consumed in excess.

Answer choice (C) is the correct answer choice. The first paragraph describes our modern-day obsession with cutting sugar at the expense of sodium (i.e. an "outlook"). By describing the deleterious effects of excessive sodium intake, the second paragraph explains why this outlook is potentially harmful.

Answer choice (D) is incorrect, because the second paragraph does not undermine the argument presented in the first paragraph. On the contrary—it supports that argument by illustrating the harmful effects of excessive sodium intake.

Answer choice (E) is incorrect, because the author does not make any recommendations until the end of the passage. There is no course of action recommended in the first paragraph.

7

Question #6: SR, Must, E. The correct answer choice is (A)

This Expansion question requires you to extrapolate ideas from the passage in order to determine what sentence or idea could follow it. The correct answer choice will be dependent upon the two or three sentences at the end of the passage, but the question is difficult because it asks you to infer the flow and direction of the passage from a somewhat limited set of rules.

Answer choice (A) is the correct answer choice. In the last paragraph, the author laments the practice of substituting one harmful additive for an equally harmful one, arguing for a more holistic approach to nutrition. This suggests that she would be critical of any dietary approach that judges food one component at a time.

Answer choice (B) is incorrect, because the author does not necessarily view all dietary regimens as harmful. Just because dietary regimens focusing on a single nutritional additive are harmful (lines 40-41) does not mean that *all* dietary regimens are potentially harmful.

Answer choice (C) is incorrect. Although our views on nutrition are clearly evolving, there is no evidence that these views are reflected in the dietary choices we make. Note that the author is critical of certain dietary choices (the so-called "fad diets").

Answer choice (D) is incorrect, because the author does not necessarily seek greater consistency in manufacturers' dietary recommendations. Such a consistency would only be preferable if these recommendations were warranted, which—according to the author—they are not. The passage is critical of manufacturers not because their recommendations are inconsistent, but because they merely substitute one harmful additive for an equally harmful one.

Answer choice (E) is incorrect, because the author does not necessarily believe that any food will ultimately be reported as *healthful*. She does not regard high-carb diets as particularly healthful, for instance. Rather, the author is critical of our obsession with specific nutritional additives as *unhealthy* (fat, sugar, etc.).

Passage #3 Analysis: Arizona Juvenile Court

The passage begins by introducing the conditions under which a 1996 Arizona statute would allow prosecutors to try juvenile offenders in criminal court as adults. In the second sentence, we learn that the author disagrees with the statute. The remainder of the passage explains why the opponents' argument is a reasonable one.

VIEWSTAMP Analysis:

There are two **Viewpoints** outlined in this passage: that of the opponents to the Arizona statute (lines 6-15), and that of the courts, who are reluctant to question the constitutionality of the statute (lines 17-19). The author clearly agrees with the opponents, who have "rightfully argued" (line 6) against the statute.

The **Structure** of the passage is as follows:

Given that the passage consists of a single paragraph, the structural analysis of the passage will be at the sentence level:

Sentence 1:   Introduce the 1996 Arizona statute.

Sentence 2:   Outline the opponents' argument against the statute.

Sentence 3:   Describe an undesirable consequence of adopting the statute.

Sentence 4:   State the legal ramifications of adopting the statute.

Sentence 5:   Question the constitutionality of these ramifications.

The author's **Tone** is critical of the Arizona statute, and skeptical toward the possibility that the courts will question its constitutionality.

The passage presents one central **Argument**—that of the opponents to the 1996 Arizona statute. Their criticism is well-founded, according to the author, because the statute would allow prosecutors to bypass juvenile court review when trying certain juvenile offenders—a discretion the author considers to be constitutionally suspect.

The **Main Point** of the passage is that the 1996 Arizona statute has certain ramifications that are constitutionally suspect.

Broadly speaking, the **Primary Purpose** of the passage is to criticize one aspect of a legal statute.

7

Question #1: SR, Must, P. The correct answer choice is (B)

To answer this Specific Reference Purpose question, a suitable prephrase is key. The author mentions armed robbery (line 13) in order to illustrate how easily the prosecution can divest the juvenile court of jurisdiction over juvenile offenders: all the prosecutor needs to do is charge the juvenile offender with a violent felony (such as armed robbery).

Answer choice (A) is incorrect, because it is perfectly possible that, up until 1996, offenders tried in juvenile court were frequently charged with armed robbery (among other violent felony offenses). Just because the new statute makes it impossible to do so does not mean that it rarely happened in the past.

Answer choice is (B) is the correct answer choice, as it is consistent with the prephrase outlined above.

Answer choice (C) is incorrect, because there is no evidence that prosecuting a juvenile offender as an adult is somehow more *difficult* than prosecuting him in juvenile court.

Answer choice (D) is incorrect. The author regrets that "many of the extenuating circumstances that would have previously been considered by a juvenile court judge are now largely irrelevant" (lines 9-11), but never explicitly states that these circumstances *must* be considered when assigning criminal responsibility to juvenile offenders. Furthermore, it is unclear how charging someone with armed robbery explains the need to consider extenuating circumstances.

Answer choice (E) is incorrect, because the author never intends to draw a line between juvenile and criminal courts with respect to the severity of the crimes being prosecuted there. In fact, up until the passage of the new statute, it is reasonable to infer that juvenile offenders charged with violent felonies were tried in juvenile court.

Question #2: GR, Must, AP. The correct answer choice is (C)

The answer to this Tone question is prephrased in our VIEWSTAMP analysis above. In lines 17-20, the author expresses regret over the court's reluctance to question the constitutionality of a statute that allows prosecutors to bypass juvenile court review. The author is both critical of the statute and skeptical toward the possibility that courts will overturn it.

Answer choice (A) is incorrect, because the author clearly opposes some of the ramifications of the recently passed statute.

Answer choice (B) is the Opposite answer, as the author's tone is skeptical, not hopeful.

Answer choice (C) is the correct answer choice. The word "regrettably" (line 17) captures the author's critical attitude towards the ability of prosecutors to bypass juvenile court review.

Answer choice (D) is incorrect, because the author is not reluctant to take a stance (the courts are).

Answer choice (E) is incorrect, because the word "divests" refers to the statute's effects on the juvenile court system and its jurisdiction over juvenile offenders, not to the author's *attitude* toward this effect.

Question #3: CR, Must. The correct answer choice is (E)

This question asks us to infer what must be true about a sixteen-year old offender charged with armed robbery in the state of Arizona *prior* to 1996. While the author does not explicitly describe the legal framework for dealing with such an offender prior to 1996, a reasonable inference can still be made.

Answer choice (A) is incorrect, because prior to 1996 the juvenile court would have had jurisdiction over the juvenile offender (the statute stripped the court of such jurisdiction). We have no reason to believe that the offender could *also* be prosecuted in criminal court.

Answer choice (B) describes a hypothetical that cannot be proven with the information available.

Answer choice (C) contains an exaggeration. While the juvenile court is likely consider many of the extenuating circumstances that would be irrelevant in criminal court (lines 10-11), we cannot prove that it would consider *all* extenuating circumstances relevant to the offender's case.

Answer choice (D) describes how the offender would be tried following the passage of the new statute, i.e. *after* 1996.

Answer choice (E) is the correct answer choice. In the fourth sentence, we learn that following the 1996 statute, "The choice of court […] rests entirely in the discretion of the prosecution" (lines 16-18). The author also observes that "courts have been reluctant to question the constitutionality of such discretion" (lines 18-20). We can therefore infer that *prior* to 1996 this was not the case, i.e. that the choice of courts did *not* rest entirely in the discretion of the prosecution.

Question #4: GR, Primary Purpose. The correct answer choice is (C)

The answer to this Main Purpose question is also prephrased in our VIEWSTAMP analysis above.

Answer choice (A) is incorrect, because the author does not defend the statute against criticism: on the contrary, she supports the criticism (line 6).

Answer choice (B) is attractive, but incorrect. The author alludes to the consequences of the newly introduced statute (lines 9-17), but we have no way of knowing if these consequences are necessarily *unforeseen*. This answer choice fails the Fact Test, and is therefore incorrect.

Answer choice (C) is the correct answer choice. The author begins by introducing a statute, which is immediately criticized ("opponents have rightfully argued that…"). The remainder of the passage explains why the opponents' argument is a reasonable one.

Answer choice (D) is incorrect, because the constitutionality of *judicial* discretion is not under question. The author only questions the constitutionality of *prosecutorial* discretion (lines 16-20).

Answer choice (E) is incorrect, because the argument in favor of the new statute is never outlined, and no reconciliation between the two positions is provided.

Passage #4 Analysis: Low-Density Lipoprotein

<u>VIEWSTAMP</u> Analysis:

The passage presents two contrasting **Viewpoints**—those of the proponents of the Paleo diet, and the views of the author who opposes it.

The **Structure** of the passage is as follows:

Given that the passage consists of a single paragraph, the structural analysis of the passage will be at the sentence level:

<u>Sentence 1</u>:   Introduce the Paleo diet and the assumptions upon which it is based.

<u>Sentence 2</u>:   Concede the correctness of an observation made by the proponents of the Paleo diet.

<u>Sentence 3</u>:   Discuss studies suggesting that the Paleo diet may be harmful.

<u>Sentence 4</u>:   Present additional evidence to substantiate the harmful effects of the Paleo diet.

<u>Sentence 5</u>:   Propose a limited solution to the harmful effects discussed in the preceding sentence.

The **Tone** is polemic and critical of the proponents of the Paleo diet. The author has a negative view toward such popular but questionable diets.

There are two **Arguments** presented in the passage:

<u>Proponents of the Paleo diet</u>:

Premise: Cholesterol intake does not directly correlate with the concentration of harmful low-density lipoprotein.

Conclusion: Increased consumption of meat and meat by-products pose minimal health risks to the human body.

<u>Counterargument (author's)</u>:

Premise: Cholesterol intake can increase LDL levels indirectly.

Premise: Consumption of saturated animal fats may cause the oxidation of LDL particles, which is itself atherogenic.

Conclusion: Increased consumption of meat and meat by-products may pose more health risks than the proponents of such diets assume.

The **Main Point** of the passage is that increased consumption of meat and meat by-products may pose more health risks than the proponents of such diets assume (Their assumption is "dubious," line 3).

The **Primary Purpose** of the passage as a whole is to debunk the assumption that the Paleo diet is entirely harmless.

Question #1: GR, Primary Purpose. The correct answer choice is (C)

The answer to this Primary Purpose question is prephrased in our VIEWSTAMP analysis above.

Answer choice (A) is attractive, but incorrect. The solution presented in the last sentence ("antioxidants and dietary fiber can help prevent oxidative modification of LDL," lines 16-19) is clearly of limited value, considering that most diets do not recommend sufficient amounts of either supplement (lines 18-19). Furthermore, the primary purpose of the passage is not to recommend a particular dietary regimen, but rather to criticize one as potentially unhealthy.

Answer choice (B) is the Opposite answer. The author opposes, rather than recommends, a particular nutritional plan.

Answer choice (C) is the correct answer choice. In the first sentence, the author describes the proponents' beliefs as "dubious," suggesting a definitive disagreement with their beliefs. The rest of the passage substantiates the author's position by describing the results of various nutritional studies.

Answer choice (D) is incorrect, because the author does not address any of the benefits of the Paleo diet. The primary focus of the passage is on the health risks posed by that diet.

Answer choice (E) is incorrect, because the primary purpose of the passage is more limited in scope. Whereas the author does criticize the shortcomings of the Paleo diet, her line of criticism does not apply to *most* modern diets. Indeed, just because the author accuses most diets of not recommending enough antioxidants and fiber does not mean that the *primary* purpose of the passage is to criticize such modern diets. The latter point was mentioned only at the very end of the passage.

Question #2: GR, Main Point. The correct answer choice is (A)

This passage opens with a critique of some popular diets, whose proponents incorrectly believe that increased consumption of meat and meat by-products pose minimal health risks to the human body. The key word here is "dubious," suggesting the author's disagreement with those views.

Answer choice (A) is the correct answer choice. The author disagrees with the proponents of the Paleo diet, suggesting that increased consumption of meat and meat by-products *may* be harmful to one's health. The remainder of the passage supports this view, which therefore represents the main point of the passage.

Answer choice (B) is incorrect. Although cholesterol intake can indeed exacerbate the negative effects of saturated fatty acids on LDL concentrations (lines 8-11), this is a *premise* for the author's conclusion that meat products may be harmful to one's health.

Answer choice (C) is incorrect, because it contains an exaggeration. While *many* of the most popular diets are not as healthful as their proponents are led to believe, we cannot reliably conclude that about *most* diets.

Answer choice (D) is incorrect, because it is a subsidiary conclusion for the main argument. Although the indirect effects of cholesterol intake are supported by the studies described in lines 8-11, these effects, in turn, serve to support a more general criticism of diets that promote increased consumption of meat and meat by-products.

Answer choice (E) is incorrect. While the author seems to believe that consuming meat and meat by-products can be harmful to one's health, no argument is made for their complete *elimination*, and no statement is made regarding which diets are the *healthiest*.

Question #3: SR, Must, P. The correct answer choice is (D)

The stem asks us to identify the role played in the argument by the claim that cholesterol intake does not directly correlate with the concentration of harmful low-density lipoprotein (lines 6-8). To answer this question correctly, it is imperative to have a solid understanding of argument structure. As described in our discussion of argumentation (above), the cited claim is simply a premise used by the proponents of the Paleo diet in support of their conclusion. Unfortunately, this prephrase does not produce a close match to any of the answer choices, as there are many ways to describe the function of any given argument part. Nevertheless, as long as you understand the broader function of the cited claim, you will be able to eliminate four of the five answer choices relatively quickly.

Answer choice (A) is incorrect, because the claim in question supports a position that the argument as a whole is directed towards discrediting.

Answer choice (B) is incorrect, because the cited claim does not *refute* the causal link between cholesterol intake and increased LDL levels. The author clearly believes that a causal link still exists.

Answer choice (C) is incorrect, because the author acknowledges that the claim in question is factually correct. As such, it only provides *support* for the position that the argument as a whole is directed toward discrediting; it is not a *summary* of that position.

Answer choice (D) is the correct answer choice. As mentioned above, the cited claim represents an observation advanced by the proponents of the Paleo diet in support of their conclusion. The author concedes that the observation is correct, but argues that their conclusion is not (cholesterol intake can still increase LDL concentrations indirectly). As such, the cited claim represents a possible objection to the recommendation put forth in the argument.

Answer choice (E): The author makes no attempt at explaining why there is no direct correlation between cholesterol intake and increased LDL levels. Instead, she argues that the two are causally related *despite* the absence of such a direct correlation.

Question #4: CR, Strengthen. The correct answer choice is (B)

The question stem asks us to strengthen the proponents' position that increased consumption of meat and meat by-products pose minimal health risks to the human body. The correct answer choice is likely to show that the consumption of meat and meat by-products somehow mitigates the ill effects of increased LDL levels, or else prevents the oxidative modification of LDL.

Answer choice (A) is incorrect, because it is an Opposite answer. If excessive consumption of salt, often found in meat by-products, is associated with increased risk of cardiovascular disease, this would strengthen the author's position that increased consumption of meat and meat by-products is harmful to one's health.

Answer choice (B) is the correct answer choice. If omega-3 fatty acids, often found in animal fat, can protect against the effects of increased LDL levels, then meat-based diets may not be as hazardous as the author believes them to be.

Answer choice (C) is incorrect, because it is an Opposite answer. If diets that exclude meat are the most protective against atherosclerosis, the author's claim that meat consumption poses certain health risks cannot be ignored.

Answer choice (D) is incorrect, because it provides further evidence that elevated cholesterol levels are associated with the risk of cardiovascular disease. One could argue that such drugs can lower the risk of consuming meat and meat by-products, but that does not mean that the consumption of meat *itself* poses minimal health risks (which is what the proponents seem to believe). Furthermore, since the drugs in question carry the risk of adverse side effects, the costs may ultimately outweigh the benefits.

Answer choice (E) is incorrect. Just because there are substances besides antioxidants and dietary fiber that can prevent oxidative modification of LDL does not mean that these substances are readily available to those who follow the Paleo diet.

Passage #5 Analysis: Andrew Blanchard

The passage outlines the critical reception of Andrew Blanchard's work, elaborating on a particularly unfavorable critical view.

Paragraph One:

In the first paragraph, we learn that Andrew Blanchard is a writer with a criminal past, which seems to bear some resemblance to the subject matter of his work. We also learn that Blanchard's scholars use his fictional world to find clues about his life. Most importantly, the first paragraph provides an insight into the author's own views regarding Blanchard and his critical reception: the judgmental attitude shared by his critics has prevented them from appreciating the "poetic brilliance" of Andrew Blanchard.

Paragraph Two:

This paragraph provides an example of a particularly negative critical view of Blanchard and his work. Mark Newman regards Blanchard as a thief as well as a bad playwright, and seems particularly bothered by the latter's penchant for meta-theater. While "meta-theater" is not explicitly defined here, you can infer that—in its ideal form—it interweaves multiple plays-within-a-play and still maintains a coherent narrative structure. Notably, according to Newman, Blanchard failed to achieve this artistic objective.

VIEWSTAMP Analysis:

There are three main **Viewpoints** expressed in the passage: The viewpoint of the scholars, who use Blanchard's fictional worlds to find clues about his life; that of Mark Newman, who illustrates this trend in its most critical form; and that of the author, who clearly believes that critics did not appreciate the poetic brilliance of Andrew Blanchard (lines 12-14).

The **Structure** of the passage is as follows:

> Paragraph 1: Introduce Andrew Blanchard's work and its critical reception.

> Paragraph 2: Exemplify a particularly negative critical view of Andrew Blanchard.

The author's **Tone** is somewhat condescending (if not overtly hostile) toward Blanchard's critics, whose "smugness" prevents them from appreciating the brilliance of Andrew Blanchard.

The only implicit **Argument** is that of the author, who regards the critics' views as smug and misguided. The author also argues that Blanchard is a brilliant playwright, but does not elaborate upon the qualities that make his work outstanding. The critics' perspective is outlined in the first paragraph and an example of it is provided in the second, but these are not arguments as much as they are mere viewpoints.

The **Main Point** of the passage is that the critics did not accord Blanchard the appreciation he deserves.

The **Primary Purpose** of the passage is to dismiss Blanchard's critical reception as unappreciative of Blanchard's poetic brilliance.

Question #1: GR, Primary Purpose. The correct answer choice is (C)

The answer to this Main Purpose question is prephrased in the VIEWSTAMP analysis above.

Answer choice (A) is incorrect, because it describes the purpose of those who criticize Blanchard (lines 7-9), which is not the author's purpose.

Answer choice (B) is incorrect, because it is Mark Newman, not the author, who seeks to "correct[…] and clarify[…] certain aspects of Blanchard's biography" (lines 16-17).

Answer choice (C) is the correct answer choice, given the discussion at the end of the first paragraph.

Answer choice (D) is attractive, but incorrect. The author clearly rejects the critics' views of Blanchard, but there is no evidence that their views amount to a "*common* misconception." The extent to which the critics' position is commonly shared remains unknown. Furthermore, we have no evidence suggesting that Blanchard was a *famous* playwright. This answer choice fails the Fact Test—twice—and is therefore incorrect.

Answer choice (E) is incorrect, because the passage makes no assertions regarding the *factual* veracity of the critics' accusations. The author takes issue with the general direction of their criticism, rather than with the historical accuracy of their observations.

Question #2: GR, Main Point. The correct answer choice is (A)

The answer to this Main Point question is prephrased in the VIEWSTAMP analysis above.

Answer choice (A) is the correct answer choice. The first paragraph outlines the negative critical reception of Andrew Blanchard's work, and the second paragraph supports this view by describing one study that exemplifies this reception. The author's own position is revealed in lines 12-14, in which she expresses regret that the critics have not appreciated Blanchard's "poetic brilliance."

Answer choice (B) is incorrect. The author neither illustrates nor elaborates on the idea that some of the themes that inhabit Andrew Blanchard's fictional world are drawn from his criminal past. Even if true, this is not the main point of the passage.

Answer choice (C) is incorrect for two reasons: First, we have no evidence that the author regards Newman's study as "well-informed." As an avid fan of Andrew Blanchard's work, the author would have little appreciation for the views expressed in the study. Second, the main point of the passage is not to discuss Mark Newman's biography of Andrew Blanchard, which is merely mentioned as an example meant to substantiate a broader claim.

Answer choice (D) is incorrect, because it describes an assumption of the "scholars [who] frequently examine Blanchard's fictional world for clues that could reveal the 'real' story of their author" (lines 7-9). This is not the author's position, let alone the main point of the passage.

Answer choice (E) is incorrect, because it presents a position most likely shared by some of Blanchard's critics, not by the author herself.

Question #3: SR, Must, P. The correct answer choice is (A)

The answer to this question should be prephrased. In lines 7-9, the author describes how scholars examine Blanchard's fictional world looking for clues that could reveal the "real" story of the author. In this context, "fictional world" refers to the body of work produced by Blanchard.

Answer choice (A) is the correct answer choice, as it correctly describes the function of the phrase in the context in which it appears.

Answer choice (B) is incorrect, because the phrase does not reflect a true belief that something is objectively false. Do not be tempted by the use of convoluted language here, unless you can definitively rule out the remaining answer choices.

Answer choice (C) is incorrect, because "fictional world" does not refer to an artistic concept as much as to an actual body of work produced by an artist.

Answer choice (D) is incorrect, because there is no evidence suggesting that Blanchard's artistic work is potentially deceptive (though the critics might have been deceived by it).

Answer choice (E) is the Opposite answer, because Blanchard is described as a writer with a scandalous life, which does bear some resemblance to the subject matter of his work (lines 1-6).

7

Question #4: MustX, SP. The correct answer choice is (C)

This Subject Perspective-EXCEPT question requires us to identify four statements about Andrew Blanchard that Mark Newman is likely to agree with. Given the structure of the passage, the second paragraph is likely to prove useful in validating the four incorrect answer choices.

Answer choice (A) is incorrect, given Newman's attempt to expose Blanchard as a "petty thief" (line 19). Clearly, Newman would regard Blanchard's work as written by someone with a criminal past.

Answer choice (B) is incorrect. Newman argues that only a highly skilled dramaturge can interweave multiple plays-within-a-play and still maintain a coherent narrative structure—something Blanchard clearly failed to do. Given Newman's negative opinion of Blanchard, it is reasonable to infer that the critic would view Blanchard's work as produced by a less than highly skilled dramaturge.

Answer choice (C) is the correct answer choice. It is Blanchard's *biography* that requires correction and clarification (lines 16-17), not Blanchard's work as a dramaturge.

Answer choice (D) is incorrect. Newman condemns Blanchard's plays as "distasteful" (line 21), which is synonymous with "offensive." It is also clear that Newman regards Blanchard's foray into meta-theater as a failure, i.e. lacking in coherent narrative structure (lines 25-26).

Answer choice (E) is incorrect, because Newman clearly dislikes Blanchard's foray into meta-theater, arguing that only a skilled dramaturge can pull it off (lines 22-28).

Passage #6 Analysis: World Trade Organization

<u>VIEWSTAMP</u> <u>Analysis:</u>

The passage presents two **Viewpoints**: the policymakers' (line 1) and the author's (lines 6-8). The policies of international regimes such as the WTO and the IMF are described in lines 16-23, but their viewpoint is not overtly stated.

The **Structure** of the passage is as follows:

Paragraph 1:   Describe a policy behavior and suggest that it adversely affects developing nations.

Paragraph 2:   Explain why developing nations are particularly affected, and present an example to illustrate this effect.

The **Tone** is critical of the implications of an economic policy.

The passage contains a single **Argument**: policymakers tend to rely on preexisting models of development, which adversely affects developing nations. The second paragraph elaborates on this position and provides an example in its support.

Main Point:

The **Main Point** of the passage is developing nations are adversely affected by the intellectual shifts typically manifested by policymakers in first-world countries.

The **Primary Purpose** of the passage is to examine the deleterious consequences of a political phenomenon.

Question #1: GR, Must, O. The correct answer choice is (B)

Before you attack the answer choices to an Organization question, it is important to have a general understanding of passage structure. As described above, the first paragraph outlines a phenomenon that adversely affects developing nations. The second paragraph explains why such nations are particularly affected, and illustrates this proposition with an example. Answer choice (B) comes the closest to matching out prephrase, and is therefore correct.

Answer choice (A) is incorrect, because the author does not examine the factors leading up to the predicament described in the beginning of the passage. We do not know, for instance, *why* policy makers tend to adopt the dominant development theory of their era. The passage is only concerned with examining the effects, not the causes, of the phenomenon outlined in the first paragraph.

Answer choice (B) is the correct answer choice. The phenomenon of policy makers adopting the dominant theory of their era is described (lines 1-6), its implication affecting developing nations is suggested (lines 6-16), and an illustration of that implication is offered (lines 16-24).

Answer choice (C) is incorrect, because no course of action addressing the problem is suggested.

Answer choice (D) is incorrect. Although the author uses evidence to explain how developing nations are adversely affected by the intellectual shifts described in the first paragraph, the observation regarding these adverse effects does not constitute a generalization. Rather, it is a specific *implication* of the generalization that policy makers tend to adopt the dominant development theory of their era. No example of this generalization is ever presented.

Answer choice (E) is incorrect. Even if the negative consequences of the worldview outlined in lines 1-6 can be described as "shortcomings," the author does not *evaluate* these shortcomings. She merely illustrates them with an example.

Question #2: SR, Must, O. The correct answer choice is (D)

This question concerns the function of the second paragraph within the passage as a whole. As previously mentioned, the second paragraph explains why developing nations in particular are adversely affected by the intellectual shifts outlined in the first paragraph. As such, the second paragraph can be said to clarify a claim made earlier. This prephrase agrees with answer choice (D), which is correct.

Answer choice (A) is incorrect, because the second paragraph makes no predictions about any future developments.

Answer choice (B) is incorrect, because the second paragraph does not *qualify* the assertion made in the first paragraph. Qualifying an assertion usually requires examining its potential limitations or applicability. In the second paragraph, the author attempts to explain, not qualify, the assertion that developing nations are adversely affected by the policy of adopting the dominant development theory of their era.

Answer choice (C) is incorrect, because it describes the function of the first, not the second paragraph.

Answer choice (D) is the correct answer choice. See discussion above.

Answer choice (E) is incorrect, because the second paragraph presents an example, not a counterexample, to the thesis outlined in the first paragraph.

Passage #7 Analysis: Plant Neurobiology

Paragraph One:

Most science passages begin by outlining some unexplained phenomenon or unresolved question, and this one is no exception. Here, the question is how vegetal behavior manages to be so sensitive and complex. The author describes various observations about the incredible complexity of plant behavior, none of which could be verified (until now). The paragraph concludes by introducing plant neurobiology as the field likely to provide an answer to all of the aforementioned questions, and we can expect to learn more about it later on in the passage.

Paragraph Two:

As predicted, this paragraph defines the academic scope of plant neurobiology, highlighting the significance of its contributions to the scientific community. The author also describes how research in plant neurobiology has prompted scientists in other fields to reevaluate their conception of "cognition."

Paragraph Three:

The third paragraph presents the author's main point: advances in plant intelligence require institutional support, which can only be provided by establishing a Department of Plant Neurobiology. The author acknowledges some of the arguments against this recommendation, but defends it by predicting a variety of research directions that can only be pursued by a department dedicated solely to plant neurobiology.

VIEWSTAMP Analysis:

There are four **Viewpoints** outlined in this passage: those of the biologists mentioned in the first paragraph, the neurobiologists discussed in the second paragraph; the opponents of establishing a department of plant neurobiology in the third paragraph, and the author's—also in third paragraph.

The **Structure** of the passage is as follows:

Paragraph 1: Describe instances of vegetal behavior that were either unknown, or impossible to prove, before the advent of plant neurobiology.

Paragraph 2: Define the scope of plant neurobiology and highlight the significance of its contributions.

Paragraph 3: Recommend the establishment of a department dedicated solely to research in plant neurobiology, and counter a possible objection to this recommendation.

7

The author's **Tone** is enthusiastic about the promise held by plant neurobiology, and forceful in his recommendation that the discipline is worthy of institutional support.

There are two **Arguments** presented here: one in favor of establishing a department dedicated solely to plant neurobiology, and one against it. The first argument is supported by observations made in the second and third paragraphs.

The **Main Point** of the passage is that recent advances in plant neurobiology warrant institutional support, which can only be provided by establishing an autonomous department of Plant Neurobiology (lines 29-32). The passage as a whole supports this recommendation.

The **Primary Purpose** of the passage is to defend an academic initiative by highlighting recent discoveries made in the field of plant neurobiology.

Question #1: GR, Main Point. The correct answer choice is (C)

The answer to the Main Point question should always be prephrased. See VIEWSTAMP analysis above.

Answer choice (A) is incorrect. While plant neurobiology may have deepened our knowledge of vegetal behavior (line 21), this observation merely supports the appeal made in the final paragraph of the passage.

Answer choice (B) is attractive, because it represents the main point of the second paragraph. However, the extent to which our understanding of cognition has evolved is not the main point of the passage as a whole.

Answer choice (C) is the correct answer choice, because the passage as a whole is intended to support the recommendation offered in the third paragraph.

Answer choice (D) is incorrect, because—while true—it is not the main point of the passage.

Answer choice (E) is also incorrect, because it only captures a point made in the second paragraph of the passage (lines 26-28), which is not the main point of the passage as a whole.

7

Question #2: CR, MustX. The correct answer choice is (C)

To answer this Must Be True/EXCEPT question, proceed by the process of elimination: four of the answer choices will contain examples of known vegetal behavior, and will be incorrect. Questions of this type are usually time-consuming, because the correct answer choice must be the one we *cannot* prove by referring to information contained in the passage.

Answer choice (A) is incorrect, because the ability of plants to process informational input is discussed in line 7.

Answer choice (B) is incorrect, because the ability of plants to communicate danger, which is a type of information, is discussed in lines 12-13.

Answer choice (C) is the correct answer choice, because experiencing pain is not an example of *known* vegetal behavior. Instead, it is discussed in line 41 as an example of something scientists are bound to discover *in the future*.

Answer choice (D) is incorrect, because the ability of plants to communicate hazards through biochemical cues, which is an example of signal-interaction behavior, is discussed in lines 13-14.

Answer choice (E) is incorrect, because the ability of plants to use biochemical cues is discussed in line 14.

Question #3: SR, Must,P. The correct answer choice is (E)

This Specific Reference/Purpose question asks us to explain why the author observes that "plants lack the neural or synaptic structures that give rise to animal cognition" in lines 27-28. Such questions almost always require a more thorough understanding of the context in which the quoted reference appears, and their answers should always be prephrased.

Answer choice (A) is the Opposite answer. The author argues that plants possess cognitive capacities even *without* exhibiting neural or synaptic structures, suggesting that such structures are *not* a necessary precondition for cognitive function.

Answer choice (B) is incorrect, because the author does not seek to *differentiate* between plant and animal cognition. On the contrary: she argues that both possess cognitive capacities, despite their physiological differences.

Answer choice (C) is incorrect, because the difficulty of attributing cognitive abilities to plants is not discussed in the second paragraph of the passage.

Answer choice (D) is incorrect, because it confuses a necessary condition for a sufficient one. The author observes that plants lack the neural or synaptic structures that give rise to animal cognition in order to show that certain physiological attributes are no longer *necessary* to prove cognitive function. The author never discusses what conditions might be sufficient to prove cognitive function.

7

Answer choice (E) is the correct answer choice. The author mentions the fact that plants lack neural structures in order to show that such physiological attributes are no longer necessary to establish cognitive function. This, in turn, supports the author's contention that plant neurobiology has prompted a critical reevaluation of "cognition" as an operative term in various fields.

Question #4: GR, Must, O. The correct answer choice is (B)

Again, we should seek to prephrase an answer based on our understanding of Passage Organization: by discussing the various contributions already made by the field of plant neurobiology, the second paragraph provides support for the recommendation offered in the third paragraph.

Answer choice (A) is incorrect. Although the final paragraph raises the issue of whether a department of plant neurobiology has a clear rationale (lines 33-35), nowhere in the second paragraph does the author *anticipate* such an objection, and no indication is given as to whether or not neurobiology is uniquely qualified to answer questions concerning vegetal behavior.

Answer choice (B) is the correct answer choice. By explaining why research in plant neurobiology is scientifically significant, the second paragraph helps justify the recommendation in favor of establishing a department of plant neurobiology outlined in the third paragraph.

Answer choice (C) is half-right, half-wrong. The final paragraph clearly suggests that establishing an autonomous department of plant neurobiology is potentially significant; however, this is the main point of the passage, not a premise in support of the argument made in the second paragraph.

Answer choice (D) is incorrect. The second paragraph does not describe a controversial view, as the cognitive capacity of plants is not under debate. The issue is whether research in plant neurobiology warrants establishing a separate academic department dedicated to that field—an issue raised in the third paragraph, not in the second.

Answer choice (E) is also half-right, half-wrong. The second paragraph describes the biological phenomenon of plant cognition, but its significance is not debated in the final paragraph. The controversy only concerns whether or not a department of plant neurobiology has a clear rationale.

Question #5: GR, MustX. The correct answer choice is (A)

To answer this Must Be True/EXCEPT question, proceed by the process of elimination: four of the answer choices will contain examples of known vegetal behavior, and will be incorrect.

Answer choice (A) is the correct answer choice, because the author only discusses the research significance of plant neurobiology, not plant physiology. No information is given as to how research in plant physiology can contribute to our future understanding of vegetal behavior.

Answer choice (B) is incorrect, because the question is answered in lines 20-24.

Answer choice (C) is incorrect, because the question is answered in line 24.

Answer choice (D) is incorrect, because the question is answered in lines 18-20.

Answer choice (E) is incorrect, because the question is answered in lines 39-46.

Question #6: GR, Must, Purpose, Tone. The correct answer choice is (D)

To answer this question correctly, you need to understand both the purpose and the tone of the passage. Both are prephrased in our discussion of VIEWSTAMP above.

Answer choice (A) is incorrect because the author's tone is not as descriptive as we would expect from a textbook. Indeed, the final paragraph advocates a course of action that is unlikely to be found in an educational source.

Answer choice (B) is incorrect, because the passage makes no mention of any experimental studies for which the author could conceivably seek funding.

Answer choice (C) is attractive, but incorrect. The polemic tone in the final paragraph may well belong to an editorial, but a national newspaper is unlikely to urge establishing a department of plant neurobiology "at our university" (line 32-33), let alone refer to other scientists as "my colleagues" (line 33). Editorials are opinion pieces written by senior editorial staff of a newspaper, not by contributing writers.

Answer choice (D) is the correct answer choice. The reference to "our university" in lines 32-33 suggests that the author is most likely a senior university administrator or a professor, whose job is to convince his or her "colleagues" (line 33) that a certain strategic initiative is worthy of institutional support. The author makes this appeal only after describing the scientific contributions made by plant neurobiologists, suggesting that the first and second paragraphs are meant to support the proposal outlined in the third paragraph.

Answer choice (E) is incorrect. The author is clearly convinced that vegetal behavior is incredibly complex (lines 1-2), a belief she supports with observations involving plant cognition, signal-interaction, biochemical communication, etc. However, the purpose of the passage is not purely descriptive, as would be the case if the passage were drawn from a study on vegetal behavior. The third paragraph clearly advocates a particular course of action, which is inconsistent with the objectives typically associated with scientific studies.

Question #7: SR, Parallel. The correct answer choice is (A)

Although a prephrased answer to this Parallel Reasoning question would be difficult to produce, examine the opponents' position closely: they object to the establishment of a department in plant neurobiology primarily because it would be redundant—the same objectives, in principle, can be achieved by plant physiologists. Apply the Test of Abstraction: your job is to identify an analogous situation in which a course of action is rejected because its objectives can be achieved by an existing process or product.

Answer choice (A) is the correct answer choice. A car manufacturer refusing to develop a new type of electric car is analogous to a scientist who refuses to support a department dedicated to plant neurobiology. The rationale in both cases is roughly the same: the objectives of plant neurobiology can arguably be achieved by plant physiologists, just like the environmental benefits of electric cars can be attained by hybrid models. In both instances, the new product or entity is made redundant by a currently existing product.

Answer choice (B) is incorrect, because the argument described in lines 33-35 does not weigh the benefits of establishing a department in plant neurobiology against its costs. No analogous relationship is presented in the passage.

Answer choice (C) is incorrect, because here the manufacturer questions the environmental benefits of electric cars, which have no clear parallel to the position discussed in lines 33-35. The value of the scientific contributions made by plant neurobiology is never under debate.

Answer choice (D) is attractive, but incorrect. Here, as well as in the passage, a course of action is rejected because of a faulty rationale. However, the premises supporting the conclusion differ. In answer choice (D), the manufacturer suspects that there is no scientific consensus on the issue of global warming, implying that electric cars may be offering a solution to an inexistent problem. No analogous argument is made in the passage, as the opponents never argue that plant neurobiologists are studying a phenomenon that may not, in fact, exist. The existence of plant intelligence or cognition is not under debate.

Answer choice (E) is incorrect, because the lack of required infrastructure to support electric cars has no analogous premise in the argument outlined in the beginning of the third paragraph. The opponents never argue, for instance, that a department dedicated to plant neurobiology should not be established because of limited technical or financial resources.

7

Passage #8 Analysis: Growth Management

Paragraph One:

The author begins the first paragraph by presenting one focal point of the passage: the importance of managing the rate of a company's growth. Management of this issue is of particular importance to small businesses, which often lack significant cash reserves and are therefore less resilient to growth mismanagement. Failure to sustain or manage growth can threaten the existence of such companies.

Paragraph Two:

In this paragraph the author presents the perspective of "a number of experts," who assert that a strong business plan is vital to the proper management of a company's growth, creating the basis for long range profit increases and planning for prospective market changes. At this point in the passage, there is a subtle shift from the opinion of "a number of experts" to the perspective of the author, who points out that a strong business plan can be helpful but does not guarantee business growth, because of rapid market change or failure to stick to the plan. Citing evidence from case studies, the author asserts that an executive with a strong understanding of the market is a more important component of successful growth management, with or without the assistance of a good business plan.

Paragraph Three:

In the final paragraph the author provides practical (though anecdotal) evidence in support of the assertion that a competent executive is more vital to growth management than a solid business plan. The example provided is that of a regional travel agency which had no basic business plan but did have an involved leader with a strong understanding of the market. In response to the advent of the internet and waning consumer travel revenues, the executive repositioned the business to focus primarily on outsourced business travel. In addition, the business improved upon its consumer services in three ways:

1. 24 hour service

2. Emergency travel specialists

3. Business concierge

The author closes the passage by recounting the predictably positive results experienced by the travel agency (over 500% annual growth following the changes), to strengthen the case that a strong leader with vision is more integral to growth management than a competent business plan.

7

<u>**VIEWSTAMP** Analysis:</u>

The **Viewpoints** reflected in this passage are as follows: The first paragraph is entirely factual, and thus viewpoint-neutral. The first sentence of the second paragraph reflects the viewpoint of "a number of experts," who believe that successful growth management depends primarily on a strong business plan. In the second sentence of this paragraph, however, there is a quick shift to the authors viewpoint (that a strong leader is more important than a strong business plan), with this perspective reflected in the remainder of the passage.

The **Structure** of the passage is as follows:

<u>Paragraph 1</u>: Discuss the notion that effective growth management is a major challenge for business executives, and why the issue is of particular concern to small businesses.

<u>Paragraph 2</u>: Present the "expert" perspective that a competent business plan is the most important factor in small business growth management, and the shortcomings of this viewpoint. Assert that a strong leader who understands the marketplace is more important than a good business plan.

<u>Paragraph 3</u>: Introduce one real-world example of a small business which thrives with a strong leader despite the fact that there was no business plan in place.

The author's **Tone** is even-handed and well reasoned. When the author takes issue with the perspective of "a number of experts," that disagreement has a reasonable basis (markets can change quickly; business plans can be ignored), and is bolstered by the the practical example provided.

The **Arguments** in the passage are those of the referenced experts who believe that the business plan is the key to effective growth management, and of the author, who provides reason and evidence to back the assertion that a business leader with a clear vision of the market is more vital to success.

The **Main Point** of the passage is that while some say a business plan is the most important component in handling growth management, a very important issue for small businesses, a strong executive who understands the market can help a business to thrive with or without a set plan.

The author's **Primary Purpose** is to discuss the importance of managing the growth of a company, debunk the notion that a business plan is a necessity, and discuss the more important factor of an executive with a clear vision, closing with an example to support this point.

7

Question #1: GR, Main Point. The correct answer choice is (B)

The main point, as stated above, is that a business plan can be helpful to managing growth, while a strong leader can help a business to thrive in the presence or absence of a business plan.

Answer choice (A): This answer references the specific example provided by the author to speak to the importance of a strong leader, but this point is provided as evidence, not as the main point.

Answer choice (B): This is the correct answer choice. Although the importance of a strong executive is not specifically mentioned in this answer, this is the choice which best reflects the author's main assertion, discussed throughout the passage.

Answer choice (C): This side point is mentioned as one potential vulnerability which exists even in the presence of a competent business plan.

Answer choice (D): This point is not the main focus, but rather speaks to the fact that proper management is of particular importance to a small business.

Answer choice (E): The argument made is that a strong leader can be more vital than a competent business plan—the author never claims that a business <u>can't</u> succeed without such a leader.

Question #2: GR, Must. The correct answer choice is (A)

Answer choice (A): This is the correct answer choice. In the first paragraph of the passage, the author discusses why proper growth management is "for small businesses...even more critical."

Answer choice (B): The author references some experts who believe that a solid business plan is vital, but the author's perspective, supported by case studies and the travel agency example, is that the business plan can be helpful but is not absolutely necessary.

Answer choice (C): While a business leader with a strong vision is more *likely* to lead a small business to success, the author never goes so far as to assert that success is guaranteed under strong leadership.

Answer choice (D): Like answer choice (C), the language here is stronger than would be justified by the passage. Improper management may jeopardize a business, but there is no implication that failure is assured by poor management.

Answer choice (E): The regional travel agency happens to be the subject of the example presented in the third paragraph, but the author does not assert that regional travel agencies provide a model for general business growth.

7

Question #3: SR, Must, O. The correct answer choice is (D)

Like Question #1, this is a question conducive to prephrasing, so we should try to get a good idea of the answer before considering the choices provided. Having already broken down the basic structure of the passage, we know the role played by the third paragraph: the author uses this paragraph to provide the travel agency example, to strengthen the general assertion that a strong leader can bring success to a business, even in the absence of a basic business plan.

Answer choice (A): The case presented exemplifies the point that a strong leader can help to foster success without necessarily requiring a business plan.

Answer choice (B): The elements of the travel agency's success are outlined to prove the point about the importance of a strong leader, not to prove a point about changing market conditions.

Answer choice (C): No assumptions are identified, so this cannot be the correct answer choice.

Answer choice (D): This is the correct answer choice. The example is presented to illustrate the point that while a business plan can be helpful, a plan is not absolutely necessary if the company's leader has a clear understanding of the marketplace.

Answer choice (E): The final paragraph is used to exemplify the main point of the passage, but the main point is stated most clearly in the final sentence of the second paragraph.

Question #4: CR, Must. The correct answer choice is (E)

The author states that "leaders with a strong personal vision can easily overcome the lack of a good business plan." The argument has reasonable basis and the author provides an example to support this assertion.

Answer choice (A): The author does not agree that business plans are essential, so this cannot be the correct answer choice.

Answer choice (B): The author does not accept the assertion.

Answer choice (C): This author is skeptical, but the skepticism is far greater than "mild," so this answer choice is incorrect.

Answer choice (D): Again, the author is not accepting of the notion that business plans are the key to effective growth management.

Answer choice (E): This is the correct answer choice. The entire passage is basically a reasoned critique of the assertion that a good business plan is the key to effective growth management.

Chapter Eight:
Test Readiness

Chapter Eight: Test Readiness

Test Readiness

The day before the test

On the day before your GMAT appointment, we recommend that you study very little, if at all. The best approach for most students is to simply relax as much as possible. Read a book, go see a movie, or play a round of golf. If you feel you must study, we recommend that you only briefly review each of the concepts covered in this book.

If you are not familiar with the location of your test center, drive by the test center and survey the parking situation. This will alleviate anxiety or confusion on the day of the test.

Eat only bland or neutral foods the night before the test and try to get the best sleep possible.

The morning of the test

Attempt to follow your normal routine on the morning of the test. For example, if you read the paper every morning, do so on the day of the test. If you do not regularly drink coffee, do not start on test day. Constancy in your routine will allow you to focus on your primary objective: performing well on the test.

Dress in layers, so you will be warm if the test center is cold, but also able to shed clothes if the test center is hot.

You should arrive at the test center approximately 30 minutes before your scheduled appointment time.

We strongly believe that performing well requires you to believe that you can perform well. As you prepare to leave for the test, run through the test in your head, visualizing an exceptional performance. Imagine how you'll react to the math problems, verbal questions, and essay prompt. Many athletes use this same technique to achieve optimal performance.

The following pages contain general notes on preparing for the day of the GMAT.

Do not study hard the day before the test. If you haven't learned it by then, that final day won't make much difference.

At the test center

Upon check-in, test supervisors will ask you for acceptable personal identification (typically a driver's license or passport). Supervisors are instructed to deny admission to anyone who does not present a photo ID with signature. They may also take a palm vein scan, photograph you, or videotape you.

The test supervisors will assign each examinee a work station. You are not permitted to choose your own station.

Once you are seated, testing will begin promptly.

Food and drink are not allowed in the testing room.

You may not leave your work station during the timed portions of the test.

If you engage in any misconduct or irregularity during the test, you may be dismissed from the test center and may be subject to other penalties for misconduct or irregularity. Actions that could warrant such consequences are creating a disturbance; giving or receiving help; removing noteboards from the testing room; eating or drinking during the test; taking part in an act of impersonation or other forms of cheating; or using books, calculators, ear plugs, headsets, rulers, or other aids. The penalties for misconduct are high: you may be precluded from attending business school.

If you encounter a problem with the test or test center itself, report it to a test administrator. Reportable problems include: power outages, computer malfunctions, and any unusual disturbances caused by an individual.

If you feel anxious or panicked for any reason before or during the test, close your eyes for a few seconds and relax. Think of other situations where you performed with confidence and skill.

After the test

At the end of the test you will see your unofficial scores from the multiple choice sections immediately, and you can print out a copy of your results. You will also be presented with the option of cancelling your score at that point, which is the only opportunity you have to cancel your score without a fee; otherwise you may cancel within 72 hours of your test's start time for a $25 fee. If you choose to cancel and later wish to reinstate your score, you may do so within five years for a $50 fee.

Official test results will be available within 20 calendar days of your GMAT exam. You will be notified via email when this occurs.

Afterword

Thank you for choosing to purchase the *PowerScore GMAT Reading Comprehension Bible*. We hope you have found this book to be both useful and enjoyable, but most importantly we hope this book helps raise your GMAT score.

In all of our publications we strive to present the material in the clearest and most informative manner. If you have any questions, comments, or suggestions, please do not hesitate to email us at:

 **gmatbibles@powerscore.com**

We love to receive feedback and we do read every email that comes in!

Also, if you haven't done so already, we strongly suggest you visit the website for this book at:

 **powerscore.com/grcb**

This free online resource area contains supplements to the book material, provides updates as needed, and answers questions posed by students. There is also an official evaluation form that we encourage you to use.

If we can assist you in any way in your GMAT preparation or in the business school admissions process, please do not hesitate to contact us. We would be happy to help.

Thank you and best of luck on the GMAT!

Alphabetical Glossary

Argument: Pages 110, 193

A set of statements wherein one statement is claimed to follow from or be derived from the others. An argument requires a conclusion.

Assumption: Page 193

An assumption is an unstated premise of an argument. Assumptions are an integral component of the argument that the author takes for granted and leaves unsaid.

Best (in Question Stems): Page 200

In order to maintain test integrity the test makers need to make sure their credited answer choice is as airtight and defensible as possible. Imagine what would occur if a question stem, let us say a Weaken question, did not include a "most" or "best" qualifier: any answer choice that weakened the argument, even if only very slightly, could then be argued to meet the criteria of the question stem. A situation like this would make constructing the test exceedingly difficult because any given problem might have multiple correct answer choices. To eliminate this predicament, the test makers insert "most" into the question stem, and then they can always claim there is one and only one correct answer choice.

Cannot Be True Questions: Page 197

Ask you to identify the answer choice that cannot be true or is most weakened based on the information in the passage. Question stem example:

"If the statements in the passage are true, which one of the following CANNOT be true?"

Cause (C): Page 141

The event that makes another event occur.

Cause and Effect (CE): Page 141

When one event is said to make another occur. The cause is the event that makes the other occur; the effect is the event that follows from the cause. By definition, the cause must occur before the effect, and the cause is the "activator" or "ignitor" in the relationship. The effect always happens at some point in time after the cause.

CE: See Cause and Effect.

Concept Reference (CR): Page 167

In Reading Comprehension, these questions refer to a specific concept discussed in the passage without reference to the location of the relevant discussion.

Conclusion: Page 222

A statement or judgment that follows from one or more reasons. Conclusions, as summary statements, are supposed to be drawn from and rest on the premises.

Conditional Reasoning: Page 141

The broad name given to logical relationships composed of sufficient and necessary conditions. Any conditional statement consists of at least one sufficient condition and at least one necessary condition. In everyday use, conditional statements are often brought up using the "if...then" construction. Conditional reasoning can occur in any question type.

Contender: Page 215

An answer choice that appears somewhat attractive, interesting, or even confusing. Basically, any answer choice that you cannot immediately identify as incorrect.

Counterargument: Page 99

A statement that actually contains an idea that is counter to the author's main argument. Counterarguments bring up points of opposition or comparison.

CR: See Concept Reference

E

Effect: Page 224

The event that follows from the cause.

Exaggerated Answer: Page 189

Exaggerated Answers take information from the passage and then stretch that information to make a broader statement that is not supported by the passage.

Except: Page 201

When "except" is placed in a question it negates the logical quality of the answer choice you seek. It turns the intent of the question stem upside down.

Expansion (E): Page 187

Expansion questions require you to extrapolate ideas from the passage to determine one of three elements: where the passage was drawn from or how it could be titled, what sentence or idea could come before the passage, or what sentence or idea could follow the passage.

F

Fact Test™: Page 181

The correct answer to a Must Be True question can always be proven by referring to the facts stated in the passage. An answer choice that cannot be substantiated by proof in the passage is incorrect.

G

Global Reference (GR): Page 167

In Reading Comprehension, Global Reference questions ask about information without specifying a location or concept within the passage (for example, "According to the statements in the passage which one of the following must be true?").

GR: See Global Reference

L

Least: Page 201

When "least" appears in a question stem you should treat it exactly the same as "except." Note: this advice holds true only when this word appears in the question stem! If you see the word "least" elsewhere on the GMAT, consider it to have its usual meaning of "in the lowest or smallest degree."

Loser: Page 215

An answer choice which strikes you as clearly incorrect.

M

Main Point: Page 119

The central idea, or ultimate conclusion, that the author is attempting to prove.

Main Point Questions (MP): Page 172

Main Point questions are a variant of Must Be True questions. As you might expect, a Main Point question asks you to find the primary conclusion made by the author. Question stem example:

"Which one of the following most accurately expresses the main point of the passage?"

Most (in Question Stems): Page 200

In order to maintain test integrity the test makers need to make sure their credited answer choice is as airtight and defensible as possible. Imagine what would occur if a question stem, let us say a Weaken question, did not include a "most" qualifier: any answer choice that weakened the argument, even if only very slightly, could then be argued to meet the criteria of the question stem. A situation like this would make constructing the test exceedingly difficult because any given problem might have multiple correct answer choices. To eliminate this predicament, the test makers insert "most" into the question stem, and then they can always claim there is one and only one correct answer choice.

MP: See Main Point.

Most Supported: See Must Be True.

Must Be True: Pages 172, 181

Must Be True questions ask you to identify the answer choice that is best proven by the information in the passage. Question stem examples:

"If the statements above are true, which one of the following must also be true?"
"Which one of the following can be properly inferred from the passage?"

N

N: See Necessary Condition.

Necessary Condition (N): Page 141

An event or circumstance whose occurrence is required in order for a sufficient condition to occur.

New Information: Page 190

Information that is not mentioned explicitly in the passage, or does not follow as a consequence of the information in the passage.

Not Necessarily True: Page 201

The logical opposite of "Must Be true." When an answer choice is not proven by the information in the passage.

O: See Organization.

Opposite Answer: Page 190

Provides an answer that is completely opposite of the stated facts of the passage. Opposite Answers are very attractive to students who are reading too quickly or carelessly and quite frequently appear in Strengthen and Weaken questions.

Organization (O): Page 186

These Reading Comprehension questions ask you to describe a characteristic of the overall structure of the passage. For example, "The second paragraph serves primarily to...," or "Which one of the following best describes the organization of the passage?" These questions are similar to the Method of Reasoning questions in the Critical Reasoning section, but are generally broader.

P: See Purpose

Parallel Reasoning: Page 196

In the Reading Comprehension section, these questions are usually broader in scope, asking you to find the scenario most analogous to an action in the passage. There is less of a focus on identifying premises and conclusions than in the Critical Reasoning section.

Passage: Pages 9, 15

GMAT Reading Comprehension passages are up to 350 words in length, based on passage topics that are drawn from a variety of subjects. Each passage is followed by questions that ask you to determine viewpoints in the passage, analyze organizational traits, and evaluate specific sections of the passage.

Premise: Page 139

A fact, proposition, or statement from which a conclusion is made. Literally, the premises give the reasons why the conclusion should be accepted.

Principle (PR): Page 202

A broad rule that specifies what actions or judgments are correct in certain situations. These are not a separate question type but are instead an "overlay" that appears in a variety of question types and the presence of the Principle indicator serves to broaden the scope of the question.

PR: See Principle.

Purpose (P): Page 119

Primary Purpose questions are quite common on the GMAT and ask what the author generally sought to accomplish when writing the passage. Local purpose questions ask why the author referred to a particular word, phrase, or idea. This is essentially an extended Method of Reasoning question, requiring you to go beyond simply identifying the argument structure, and asking you the reasons behind the author's use of words or ideas.

Question Stem: Page 165

Follows the passage and poses a question directed at the passage. Make sure to read the question stem very carefully. Some stems direct you to focus on certain aspects of the passage and if you miss these clues you make the problem much more difficult.

Reverse Answer: Page 191

Occurs when an answer choice contains familiar elements from the passage, but rearranges those elements to create a new, unsupported statement.

S

S: See Sufficient Condition

Scope: Page 194

The range to which the premises and conclusion encompass certain ideas. An argument with a narrow scope is definite in its statements, whereas a wide scope argument is less definite and allows for a greater range of possibility.

Shell Game: Page 190

An idea or concept is raised in the passage, and then a very similar idea appears in the answer choice, but the idea is changed just enough to be incorrect but still attractive. This trick is called the Shell Game because it abstractly resembles those street corner gambling games where a person hides a small object underneath one of three shells, and then scrambles them on a flat surface while a bettor tries to guess which shell the object is under.

SN:

Abbreviation for Sufficient and Necessary Conditions. May be seen separately in diagramming as "S" and "N." See also Sufficient Condition and Necessary Condition.

Specific Reference (SR): Page 166

These Reading Comprehension questions provide you with the specific location of a given term or phrase within the passage. To attack the question, refer to the location of the word or phrase and then begin reading about 5 lines above the reference. Note that in the Official Guide, Specific Reference questions provide the location of the referenced term or phrase by line number, while on the actual GMAT the relevant word or phrase is highlighted within the passage.

SR: See Specific Reference.

Strengthen/Support Questions: Page 173

These questions ask you to select the answer choice that provides support for the author's argument or strengthens it in some way. Question stem examples:

"Which one of the following, if true, most strengthens the argument?"
"Which one of the following, if true, most strongly supports the statement above?"

Structure: Page 92

The order in which things are presented in the passage.

Sufficient Condition (S): Page 141

> An event or circumstance whose occurrence indicates that a necessary condition must also occur. The sufficient condition does not make the necessary condition occur; it is simply an indicator.

T

Tone/Attitude: Page 99

> Identifying the tone or attitude of each group can sometimes be more challenging. Attitude is the state of mind or feeling that each group takes to the subject matter at hand, and for our purposes, "attitude" and "tone" will be used interchangeably. In most passages, GMAT authors tend not to be extreme in their opinions.

V

VIEWSTAMP: Page 65

> This acronym helps you remember the critical elements to track in Reading Comprehension passages:

> | | | |
> |---|---|---|
> | **VIEW** = | the different **VIEW**points in the passage |
> | **S** = | the **S**tructure of the passage |
> | **T** = | the **T**one of the passage |
> | **A** = | the **A**rguments in the passage |
> | **M** = | the **M**ain Point |
> | **P** = | the **P**rimary Purpose of the passage |

Viewpoint: Page 77

> A viewpoint is the position or approach taken by a person or group. On the GMAT, Reading Comprehension passages typically contain anywhere from one to six different viewpoints. These viewpoints can be the author's or those of groups discussed by the author.

W

Weaken Questions: Page 195

Weaken questions ask you to attack or undermine the author's argument. Question stem example:

"Which one of the following, if true, most seriously weakens the argument?"